Autism and Asperger's Conditions
A practical guide for nurses

Note

Healthcare practice and knowledge are constantly changing and developing as new research and treatments, changes in procedures, drugs and equipment become available.

The author and publishers have, as far as is possible, taken care to confirm that the information complies with the latest standards of practice and legislation.

Autism and Asperger's Conditions
A practical guide for nurses

by

Christopher Barber

A division of MA Healthcare Ltd

Quay Books Division, MA Healthcare Ltd, St Jude's Church, Dulwich Road, London SE24 0PB

British Library Cataloguing-in-Publication Data
A catalogue record is available for this book

ISBN-10: 1-85642-411-1
ISBN-13: 978-1-85642-411-0

Edited by Jessica Anderson

Cover design by Louise Cowburn, Fonthill Creative

Publishing Manager: Andy Escott

Printed by Mimeo, Huntingdon, Cambridgeshire

Contents

Acknowledgements

I would like to take this opportunity to thank all those who have encouraged me throughout the writing of this book. First of all, I would like to thank my dear wife Jean and son Freddie for being long-suffering and patient with me throughout the past two years. Without you, this book would not have been written.

Secondly, I would like to thank all friends and colleagues who have likewise encouraged and supported me.

Thirdly, I would like to extend a very big thank you to two friends, Jo Delrée and Karen Sanders for writing *Chapters 19 and 20*, respectively

CHAPTER 1

Introduction

'So, what exactly is this 'disease' called Asperger's syndrome?'

Let me explain. At the Royal College of Nursing's Annual Congress at Harrogate in 2005 there was a resolution debate around learning disability services. During a two minute verbal contribution to the debate a nurse mentioned that his then 12-year-old son had Asperger's syndrome and that there was a possibility that he, too, might also have the condition. His self-diagnosis was based upon a reflective reading of the first two chapters of *Autism and Creativity* by Michael Fitzgerald (2004). The more this nurse read of Fitzgerald's book, the more certain aspects of his own life story finally started to make sense. He had reached the 'eureka' moment of understanding who he was.

During a coffee break later that day the nurse was approached by a nursing colleague who asked him, in all seriousness and with an apparent lack of knowledge regarding Asperger's and similar conditions on the autism spectrum, what this 'disease' called Asperger's was. To say the nurse was stunned is an understatement. He mumbled something vague and unhelpful about Asperger's syndrome being a form of autism before self-consciously disappearing into the crowd. He had hoped that someone would ask him intelligent questions about the syndrome and his experience of it or to use his knowledge, which he had gained not only from completing a master's degree in the subject, but also from working with service users in a professional capacity and from being his son's 'informal carer', but no one did. So much for 'coming out' and his five minutes of fame. The Congress resolution debate and his contribution to it were, however, reported briefly in the *Nursing Times* (2005). The nurse who spoke during that Congress debate was me, and the 'self-diagnosis' was later confirmed after a period of assessments.

The question still stands, despite the initial phrasing of it being somewhat inelegant and betraying a serious lack of knowledge on the part of the nurse asking it. I spent the following year repeatedly asking myself and others what an appropriate response to this question should be. Clearly, a few information 'sound bites' would not suffice even to cover the essential basics of what autism and Asperger's syndrome are, let alone anything approaching an in-depth discussion surrounding its causes, presentation, assessment, effects and interventions. Numerous discussions were held with a wide number of interested people including parents of people with Asperger's syndrome and autism, fellow nurses, social workers and teachers. The suggestion of a book about Asperger's syndrome and autism aimed specifically at nurses was raised as a possible solution to the question. As the year progressed the idea of writing such a book took root and grew. So this is where we are now: a book about Asperger's syndrome and autism aimed specifically at nurses.

Purpose

What, then, is the purpose of this book? Is there not already enough written material about autism and Asperger's syndrome? Why the need for more?

Agreed, there are whole libraries of books, journal articles and internet formats on autism and Asperger's, with more being added almost weekly. However, the conversation that I had with my nursing colleague at Harrogate and subsequent conversations have convinced me that this information, although both available and plentiful, is not getting through.

As nurses we do not appear to be as informed and aware as perhaps we should be about Asperger's syndrome and autism. This lack of awareness is evident each time I take my son, who is now 17 years old and who has Asperger's syndrome, to our local A & E department. Both myself and my son are met by silence when I ask the nurses how much they know about Asperger's syndrome and autism. 'Well, I did once watch the movie Rain Man with Dustin Hoffman. Wasn't that about autism?' seems to be the stock answer and also seems to be the limit of many nurses' knowledge about these two conditions. Such lack of knowledge is further hampered by the use of a biological, medical and disease model to understand autism and Asperger's syndrome; hence the idea of Asperger's being a disease, which actually it is not. In his Masters of Education dissertation, a shortened version of which can be found in Barber (2001), Barber investigated the need for an accredited course in autism spectrum conditions (ASCs) specifically for nurses and makes the point that registered nurses are generally poorly served by existing opportunities for in-depth training in the field. In this study many parents expressed the belief that nursing interventions aimed at either themselves or their ASC children would have been better if the nurse had had some knowledge and understanding of ASC issues. This finding was supported by those with ASC who were questioned as part of Barber's dissertation. Those with ASC suggested a need for specific courses for all nurses who come into contact with this group of people.

Barber echoed a number of writers who suggest that those with an ASC are as much prone to physical health problems and illnesses as are the general population, and in the areas of mental health and learning disabilities, possibly more so. Clarke (1996) suggests that anxiety, depression, bipolar mood disorders, schizophrenia and related forms of psychosis are heightened in those with autism. Midence and O'Neill (1999) highlighted the need for all healthcare professionals, especially doctors, to have a vastly improved awareness and understanding of developmental problems such as autism and Asperger's syndrome. Green-Allison (1999), the founder of the National Autistic Society (NAS), supported by Peeters and Jordon (1999) agreed that a core autism-specific training system is needed.

In order even to get to first base in terms of understanding autism and Asperger's syndrome, rigid, narrow and regimented biological and medical thinking needs to be ditched in favour of holistic and social models. Asperger's and autism are complex conditions and knowledge about them is evolving as people's understanding of their causes and presentation and therapeutic interventions for them changes and improves over time.

Barber (2001) suggested that, since adults and children with ASC require access to a whole range of healthcare services, better educated nurses should lead to enhanced service provision and may also lead to enhanced recruitment and retention of key qualified healthcare professionals. Such recruitment and retention is essential and access can only be achieved if these healthcare professionals are empowered by more knowledge about the health needs of this patient group.

There also appears to be an assumption that Asperger's syndrome and autism are childhood conditions and once people reach adulthood the conditions will either improve drastically or even disappear. Such thinking appears to be reinforced by the vast number of published articles about children with Asperger's and autism but the relatively few about adults. On that assumption, as the parent of a child with Asperger's syndrome, I can, in a year's time when he reaches 18, look forward to my son suddenly 'getting better'. This is highly unlikely – autism and Asperger's is for life; I should know, having recently been diagnosed with high functioning autism/Asperger's syndrome myself.

So, what then is the purpose of this book? The short answer is to raise awareness, understanding and the profile of Asperger's syndrome and autism – and not just among nurses. The questionnaires distributed by Barber (2001) on the autism training and learning needs of registered nurses were also completed by the doctors in a local GP practice. The findings indicated a similar lack of knowledge and need for training among the GPs surveyed. However, since only three GPs completed the questionnaire, it is not possible to generalise the findings, although they do point to the need for cross-professional awareness of ASC.

However, it is not the intention of this book to be merely an academic exercise in raising consciousness and awareness. There are already books and journal articles available on many aspects of Asperger's syndrome and autism, the most important and accessible being Wing (1999), Jackson (2002) and Morgan (1996), others, including Fitzgerald (2004) and Hobson (1993), and, looking at ASC from a parents' perspective, Maurice (1993). It is hoped and intended that the information contained in this book will contribute not only to nurses' understanding but also to their nursing practice when working with and for those with Asperger's syndrome and autism and their families and significant others.

It is also hoped that some nurses, and possibly even some of our medical colleagues, may become sufficiently interested in Asperger's syndrome and autism to study these conditions in greater depth (see the Resources section at the end of the book for information on books and courses available). It is even hoped that some may consider becoming involved in a more overt political arena.

What is meant by this? For far too long mainstream service provision for those with Asperger's syndrome and autism and their families have been hampered by a lack of knowledge, understanding and funding, and this group has lost out as a result. Mainstream service provisions have often lagged behind initiatives proposed and actioned by those with autism and ASCs and their families. The NAS is a case in point. The NAS is a voluntary sector organisation set up by the parent of a person with autism to meet the needs of other such parents and people on the autism spectrum. In an ideal world such a service need should have been recognised and acted upon by care professionals and care agencies such as the NHS long before parents recognised the need, thus pre-empting any call for action by parents, family members and those with autism or ASC. This has arguably not been the case and autism services are not alone. Many other health conditions have been recognised and provided for by voluntary sector organisations before mainstream services recognised them.

In the case of autism this may have been as a result, either directly or indirectly, of 'victim blaming', i.e., the so-called 'refrigerator mother' theory of causation much favoured in the late 1960s (Bettleheim 1967). Indeed, Caiseal Mor, an Australian who has autism, was subject to excruciating physical, sexual, psychological and emotional abuse throughout his early years during the 1960s because it was claimed that autism could be 'cured' through the application of such measures (Mor 2007). Whilst such archaic thinking may have been consigned to the scrap heap of history, discrimination against those with autism and ASC has, unfortunately, not. This discrimination will be further discussed later. It is the duty and responsibility of all health, and, indeed, social care and education professionals to recognise and challenge the causes and effects of such discrimination on those with ASC. Health and social care staff have a duty to stand with those with autism and ASC even including facilitating them to participate in 'political' activity such as the so-called 'mad pride' events if that is what they want. On a more everyday level, health and social care staff have a duty to ensure that services and information which those with autism and ASC and their families and 'informal carers' need are available and accessable. They should also make sure that the days when those with autism and their families have to fight for appropriate information and services, and for basic respect and dignity are consigned to the past. In order to fulfil this duty, staff have a responsibility to be aware of and understand what autism and ASC are and what they are not. This is the purpose of this book: to help raise and improve such awareness and understanding; to provide nurses, doctors and other health and social care staff with the necessary information to enable them to 'be with' those with autism and their families and, through this, to raise awareness to improve service provision and nurses' interactions with those with ASC.

Aims and objectives

As has already been noted, the intended aim of this book is to improve nurses' professional interactions with those with autism and ASC through improved awareness, knowledge and understanding of:

- What autism and ASCs are and are not.
- Diagnostic issues.
- The history of autism.
- The possible causes of autism and ASCs.
- Issues affecting children, adolescents and adults with autism and ASCs and their families.
- Nursing interventions for children, adolescents, adults, and informal carers.

In order to achieve these aims the reader will be able to:

- Define both autism and Asperger's syndrome and discuss the various definitions available.
- Assess the value and appropriateness of the various diagnostic tools available.
- Place autism and Asperger's syndrome within a historical context.

- Understand and discuss the possible causes of autism and Asperger's syndrome.
- Understand and discuss the effects of autism and Asperger's syndrome from early childhood through to adulthood.
- Understand and discuss the effects of autism and Asperger's syndrome to the wider family.
- Apply the above understanding in the professional work environment.

Whilst the above aims and objectives are not exclusive, the intention is for the reader's awareness and understanding of autism and Asperger's syndrome to be challenged and changed. It is intended that this will lead to an improved way of working with this group of people.

Chapter overview

This book covers all the major stages of the life of a person with autism or an ASC from early childhood diagnosis through to adulthood.

Chapter 2 investigates what autism, Asperger's syndrome and other forms of ASC actually are and are not. There is a lot of confusion regarding the meanings of the different terms, a confusion not helped by looking at these conditions from a rather reductionist 'medical model'. It could be that an unconscious adherence to such a model led to the phrasing of the question: 'What is this disease called Asperger's syndrome?'. Therefore this chapter focuses on the main signs of autism and Asperger's syndrome and how, through the variety of assessment tools available, these signs lead to a diagnosis.

Chapter 3 considers the history of autism and Asperger's syndrome within social, medical and religious contexts.

Chapter 4 focuses on some of the causes of autism, Asperger's syndrome and other ASCs. There has recently been controversial and often heated discussion about the role that the MMR (measles mumps and rubella) vaccine has played, and the relationship between mother and child as a possible cause of autism and Asperger's syndrome. This debate, along with an investigation into genetic and other environmental causes of autism, will be highlighted.

Chapter 5 focuses on diagnostic issues in both childhood and adulthood. Diagnostic differences between autism and Asperger's syndrome are highlighted as are the differences and appropriateness of the various diagnostic tools applied to children and adults. *Chapter 6* focuses on an adult's journey towards, through and beyond diagnosis.

The next three chapters (*Chapters 7, 8 and 9*) explore the differences in presentation and lived experience of autism and Asperger's syndrome from early childhood through to adulthood. The focus of many books and articles tends to be on young children, with the implication that these are childhood conditions which magically disappear once the person hits adulthood. However, over the past few years there have been an increasing number of publications that deal with the adolescent with autism and Asperger's syndrome in relation to sexuality, relationships and social skills (Jackson 2002, Willey 2003, Wrobal 2003, Harpur et al 2006, Painter 2006, Larkey 2007, Yoshida 2007). There still, however, appears to be little that focuses on adults with these conditions. Morgan (1996) is one of the few exceptions to this. *Chapter 8* also revisits diagnostic issues as applied to adults, and investigates the phenomenon of 'self-diagnosis' of autism and Asperger's syndrome and self-disclosure and the risk of being 'outed', which many people with autism and Asperger's syndrome face. Alongside this, mental health issues and adults with ASC, which, up until now, have been unfairly neglected will be highlighted.

Chapter 10 focuses on the links between mental health issues and autism and Asperger's syndrome. A recent survey carried out by the National Autistic Society regarding the experiences of adults with ASC and the services available to them (NAS 2008) indicates that one in three also experiences mental health issues, mainly depression, as a result of social isolation. Possible treatments and solutions to mental health problems (Dubin 2009) are highlighted. *Chapter 11* discusses autism and the criminal justice system and the implications of this for those who work within the system.

The next six chapters (*Chapters 12–17*) investigate nursing interventions from a number of perspectives. The first of these is historical and focuses on nursing and, where relevant, medical and social interventions practised in the past (ranging from downright weird through useful to brilliant), the present, and a bit of 'crystal ball' gazing, for the future.

Chapters 13 and 14 discuss person-centred planning and personalisation as applied to those with autism, and *Chapter 15* focuses on the sensory issues which are believed to influence many if not most aspects of autism.

Nursing interventions for 'independent adults' with ASC form the focus of *Chapter 16*. Whilst many adults with ASC are able to find and keep meaningful and paid employment, live independently on their own, have a meaningful social life, connect with others and even marry and have children, many do not and will need support to achieve 'reasonable' independence. Even those who are able to live independently may need a range of nursing interventions to maintain that independence. These interventions include the skilful and sensitive use of diagnostic assessments for adults who consider themselves or are considered by others to be on the autistic spectrum, support for those who as yet have not had a formal diagnosis, support for those who wish to disclose their autism status to significant others such as employers and colleagues, and support for adults with ASC when they need to access healthcare services.

The final chapter in this section (*Chapter 17*) focuses on the largely neglected area of the nursing, health and social care needs of informal carers of those who have autism and Asperger's syndrome, be they parents, siblings, partners, children or friends. It is arguably and sadly often forgotten that informal carers will also have needs, needs that often go unmet with sometimes tragic consequences for the family and wider society. The role of the nurse and other healthcare professionals in meeting these needs is highlighted.

Chapter 18 focuses on the various welfare benefits that are available to those on the autism spectrum and their families.

Chapters 19 and 20 discuss specific legislation. *Chapter 19* discusses the Autism Act 2009 in terms of what it says, what it doesn't say and its implications for service provision, and *Chapter 20*, whilst not referring to those with ASC, discusses the implications of the Mental Capacity Act 2008.

Chapter 21 provides a very brief summary and draws together emerging strings of thought such as the use of labelling and language as power constructs which may lead to inadequate and inappropriate services being offered to those with autism or Asperger's syndrome.

A selection of resources including books, journals, multi-media and courses is provided at the end of the book.

Conclusion

I hope that your curiosity and interest in autism, Asperger's syndrome and ASC has been aroused and that, rather than being put off the subject, you are beginning to question the idea of autism and Asperger's syndrome as diseases or are disuaded from using an illness or disease model of thinking. Autism and Asperger's syndrome are not diseases but rather a different way of life, of thinking, and of receiving and processing sensory information, a different way of viewing, understanding and interacting with the world and other people.

Both anecdotal and research evidence suggests that nurses' knowledge of autism and Asperger's syndrome is not what it perhaps could and possibly should be. The purpose of this book, therefore, as has already been stated, is to help fill this gap in nurses' knowledge and understanding and through this to change attitudes towards and ways of working with those with autism and Asperger's syndrome. Through this change it is hoped to improve the delivery of health and nursing services and to change negative experiences on the part of both those on the autistic spectrum and those who provide health, medical and nursing services.

Key points

- The purpose of this book is to raise awareness and understanding of people with an autism condition among nurses and other healthcare professionals.
- This book came about as a response to just such a lack of understanding expressed by a nurse.
- Autism and Asperger's Conditions: A practical guide for nurses covers a wide range of issues relating to the care and support of those with an autism spectrum condition from a variety of perspectives.

References

Barber C (2001) The training needs of registered nurses engaged in work with people with an autistic spectrum disorder. *Good Autism Practice* **2**(2): 86–96

Bettleheim B (1967) *The Empty Fortress*. The Free Press, New York

Clarke D (1996) Psychiatric and behavioural problems and pharmaceutical treatments. In Morgan H (ed) *Adults with Autism: A guide to theory and practice*. Cambridge University Press, Cambridge

Dubin N (2009) *Asperger's Syndrome and Anxiety*. Jessica Kingsley Publishers, London

Fitzgerald M (2004) *Autism and Creativity*. Brunner-Routledge, Hove

Green-Allison H (1999) Valuing residential care staff in services for adults with autism. *Good Autism Practice* **April**: 91–7

Harpur J, Lawlor M, Fitzgerald M (2006) *Succeeding with Interventions for Asperger Syndrome Adolescents*. Jessica Kingsley Publishers, London

Hobson P (1993) *Autism and the Development of Mind*. Laurence Erlbaum Associates, Hove

Jackson L (2002) *Freaks, Geeks and Asperger Syndrome*. Jessica Kingsley Publishers, London

Larkey S (2007) *Practical Sensory Programmes for Students with Autism Spectrum Disorder and Other Special Needs*. Jessica Kingsley Publishers, London

Maurice C (1993) *Let Me Hear Your Voice*. Robert Hale Ltd, London

Midence K, O'Neill M (1999) The experience of parents in the diagnosis of autism. *Autism*

3(3): 273–85

Mor C (2007) *A Blessing and a Curse: Autism and Me*. Jessica Kingsley Publishers, London

Morgan H (1996) *Adults with Autism: A Guide to Theory and Practice*. Cambridge University Press, Cambridge

National Autistic Society (2008) *I Exist*. Available from: http://wwww.nas.org.uk/nas/jsp/polopoly.jsp?d=1558 [Last accessed 21 February 2008]

Nursing Times (2005) Decline of learning disability nurses. *Nursing Times* **101**(18): 3

Painter K (2006) *Social Skills Groups for Children and Adolescents with Asperger's Syndrome*. Jessica Kingsley Publishers, London

Peeters T and Jordon R (1999) What makes a good practitioner in the field of autism? *Good Autism Practice* **April**: 85–9

Willey L H (2003) *Asperger's Syndrome in Adolescence* Jessica Kingsley Publishers, London

Wing L (1999) *The Autistic Spectrum*. Constable, London

Wrobel M (2003) *Taking Care of Myself*. Future Horizons, Texas

Yoshida Y (2007) *How to Be Yourself in a World That's Dfferent*. Jessica Kingsley Publishers, London

CHAPTER 2

What autism and Asperger's syndrome are and are not

Not everything that steps out of line, and is thus 'abnormal', must necessarily be inferior.

Hans Asperger (1938)

In this chapter the meanings of autism and Asperger's syndrome will be briefly investigated and defined using the various diagnostic criteria available and the experiences and lives of a small number of people with the conditions. Although it is intended that people's experiences should support the diagnostic criteria, there are a few contradictions along the way.

This chapter will also consider the following:

- What autism is not.
- The prevalence of autism and Asperger's syndrome in the UK.
- What autism and Asperger's syndrome actually are.
- Whether or not there any differences between the two conditions.
- Autism and Asperger's syndrome as 'different but equal', autism as 'deviance' and autism as 'abnormal' (see the quote from Hans Asperger above).

What autism is not

First of all, perhaps the obvious needs to be stated. Autism is not:

- A disease.
- Catching.
- A childhood condition that magically improves or disappears once the person becomes an adult.
- A form of infantile psychosis.
- A form of negative or social deviance.
- A negative life sentence.

Many healthcare professionals, including nurses, still work from a reductionist 'medical' rather than a 'social' model of care which, to put it rather simplistically, sees most if not all health conditions as 'illnesses' or 'diseases' and regards those with a health condition as 'ill' or 'diseased'. Therefore, autism or Asperger's syndrome are seen as diseases. This alters the person's social, psychological and emotional behaviour; people are disabled due to their condition and not the environment. Implicit in this approach is the idea that, as a disease, autism and Asperger's can be cured and possibly eradicated. Lucy Clark, in her foreword to Lawson (2008) suggests that:

> *The medical model remains all too evident in much of the current literature on autism and subsequently informs the way that support services are constructed for autistic people.*
>
> Lawson (2008: 9)

It could be suggested that 'normalisation' is one goal of the medical model which seeks to make the disabled person as 'near normal as possible' and therefore less deviant and inferior. It does this by decreasing the person's disability through behaviour modification rather than challenging and changing other people's perceptions of and attitudes towards the disabled person. 'Normalisation', however, could be argued to equate disability with the power constructs of 'normal' equals good and 'abnormal' equals bad. Those so characterised as abnormal become deviant and may be treated accordingly.

A social model does not seek to deny or play down the very real difficulties and problems that many people with autism face every day. However, it places the cause of these problems or difficulties not within the person but within the environment and other people's lack of understanding and acceptance both of the individuals and their issues. Therefore, barriers erected by other people who do not understand autism cause many of the problems that those with autism face. However, this is not to imply that autism will disappear once care professionals, the public and society stop erecting barriers.

The idea that certain forms of 'learning disability' are 'catching' has a long history and arguably results from a 'medical' or 'disease' philosophy. Even as recently as the late 1980s in learning disability services it was not unusual to observe staff refusing to use the same crockery or cutlery or sit in the same chairs as service users for fear of 'catching' their learning disability. There is, possibly, an unconscious idea that autism is a 'childhood condition' in much the same way as measles, mumps and chickenpox. Hence early research into autism and interventions for those with autism or Asperger's syndrome focused on children. It was only during the mid-1990s that publications began to appear that focused on adolescents and adults with autism, one of these being Morgan (1996). The idea that autism is a childhood condition could be based on the fact that one of the key diagnostic criteria for autism and Asperger's is that the signs and symptoms have to be present in the person from early childhood. However, implicit in this is the idea that the person with autism will 'grow out of' this condition as he or she gets older.

Autism and Asperger's syndrome are not mental illnesses as such and are definitely not a form of psychosis, infantile or otherwise, although there are various forms of mental health issues such as depression that may have a higher than average prevalence among people with autism and Asperger's syndrome. However, autism was often called 'infantile psychosis' during the 1960s and 1970s.

Autism as deviance will be discussed later. Deviance can have both positive and negative aspects; the word being both socially and politically loaded. However, autism is not a negative 'life sentence' either for people with this condition or their families and friends. Autism is a different and unique way of interacting and communicating with the self, others and the environment and is thus not to be treated as abnormal.

Prevalence of autism and Asperger's syndrome

There are currently around 60 million people living in the UK (the UK comprises England, Wales, Scotland and Northern Ireland).

Gender

There appear to be more females with autism or Asperger's syndrome than males, possibly in the region of 4:1 (f:m). The reason for this is uncertain. However, regardless of gender, those with autism appear to have a more 'systemising' (male) and less 'empathising' (female) brain (Baron-Cohen 2005).

Autism

Various authors report different prevalence rates for autism:

- According to Yoshida (2007) around 1% of the world's population has autism. This equates to around 600 000 people in the UK.

- Morgan (1996) suggests that there are around 300000 people with autism spectrum disorders in the UK.
- Lawson (2008) suggests that there could be as many as one person in every 58 that is somewhere on the autism spectrum. Currently, this equates to around one million people in the UK.
- According to Aylott (2010) around 1% of all children and adults have an autism spectrum condition. However, she also suggests that a lack of formal diagnosis in the adult population may mean that the correct prevalence for adults may not be recorded.

Asperger's syndrome

- Attwood (2006) suggests that the prevalence rate of Asperger's syndrome varies due to the different ways that the DSM-IV and ICD-10 classification systems utilise diagnostic criteria. Research and data gathering and analysis methods may also produce different figures. Prevalence data varies between 0.3 and 8.4 per 10000. This would give a prevalence rate of between 1800 and 50400 people with Asperger's syndrome.
- Fitzgerald (2004) suggested a total prevalence rate of all ASDs as 91 per 10000 which would give a UK prevalence of 546000. Fitzgerald breaks this down further to: (a) 'Classic autism' – those with an IQ level below 70 (learning disability): 5 per 10000 (30000 people) and (b) Asperger's syndrome/high functioning autism – those with an IQ above 70 ('normal intelligence'): 35 per 10000 (210000 people).

The difference in the numbers of people with autism as recorded by Morgan and Yoshida could be due to the 11-year time gap between the two studies. The different research methodology used and philosophical standpoints held by the two writers may also produce different sets of figures, hence the wide difference in reported prevalence from around 300000 to one million people with some form of autism.

However, as with all statistics, caution must be exercised in looking at the results. Does the 1% mentioned by Aylott represent only those people who have received a formal diagnosis or does it include those who are 'self-diagnosed' or those who may, due to either a balance of probabilities or signs presented by certain people, have autism but are undiagnosed? Again, as suggested above, to what extent, if any, does the use of different diagnostic tools, methods and criteria provide different results? To what extent do the statistics refer to different conditions? Is the same 'autism' being measured? If not, that will have a bearing on the statistics given. Therefore, investigating the exact numbers of people with autism or Asperger's syndrome can never be an exact science and will always be a best guess.

What are autism and Asperger's syndrome?

So, what exactly are autism and Asperger's syndrome? There are many answers to this: The first is that autism is not a static single condition but is a range or spectrum of conditions. This is the reason why one will often see references to 'autism spectrum disorder' or 'ASD'. Autism ranges from:

- 'Mild' where the person is able to function relatively well in mainstream society and does not require a great deal of professional support, to
- 'Severe' where most, if not all, aspects and areas of the person's life are affected and he or she requires a large amount of possibly complex support in order to function within society.

Again, some people with ASD will have very high IQ levels whilst others may have below or significantly below average levels and will thus be seen as 'learning disabled' in the same way as people who have Down's syndrome, for example. Those with a higher than average IQ will probably be labelled as having Asperger's syndrome (AS) or high functioning autism (HFA). There are also 'idiot savants', people who have major problems with most aspects of life, who may not know how to wash or dress themselves or use a knife and fork, for example, but who will have incredible ability in one specific, narrow and isolated skill. Such skills may include mathematics, feats of memory (being able to remember dates, sequences or facts), music or art. Many people in public life are said to have AS/HFA. These include, among many others:

- Bill Gates (the founder of Microsoft).
- Sir Patrick Moore (the astronomer).
- Lord Keith Joseph (the Conservative politician who was Secretary of State for education in the early 1980s under Prime Minister Margaret Thatcher).
- Peter Sellers (the comedian).
- Lewis Carroll (author of *Alice in Wonderland*).
- William Butler Yeats (the poet).
- Eamon de Valera (the Irish politician and first Teasach).

- Ludwig Wittgenstein (the philosopher).
- Temple Grandin (American professor of bovine care).

Autism

The condition known as autism has still not been defined, however. This could, in part, be due to the plethora of somewhat confusing 'labels' that exist, such as autism, Asperger's syndrome, classic autism, high functioning autism, autism spectrum disorder, atypical autism, autistic disorder, Asperger disorder and pervasive developmental disorder. Many of these refer to either the same or similar conditions. Throughout the rest of this book the words autism, high functioning autism, Asperger's syndrome, autism spectrum disorders and autism spectrum conditions will be used to, hopefully, avoid any confusion regarding the condition known as autism. Many people with and without an autism condition prefer the term 'condition' rather than 'disorder' as they consider the word 'disorder' to be a negative term. So, again, what is autism?

Autism is a life-long condition comprising the three specific areas of social communication, social interaction and social imagination where the person can experience major problems in life. Wing (1981) calls this the 'triad of impairment'. I am indebted here to the National Autistic Society (NAS) for the following information that was downloaded from their website.

Communication

For people with autistic spectrum conditions, 'body language' can appear as foreign as someone speaking Greek. See *Box 2.1* for an example of the sort of problem a person with autism can encounter.

People with autism have difficulties understanding both verbal and non-verbal language. This could mean several things:

- The subtlety of spoken language is often missed. Many of those with autism do not understand sarcasm, idioms, much humour and common phrases such as, 'It's cool'. To many, 'It's cool' would mean that something is good or fashionable and trendy. To those with autism it would mean that it's a bit cold. Many people with autism will have a straightforward and literal understanding of language. So don't ask a person with autism/Asperger's 'Does my bum look big in this?' unless you really want to know the truth.
- Many people with autism have problems using personal pronouns such as

Box 2.1. Case example

A person with autism, Vicky, in her mid-40s, had an appointment with a disability advisor at the local Job Centre Plus. Unfortunately, she went to the wrong office, there being two job centres in the town.

Vicky asked for directions from the member of staff who was acting as 'gate keeper'. This staff member pointed in a rather vague manner in a general direction. When Vicky asked her to be more specific, she complained that Vicky was shouting at her and that she was not there to be shouted at. Vicky apologised to her and left.

Vicky tried to find the appropriate job centre by following the directions but could not find it. She returned to the office wet and cold (it was snowing at the time) and repeated her request for directions. Again the 'gate keeper' replied by waving her finger in a very vague way, this time in a different direction. Vicky again tried to find the correct building but came back even more wet and frustrated, not having found it. By this time, Vicky was anxious as she was late for her appointment, and was nearly in tears due to frustration and anger.

She informed the 'gate keeper' that she had autism and needed very clear and precise verbal directions to the correct building and that vague finger pointing would not suffice. The 'gate keeper' replied that she should have had someone with her to help and that she should not have been out on her own.

Vicky left the building in tears of rage and frustration at having been treated in such an unprofessional and shoddy manner. All this member of staff had to say was, 'Turn right out of this building, cross the road, turn left and then right. Continue to the end of the road (the main dual carriageway will be facing you) and then turn right. The building you want will be on the right hand side about five minutes walk. It is also nearly opposite the police station.' Giving such simple directions seemed to be beyond her ability as was the use of correct and appropriate de-escalation techniques when working with anxious members of the public.

'me' and 'you'. Concepts such as 'now', 'later', less' and 'more' may also pose problems.

- Whilst it is acknowledged that the vast majority of human communication takes place on the 'non-verbal' level, such as gestures, facial expressions and tone of voice, many if not most people with autism would be unable to pick up and understand these. For example, non-verbal cues as to when the listener is bored, wants to change or end the conversation or dislikes the contents of the conversation would be missed.

- Some people with autism may be unable to speak or have very limited speech and whilst they may be able to understand what someone is saying to them may prefer to use other forms of communication such as sign language. Other people with autism may have good verbal communication skills but repeat either key words or phrases or the comments of others. This is known as 'echolalia'.

Social interaction

Socialising is not something that comes naturally – we have to learn it. I can stand up in front of hundreds of my nursing colleagues at RCN Congress and have no fear about addressing a particular agenda item at the podium/ microphone. However, place me at any of the Congress social events during the evening and I freeze. I just can't handle informal socialising, particularly in large groups.

People with autism often find interacting and socialising with others in any setting difficult as they may experience problems in recognising or understanding other people's emotions and feelings. They may also find it more difficult to express their own feelings appropriately. People with autism may:

- Not understand the unwritten social rules which most of us pick up without thinking.
- Stand too close to other people, thus invading the other person's 'personal space'.
- Start an inappropriate subject of conversation.
- Use strange facial expressions and gestures.
- Appear to be insensitive because they have not recognised how someone else is feeling.
- Prefer to spend time alone rather than seeking out the company of other people.
- Not seek comfort from other people.
- Appear to behave 'strangely' or 'inappropriately', as it is not always easy for them to express feelings, emotions or needs.

Many people who have autism find it hard to form friendships because of these difficulties in social interactions. Some may want to interact with others and make friends but do not know how to go about it. However, this is not to say that all those with autism are going to be lonely (although some will be) as many will be happy being on their own.

Imagination

People with autism have trouble working out what other people know, and have difficulty guessing what other people are thinking (theory of mind).

For most people, social imagination allows them to understand what other people know, think and even feel. Social imagination is part of what oils social interaction and social communication. It allows the person to predict the behaviour of others, make sense of abstract ideas, and to imagine situations outside the immediate daily routine. People with autism have trouble:

- Understanding and interpreting other people's thoughts, feelings and actions.
- Predicting what will, or could, happen next in any sequence of events or actions.
- Distinguishing between what is and is not real.
- Understanding the concept of danger.
- Engaging in imaginative play and activities, preferring set routines even when engaging in play or leisure activities.
- Preparing for change.
- Planning for the future.
- Coping in new and unfamiliar situations or settings.

However, difficulties with imagination do not mean a lack of imagination, as many artists, actors, writers and musicians have autism.

Asperger's syndrome

In many ways, Asperger's syndrome is very similar to autism as it, too, can be defined in terms of the 'autism triad'. However, people with Asperger's syndrome tend to have fewer problems with speaking and also tend to be of average to very high intelligence. They tend not to have the associated learning disabilities that may be linked to autism. However, some people with Asperger's syndrome may have forms of dyslexia, dyspraxia and attention deficit hyperactivity disorder (ADHD).

Communication

If you have Asperger's syndrome, understanding conversations is like trying to understand a foreign language. In addition to the communication difficulties faced by people with autism, those with Asperger's syndrome tend to:

- Experience difficulty understanding gestures, facial expression or tone of voice.
- Have difficulty knowing when to start and end a conversation and choosing topics to talk about.
- Use complex words and phrases but may not fully understand what these words and phrases mean.
- Be very literal in what they say and can have difficulty understanding jokes, metaphor and sarcasm.
- Process and retain verbal information.

Social interaction

People with Asperger's syndrome have difficulty picking up social cues, and difficulty knowing what to do when they get things wrong. In addition to the social interaction difficulties faced by people with autism, those with Asperger's syndrome tend to:

- Experience difficulties in making and maintaining friendships.
- Be unable to understand the unwritten social rules regarding many, most or perhaps all aspects of social interactions.
- Find other people unpredictable and confusing.
- Experience social withdrawal and isolation.
- Lack interest in other people which may lead them to appear to be rather aloof.
- Behave in ways that may appear to be inappropriate.
- Be able to cope with and manage unstructured parts of the day.
- Be able to work co-operatively with other people.

Imagination

People with Asperger's syndrome have trouble working out what other people know and have difficulty guessing what other people are thinking.

In addition to the imagination difficulties faced by people with autism, those with Asperger's syndrome tend to experience difficulties in:

- Imagining alternative outcomes to situations.
- Empathising with others.
- Transferring learning and learnt skills and abilities from one situation to another. For example, Jo may be an excellent swimmer at her local swimming baths but be totally unable to swim at another swimming bath a few miles down the road or at a seaside because they are not environments with which she is familiar.
- Predicting what will happen next.
- Understanding or interpreting other people's thoughts, feelings or actions. The subtle messages conveyed by facial expression and body language may often be missed.
- Using their imagination. They may have a limited range of imaginative activities which are pursued rigidly and repetitively (such as lining up toy cars).

Other related characteristics may include:

- A love of routines. Some people with Asperger's syndrome will become anxious if their routines are changed or disrupted in any way. Some need to have a fixed timetable that allows them to see and predict what will happen next during the day.
- Some people with Asperger's syndrome (and autism) will experience sensory difficulties which may include a dislike of being touched or held, or not liking particular sounds, colours, smells, tastes and textures. They may react to these stimuli in ways that may not seem appropriate.
- An intense, sometimes obsessive, interest or hobby which may be short-lived to be replaced with another intense interest or long-term and even life-long hobby or interest that could become a future job or career.

Yoshida's triad of impairment

However, Yoshida (2008) has a slightly different take on the autism and Asperger's 'triad of impairment'. She sees the triad in terms of 'advantages' and 'disadvantages' which includes the following:

Communication

Advantages:

- Pleasure in using words and conveying facts accurately.
- Interest in, and wide knowledge of, 'sophisticated and technical language'.
- A tendency to memorise facts and written texts.
- A sincere respect for language.
- A tendency to be highly diligent regarding use of language.

Disadvantages:

- Difficulty conveying one's own thoughts with words and a tendency to be misunderstood.
- A tendency to make one-sided, tedious or hard to understand conversation.
- Although hearing every word, a tendency not to be able to put the words together to form a coherent whole.
- Occasional bizarre misunderstanding of social conversations.
- A frequent inability to use or understand body language.
- A frequent tendency to be left out of conversation.

Social interaction

Advantages:

- Unique ideas that would never occur to people bound by 'common sense'.
- A strong inclination to take social rules seriously.
- A tendency to be un-biased or non-judgemental regarding other people.
- A strong sense of equality and social, political and economic justice.
- Loyalty to friends.
- A tendency to be kind and gentle.
- A determination to follow plans to completion.
- An ability to enjoy time spent alone.

Disadvantages:

- A lack of common sense.
- Trouble related to an inability to understand what other people may be thinking or feeling.
- Difficulty making friends and getting on with people.
- A tendency to be left out of social circles and activities despite trying hard to be liked.

Social imagination

Advantages:

- Having unique ideas that would never occur to other people.
- A tendency to have interests that are 'narrow and deep'.
- A great thirst for knowledge and research. An ability to get absorbed in reading texts that are of interest to them.
- An ability to accomplish goals in areas they enjoy.
- An appreciation of the value of following rules and procedures.
- An ability to go to and enjoy 'imaginary worlds' and use this for relaxation.

Disadvantages:

- Problems resulting from having to follow rules and routines.
- Trouble switching from one activity or thought to another.
- Difficulty generalising.
- A tendency to get upset when confronted with anything unplanned.
- Trouble predicting possible outcomes before engaging in activities.
- Trouble seeing the point of fiction writing or television.
- A tendency to get absorbed in their own 'fantasy world'.

As can be seen, some of the issues Yoshida mentions can be seen as an advantage or a disadvantage or both, depending on the context in which these characteristics are expressed.

In the scenario involving Vicky (*Box 2.1*) a number of traits in all three areas of communication, interaction and imagination came into play.

Key points

- Between 300 000 and 1 million people living in the UK have some form of autism.
- There are more females than males with an autism spectrum condition.
- Autism and Asperger's syndrome are life-long conditions.
- There are a number of well-known people who have some form of autism.
- Autism and Asperger's syndrome are very similar in terms of how they present.
- The major diagnostic and life issues around autism and Asperger's syndrome are social communication, social interaction with others, and social imagination.
- Many of these could be either an advantage or a disadvantage.

References

Asperger H (1938) Das psychisch abnorme kind. *Wiener Klinische Wochenschrift* **49**: 1–12

Attwood T (2006) *The Complete Guide to Asperger's Syndrome*. Jessica Kingsley Publishers, London

Aylott J (2010) Improving access to health and social care for people with autism. *Nursing Standard* **24**(27): 47–56

Baron-Cohen S (2005) The empathizing system: A revision of the 1994 model of the mindreading system. In B Ellis, D Bjprklund (eds) *Origins of the Social Mind*. Guilford, New York

Fitzgerald M (2004) *Autism and Creativity*. Brunner-Routledge, Hove

Lawson W (2008) *Concepts of Normality*. Jessica Kingsley Publishers, London

Morgan H (1996) *Adults with Autism*. Cambridge University Press, Cambridge

National Autistic Society (2011) Information for autism available from: http://www.nas.org.uk/nas/jsp/polopoly.jsp?d=211; for Asperger's syndrome: http://www.nas.org.uk/nas/jsp/polopoly.jsp?d=212

Wing L (1981) Asperger syndrome: A clinical account. *Psychological Medicine* **11**: 115–29

Yoshida Y (2008) *How to be Yourself in a World That's Different*. Jessica Kingsley Publishers, London

CHAPTER 3

A history of autism and autism spectrum conditions

Introduction and aims

Autism and Asperger's syndrome have a long history, although their existence has only been documented in the past 70 years, commencing with the work of Kanner (1943) and Asperger (1944). The aim of this chapter is to enable the reader to:

- Be able to track and have a basic knowledge of the history of autism and Asperger's syndrome.
- Have a basic knowledge of the development of ideas and philosophy associated with autism and Asperger's syndrome.

This chapter is divided into the following eras:

- Up to 1860
- 1860–1940
- 1940–1960
- 1960–1980
- 1980–1995
- 1995–2010
- 2010 and beyond.

Autism and Asperger's syndrome could be described as being on a journey of discovery that has by no means reached its end. The history of autism spectrum conditions is very similar to that of learning disability and mental health issues in relation to social thinking, legislation and Government policy. Some of this legislation is included here in order to provide a policy and legislative context.

Time line 1: Up to 1860

Autism, as an identifiable condition was unknown prior to about 1870. That is not to say, however, that autism spectrum conditions (ASCs) did not exist before

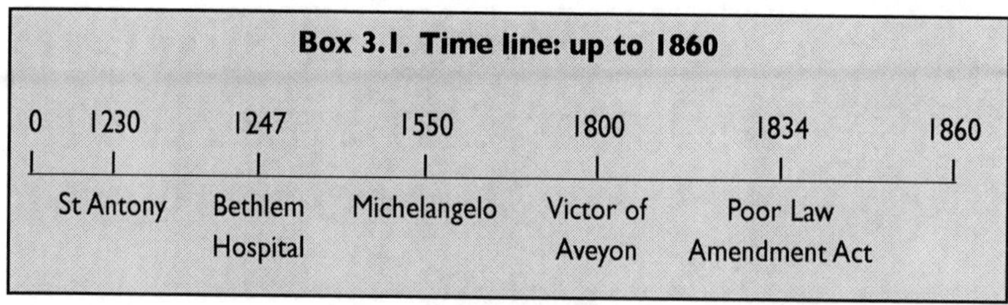

this date. It is highly probable that those who had autism or Asperger's syndrome would have been seen as 'possessed' or tried as witches or wizards (as evidenced by the Salem witch trials, which inspired Arthur Miller to write *The Crucible*). Medicine in the Middle Ages was largely based on superstition and it is highly likely that those with ASCs would have been seen as 'holy' or 'wise fools', either feted by the Church or locked up.

Those who could possibly have had autism or Asperger's syndrome, based on available archival records, include St Antony, an early Franciscan friar and contemporary of St Francis of Assisi, and the artist Michelangelo.

Michelangelo (1475–1564), considered to be one of the greatest artists of all time, could have had Asperger's syndrome or high-functioning autism (*Medical News Today* 2004). In terms of social interaction, Michelangelo was known to be 'aloof, a loner, and had few friends'. He apparently found it difficult to maintain social relationships. Although this was perceived at the time as a necessary condition to being able to create works of art, even when Michelangelo needed help on a project he always preferred to work independently. Michelangelo's failure to attend his brother's funeral underlined his 'inability to show emotion' and as a boy he was unsure about himself outside of his talent as an artist. In 1505, he wrote, 'Anything might happen to shatter my world'. Michelangelo was obsessed with work and controlling everything in his life – 'family, money, time and much else'. He was self-absorbed and gave his undivided attention to his masterpieces; a feature of autism. He was also obsessed with money and nudity and was so focused on his work that he toiled eight years over The Last Judgement. In terms of social communication, Michelangelo was noted 'not to be a great public speaker' and had difficulty holding up his end of a conversation, often walking away in the middle of an exchange.

In the last few years of the 18th Century, Victor of Aveyron (also known as the Wild Boy of Aveyron) (Autism Resources 2004) was a feral child who apparently lived his entire childhood naked and alone in the woods before being found wandering near Saint-Sernin-sur-Rance, France. He was captured and displayed in the town, but soon escaped and was periodically spotted between 1798 and 1799. However, on January 8, 1800, he emerged from the forests on his own. His age was unknown but citizens of the village estimated that he was about 12 years old. His lack of speech, as well as his food preferences and the numerous scars on his body, indicated that he had been in the wild for the majority of his life. Victor is thought to be the first documented example of a person with autism. However, it is unsure whether Victor was truly autistic or whether he displayed certain autism-like behaviour due to the environment in which he had lived.

Time line 2: 1860–1940

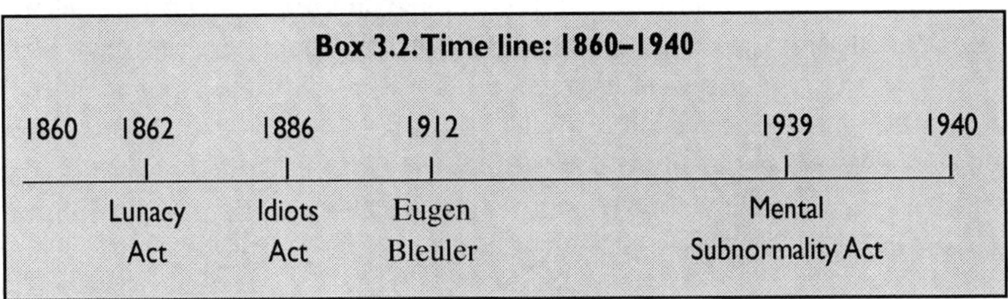

From the 1860s onwards there was a wide range of 'social legislation', including the Lunacy Act of 1862 and the Idiots Act of 1886 which, Gilbert (2009) suggests, would have affected most of those with an ASC. These Acts paved the way for the Victorian asylums which became home for many within society. These included those who had mental health problems and/or learning disabilities, unmarried mothers and, with the 'poor laws', the destitute and 'undeserving poor'. These asylums and 'colonies' survived until the 1990s.

Eugen Blueler (1857–1939) was a Swiss psychiatrist who invented the term 'schizophrenia' in 1908 and 'autism' in 1912 (Doctors Independent Network 2004). Originally, autism meant 'escape from reality' and nearly 30 years later Kanner borrowed Bleuler's term.

Apart from Bleuler's coining of the word 'autism', little else was recorded about autism conditions or their treatments. The only possible exception to this was the Mental Subnormality Act of 1939 which introduced such terms as retardation and subnormality into common language and understanding. These terms were legally defined, perhaps for the first time. As autism was not then recognised or accepted either as a concept or as a condition in the way it would later become, the history, treatment and fate of those with autism would have been very similar to those with a learning disability.

Time Line 3: 1940–1960

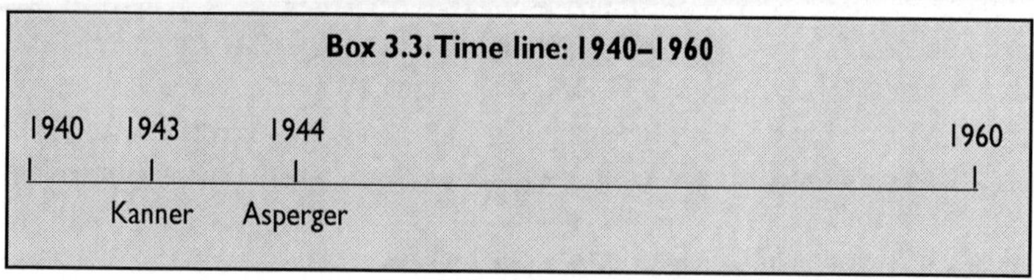

The 1940s to 1960s were dominated by two psychiatrists, one working in America and the other in Austria who, unknown to each other, described very similar phenomena.

Leo Kanner was a child psychologist working in Boston, USA who recognised an unusual pattern of behaviour in a number of children referred to his clinic. Kanner named the children's condition 'early infantile autism' and in 1943 published his findings (Kanner 1943). In the paper, Kanner gave detailed descriptions of the children's behaviour but selected certain features he felt were essential for diagnosis. These features included:

- *Extreme autistic aloneness*: the children failed to relate to other people normally and appeared to be happiest when left alone. This lack of social responsiveness appeared to Kanner to start very early in life.
- *Anxiously obsessive desire for the preservation of sameness*: the children were extremely upset by changes of routine or surroundings. A different route to school or a rearrangement of furniture, would cause a tantrum.
- *Excellent rote memory*: many of the children could memorise large amounts of material that seemed to have no practical use. This was seemingly out of line with their apparent learning difficulties in other respects.
- *Delayed echolalia*: the children tended to use repeated words and phrases they had heard, but failed to use words correctly and appropriately to communicate beyond their immediate needs.
- *Over-sensitivity to stimuli*: Kanner noticed that many of the children reacted strongly to certain noises or objects, such as elevators, vacuum cleaners, even the wind. Some also exhibited feeding problems or food fads.
- *Limitation in the variety of spontaneous activity*: this was shown in the children's repetitive movements, speech and interests. However, Kanner noted that the children often showed a good relation to objects, sometimes displaying surprising dexterity in spinning things or completing jigsaw puzzles.

- *Lack of speech*: some people with severe or profound autism may be 'pre-verbal' and thus unable to speak.

Before Kanner noticed and recorded this pattern of symptoms, such children would be classified as emotionally disturbed or learning disabled. Kanner observed that these children often demonstrated capabilities that showed they were not slow learners, yet they did not fit the patterns of emotionally disturbed children. Thus he invented a new category, which he called 'early infantile autism', which has since sometimes been called Kanner's syndrome.

Hans Asperger essentially made the same discoveries at the same time, independently of Kanner. Asperger's name is associated with one of the autism spectrum disorders in which there is no language delay, but significant social impairment, so the term Asperger's or Asperger syndrome is sometimes used to label autistic people who have speech. The two psychiatrists never met. Asperger (who published in German) and Kanner (who published in English) apparently knew nothing of each other, perhaps because of the absence of communication between the US and Austria prior to and during World War II. Asperger apparently did little work on the subject after his laboratory was destroyed by Allied bombing. This was unfortunate because he, much more than Kanner, believed that autism was a spectrum of disorders and it took another 35 years for this idea to take off in the US and the UK.

Time Line 4: 1960–1980

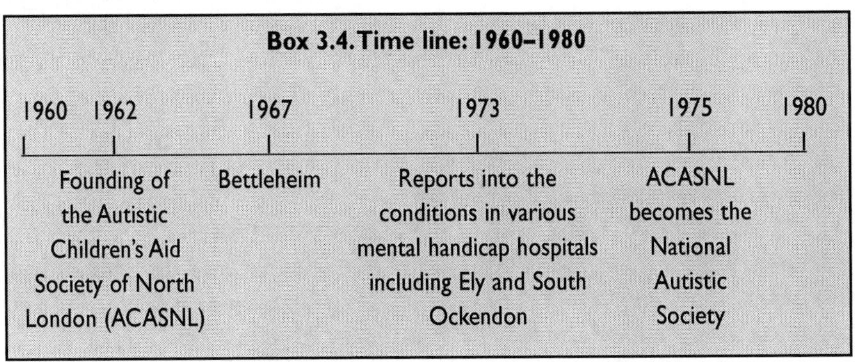

Box 3.4. Time line: 1960–1980

The Autistic Children's Aid Society of North London was founded on 23 January 1962 by parents of autistic children living in the area, with the assistance of a member from The Spastics Society (later Scope). The current name of the

National Autistic Society was adopted in 1975 when the charity extended its interest to the whole of the UK.

Bruno Bettelheim's work on autism has proven controversial. Initially Bettelheim believed that autism did not have an organic basis, but resulted when mothers withheld appropriate affection from their children and failed to make a good connection with them. The most extreme expression of this was the suggestion that mothers literally did not want their children to exist. Bettelheim also blamed absent or weak fathers. One of his most famous books, *The Empty Fortress* (Bettelheim 1967), contains a complex and detailed explanation of this dynamic in psychoanalytical and psychological terms. He derived his thinking from the qualitative investigation of clinical cases. He also related the world of autistic children to conditions in concentration camps. In *A Good Enough Parent* (Bettelheim 1987), he had come to the view that children had considerable resilience and that most parents could be 'good enough' to help their children make a good start.

Bettelheim subscribed to and became a prominent proponent of the 'refrigerator mother' theory of autism — the theory that autistic behaviours stem from the emotional frigidity of the child's mother — a view which enjoyed considerable influence into the 1960s and 1970s in the United States and elsewhere. This theory soon became the accepted explanation for autism in popular culture and, to a considerable extent, in professional circles. However, some indications suggest that he later changed his thinking.

Subsequently, medical research has provided greater understanding of the biological bases of autism and other conditions. Scientists have largely discredited Bettelheim's views on autism, although the 'refrigerator mother' theory still retains some supporters.

During the early 1970s, there were repeated calls from UK politicians to close down the old psychiatric and mental subnormality (as learning disabilities were then known) asylums and phase in what is now known as 'community care'. These calls resulted from a number of enquiries into allegations of poor care and abuse at certain mental subnormality hospitals including Ely in Cardiff in 1969, Farleigh in 1971 and South Ockendon Hospital in Essex in 1974. However, these calls for a possibly more humane form of care were largely ignored and the asylums and institutions were left open. Indeed, learning disabilities nurse training was still taking place at South Ockendon in the late 1980s and early 1990s.

At the same time as the existing hospital system was being discredited, the concept of 'normalisation' (Wolfensberger 1972) was being imported from Canada and indicated the direction of change in care philosophy and systems. Normalisation initially focused on the search for a new residential model to accommodate people living in the large hospitals. This included providing a more humane living environment, the end to dormitories and gender segregation, a more socially valued lifestyle and a physical presence in the local community.

Around the time that Wolfensberger was working on his theory of normalisation, within the UK the Department of Health and Social Security (DHSS 1971) was also working to improve the lives of those with a learning disability (which would also have included those on the autism spectrum, although those with autism would not have been seen as a separate category). The decade ended with the Jay Committee Report which recommended the ending of the mental subnormality nurse specialism to be replaced with a new care professional (DHSS 1979). Although this has yet to happen, the ending of learning disabilities as a nursing specialism is still a perennial favourite for debate as we enter the second decade of the 21st century.

Time Line 5: 1980–1995

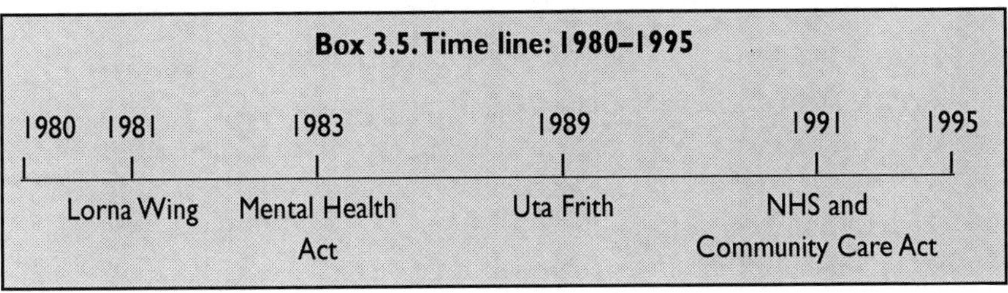

The new decade of the 1980s started with a right wing libertarian Government in the UK headed by Margaret Thatcher as Prime Minister. This coincided with an interesting combination of issues:

- Emerging user self-advocacy and empowerment movements such as 'People First' involving those with a learning disability, mental health and autism spectrum conditions.
- An emerging social model of care which suggested that handicap and disabilities were results of societal barriers and prejudices.
- 'Anti-professional' thinking by certain academics from both the political right and left, including the Austrian Catholic priest, Ivan Illich (see, for example, Illich 1974). Less State involvement in the lives of people was in vogue on both sides of the Atlantic.

During the 15 years between 1980 and 1995, a number of changes affected the lives of those with a learning disability or mental health issue. These changes included the 1983 Mental Health Act, the closure of the large learning disability and psychiatric hospitals, the growth in community care/care in the community and the 1991 NHS and Community Care Act. The debate into the future of learning disability nurses and nursing continued. These changes affected many of those with autism and Asperger's syndrome as they lived or were patients/service users in these old hospitals or were known to community mental health or learning disability teams. However, some people on the autism spectrum during this time (and since) would, almost certainly, have fallen through gaps in learning disability and mental health services since they saw themselves as having neither a learning disability nor a mental health issue. Thus the needs of such people would not have been recognised, assessed or met, sometimes with disastrous results for those concerned and their families.

This 15-year period also gave rise to the growth in two types of writers in the field of ASCs:

- 'Professional academics' including Lorna Wing, Uta Frith, Tony Attwood, Simon Baron-Cohen and Francesca Happe, most of whom were psychologists, with the exception of Wing who was a psychiatrist. Some of these academic psychologists were also parents of people with autism or Asperger's syndrome.
- Those with an ASC including Temple Grandin and Donna Williams, the latter having written a number of autobiographies including *Nobody Nowhere* (1992) and *Somebody Somewhere* (1994). These writers, perhaps even more than the professional academics, were to have an increasing influence on how autism and Asperger's syndrome was to be understood.

In 1981, Lorna Wing (a psychiatrist who had a daughter with autism) wrote a seminal paper which brought the work of Hans Asperger to a wider English-speaking readership (Wing 1981). One of the major points that Wing suggested was that autism was not a static, single condition but was a dynamic spectrum of conditions including 'Kanner's autism' and Asperger's syndrome. Indeed, it was Wing who first used the term 'Asperger's syndrome'. This seminal paper was to influence much of the debate around autism and Asperger's throughout the 1980s and beyond.

Time Line 6: 1995–2010

The years between 1995 and 2010 were characterised by legislation, Government White Papers and independent reports that focused on the lives

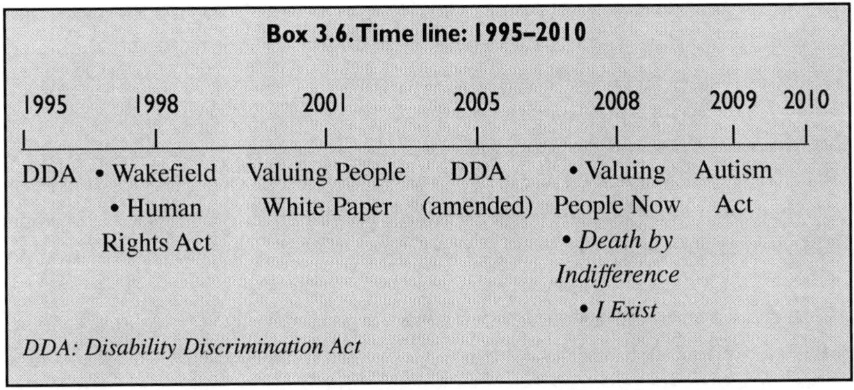

and needs of people with disabilities and which followed a 'New Labour' agenda. Whilst people with autism and Asperger's syndrome were not specifically mentioned nor their needs focused upon or met, the Disability Discrimination Act (DDA), the Human Rights Act, the Autism Act, and the Government White Paper, with its review and two reports, had both a direct and indirect impact on their lives. There was also a major controversy around the measles, mumps and rubella (MMR) vaccine and its possible link to autism.

The DDA (Department of Health 1995) defines disability, protects disabled people from discrimination and promotes civil rights. The DDA 1995 (and its amendments passed in 2005) aims to end the discrimination that many disabled people faced in most aspects of their lives including:

- Employment.
- Education.
- Access to goods, facilities and services, including larger private clubs and land-based transport services.
- Buying or renting land or property, including making it easier for disabled people to rent property and for tenants to make disability-related adaptations.
- The functions of public bodies, for example, issuing of licences.

The Act requires public bodies to promote equality of opportunity for disabled people. It also allows the Government to set minimum standards.

In 1998 the Human Rights Act was passed. It enshrines in UK law certain basic human rights. These include, amongst others, the right to life, the right to respect for private and family life, freedom of expression, the right to marry and to start a family, the right to an education and the right not to be discriminated against in respect of these rights and freedoms.

It was also in 1998 that the controversy around a possible link between the MMR vaccine and ASCs as proposed in *The Lancet* by Andrew Wakefield (Wakefield et al 1998). Wakefield et al's article resonated with the experiences of many parents of children and young people with autism and Asperger's syndrome but it also had a great many critics. The debate (which is still raging) focused on the research methodology, the sample and the sample size used by Wakefield in his study. Research ethics along with issues around parental choice and vaccine safety (both the MMR and vaccines in general) also featured. This debate resulted in the article being formally retracted in February 2010 and Wakefield being disciplined by the General Medical Council in April of the same year. However, Wakefield has become something of a folk hero for many parents of those with autism or Asperger's syndrome and he has promised to continue his research in the USA.

In 2001 *Valuing People* (Department of Health 2001) was published. This was the first White paper for decades to focus on the needs and lives of those with a learning disability. Those with autism are mentioned briefly but within the context of learning disabilities. What is important about *Valuing People* is the introduction of person-centred care and health action plans.

Two major reports were published in 2008. The first, *Death by Indifference* (Mencap 2008), highlighted the needless deaths of people with a learning disability while accessing acute general hospitals. This was as a result of a lack of knowledge and understanding of the needs of those with a learning disability on the part of nursing staff. *Death by Indifference* called for learning disability liaison nurses to be established in all acute general hospitals to act as advisors to ward staff. The second report, *I Exist* (National Autistic Society 2008), highlighted the problems and difficulties experienced by adults with autism and Asperger's syndrome. It led directly to the 2009 Autism Act and the 2010 Adults with Autism Strategy (Department of Health 2010).

The final year of this decade brought about a real change in the understanding of, attitudes to and way in which services are to be delivered to adults with autism and Asperger's syndrome. After years of campaigning, both Houses of Parliament debated and passed the Autism Bill, which became the Autism Act in 2009 (Department of Health 2009). A discussion of the history, contents and implementation of the 2009 Autism Act and its accompanying strategy for adults are discussed in *Chapter 19*.

Time Line 7: 2010 onwards

Box 3.7. Time line: 2010 onwards

2010

Autism Strategy for Adults

At last ASCs have come of age. It has taken a long time but there is a real acknowledgement of the varied needs and strengths of adults with autism and Asperger's syndrome in the form of a Government-sponsored strategy document that focuses on the needs of adults with these conditions. The strategy, *Fulfilling and Rewarding Lives* (Department of Health 2010) is the result of years of pressure and campaigning on the part of those with autism and Asperger's syndrome, their families and friends and those who support them, including the National Autistic Society. Much of the Strategy was informed by the consultation exercise sponsored by the Department of Health between September and October 2009 and engaged in by many both within and outside the 'autism world' including, the Royal College of Nursing.

The contents of *Fulfilling and Rewarding Lives,* which has a foreword by the Secretary of State for Health, includes:

- Executive summary.
- Explanation of terminology.
- Increasing awareness and understanding of autism.
- Developing a clear, consistent pathway for diagnosis of autism.
- Improving access for adults with autism to the services and support they need to live independently within the community.
- Helping adults with autism into work.
- Enabling local partners to develop relevant services for adults with autism to meet identified needs and priorities.
- The next steps.
- Summary of actions.
- List of policies that apply to adults with autism.

Since this chapter was written, the NAS has been asked by the Department of Health to develop an online resource for information regarding the Autism Strategy. This resource has been developed to support health and social care professionals in the implementation of the strategy.

Also, to monitor progress, the NAS launched a survey asking people to email their local authority in England to ask them what they are doing to implement the strategy and statutory guidance (NAS 2011). A number of local authorities have yet to inform the NAS as to their progress.

This strategy, follow up guidelines and subsequent evaluations, will be treated to a greater scrutiny in *Chapter 19*.

Conclusion

Those with autism and Asperger's syndrome have come a long since being considered witches and wizards in the Middle Ages. They are becoming part of 'mainstream' society; they have their own specific legislation and Government strategy and are highlighted in an increasing number of television programmes. This journey has included being:

- Lumped in with those with a learning disability and/or mental health problem despite not really fitting in, feeling comfortable or even accepted in either group.
- Seen as tortured geniuses.
- Made subject to mental health legislation that did not take into account their specific issues and needs.
- Seen as the result of poor or non-existent parenting.
- Subject to a eugenics agenda.
- Subject to or involved in changing attitudes on the part of politicians, health and social care providers and the general public.
- Involved in the user self-advocacy movement, partly through an increasing number of articulate people with autism spectrum conditions writing books on the subject.

The question here is whether we have finally arrived at a society that fully welcomes as equals those with autism or Asperger's syndrome. Or is the point we are at now just another stage in the development of understanding of the services for those with an autism spectrum condition?

Key points

- Although autism has only been recognised as a condition since the mid 1940s, it is likely that it has existed for hundreds of years.
- Much of the history of autism has been interlinked to the poor laws of the 19th century and the mental health laws of the late 19th and early 20th centuries.
- The history of autism since the 1940s have been dominated by the work of Kanner and Asperger.
- The last quarter of the 20th century saw a growth in support organisations such as the NAS and the user, self-advocacy and human rights movements. Published work about autism both by academics and those with an ASC 'exploded'.
- The first decade of the 21st century saw improved services for those on the autism spectrum who also have a learning disability through the Department of Health's *Valuing People*.
- Autism came of age with the Autism Act of 2009 and the Autism Strategy and Guidance of 2010.

References

Asperger H (1944) Die 'aunstisehen Psychopathen' im Kindesalter. *Archiv fur psychiatrie und Nervenkrankheiten* **117**: 76–136.

Autism Resorces (2004) *Autism FAQ and History*. Available from: http://www.autism-resources.com/autismfaq-hist.html [Last accessed 27 June 2010]

Bettelheim B (1967) *The Empty Fortress: Infantile autism and the birth of the self*. Free Press, New York

Bettelheim B (1987) *A Good Enough Parent: A Book on Child-Rearing*. Knopf Books, New York

Department of Health (1995) *Disability Discrimination Act*. Available from: http://www.direct.gov.uk/en/DisabledPeople/RightsAndObligations/DisabilityRights/DG_4001068 [Last accessed 31 May 2010]

Department of Health (2001) *Valuing People: A new strategy for learning disabilities for the 21st Century*. The Stationary Office, London

Department of Health (2009) *Autism Act*. The Stationary Office, London. Available from: www.opsi.gov.uk/acts/acts2009/pdf/ukpga_20090015_en.pdf [Last accessed

25 June 2009]

Department of Health (2010) *Fulfilling and Rewarding Lives: The strategy for adults with autism in England*. Available from: http://www.dh.gov.uk/prod_consum_dh/groups/dh_digitalassets/@dh/@en/@ps/documents/digitalasset/dh_113405.pdf [Last accessed 1 June 2010]

Department of Health and Social Security (1971) *Better Services for the Mentally Handicapped*. HMSO, London

Department of Health and Social Security (1979) *Report of the Committee of Enquiry into Mental Handicap Nursing and Care* (Report of committee chaired by Peggy Jay). HMSO, London

Doctors Independent Network (2004) *Autism 1836–1917*. Available from: http://www.din-web.org/dinweb/DINMuseum/Autism.asp [Last accessed 27-06-2010]

Gilbert T (2009) From the workhouse to citizenship: Four ages of learning disabilities. In: Jukes M (ed) *Learning Disability Nursing Practice*. Quay Books, London

Illich I (1974). *Medical Nemesis*. Calder & Boyars, London

Kanner L (1943) Autistic disturbances of affective contact. *Nervous Child* **2**, 217–50

Medical News Today (2004) *Was Michelangelo Autistic? asks the Royal Society of Medicine, UK*. Available from: http://www.medicalnewstoday.com/articles/8702.php [Last accessed 26 June 2010]

Mencap (2008) *Death by Indifference*. Available from: http://www.mencap.org.uk/document.asp?id=284 [Last accessed 15 June 2010]

Miller A (1953) *The Crucible*. Viking Press, London

National Autistic Society (2008) *I Exist: The message from adults with autism*. Available from: http://www.autism.org.uk/iexist [Last accessed 15 June 2010]

NAS (2011) Progress towards implementing Adult Autism Act 2009. Available from: http://www.autism.org.uk/en-GB/Get-involved/Campaign-for-change/Campaigning-by-issue/Adult-social-care/Adult-social-care-in-England/

Wakefield A, Murch S, Anthony A et al. (1998). Ileal-lymphoid-nodular hyperplasia, non-specific colitis, and pervasive developmental disorder in children. *Lancet* **351**(9103): 637–41.

Williams D (1992) *Nobody Nowhere: The extraordinary autobiography of an autistic*. Times Books, New York

Williams D (1994) *Somebody Somewhere*. Jessica Kingsley, London

Wing L (1981) Asperger syndrome: A clinical account. *Psychological Medicine* **11**: 115–29

Wolfensberger W (1972) *The Principle of Normalisation in Human Services*. National Institute of Mental Retardation, Toronto

CHAPTER 4

Causes of autism and Asperger's syndrome

Introduction

One question that is frequently asked by care professionals, parents, siblings and those with autism and Asperger's syndrome is, 'What causes autism and Asperger's syndrome?' The answer is that there is no answer. While this may seem to be a bit of a cop-out, actually no one knows for sure what the cause might be. Most 'experts' will say that autism is probably caused by a combination of genetic and environmental factors. Even here, there are endless debates and a certain amount of professional and philosophical infighting as to the precise causal mechanisms and the probable proportion or balance between genetics and environmental factors.

For many, including care professionals, academics, carers and service users, this causal uncertainty can be extremely frustrating for a whole host of reasons. This frustration is further exacerbated by a lingering feeling on the part of many parents and some care professionals that autism and Asperger's syndrome are caused by 'bad parenting'.

In order to try to provide not necessarily answers to these questions but the basis for informed debate this chapter considers the following issues:

- Autism as a quirk of nature.
- Autism due to bad parenting.
- Autism due to brain trauma.
- Possible areas of the brain affected in those with an autism spectrum condition (ASC).
- Autism caused by vaccine damage.
- Autism caused by genetic traits.
- Genetic counselling and testing.

By the end of the chapter the reader will be able to:

- Understand the various possible causes of autism and Asperger's syndrome.
- Weigh up the merits and demerits of each possible cause.
- Have enough basic information regarding each possible cause to be able to contribute to discussions and debates around ASCs and their causes.

- Have enough basic information regarding each possible cause to be able to reassure parents, siblings and service users.

Idiopathic origin

Idiopathic simply means that a disease, illness, or genetic or health condition is of unknown origin; nobody knows for sure what causes it or where it came from. Idiopathic conditions are those that are self-originated or self-generated. The term is used primarily in medicine, meaning arising spontaneously or from an obscure or unknown cause. It comes from the Greek words 'idios' (one's own) and 'pathos' (suffering) and means approximately 'suffering originating from one's own' or 'a disease of its own kind'.

A root cause cannot always be established for a medical condition, however, as medical and scientific advances are made, the percentage of conditions designated as idiopathic shrinks.

The term 'idiopathic', however, could be considered to conceal ignorance; in the American television drama, *House*, the title character remarks that it means, 'We're idiots, because we don't know what's causing it.'

Thus, autism and Asperger's syndrome generate or originate themselves. They are effectively 'quirks of nature'; the unforeseen outcomes of the subtle and complex interplay between genetic and environmental forces, the 'next stage in human evolution' and, regardless of the amount of debate and the plethora of published journal articles and books, no-one knows what causes them. However, just because many autism and Asperger's syndrome researchers and professionals believe that there may be no known cause does not mean that there are no causes or possible contributory factors. An acceptance of the 'no known causes' position does not excuse us from engaging in the search for a possible and proven cause of autism and Asperger's.

Refrigerator mothers

The term 'refrigerator mother' originated in the 1940s when Leo Kanner used it as a label for mothers of children diagnosed with autism. These mothers were often blamed for their children's behaviour, which included rigid rituals, difficulties in speaking, and self-isolation. In his 1943 article that first identified autism, Kanner called attention to what appeared to him to be a lack of warmth among the fathers and mothers of autistic children. In 1949, Kanner suggested autism may be related to a 'genuine lack of maternal warmth'. He noted that fathers rarely stepped down to indulge in children's play, and observed that children were exposed 'from the beginning to parental coldness, obsessiveness, and a mechanical type of attention to material needs only.... They were left neatly in refrigerators which did not defrost. Their withdrawal seemed to be an act of turning away from such a situation to seek comfort in solitude' (Kanner 1949). In a 1960 interview, Kanner bluntly described parents of autistic children as 'just happening to defrost enough to produce a child' (Kanner 1960).

The label was based on the assumption, now discredited among most, although not all, healthcare professionals, that autistic behaviours stem from the emotional frigidity of the child's mother. As a result, many mothers of children on the autistic spectrum suffered from blame, guilt, and self-doubt from the 1950s to the 1970s and beyond, when the prevailing medical belief that autism resulted from inadequate parenting was widely assumed to be correct. Some care professionals continue to maintain that autism is a result of poor parenting. Others point out that some conditions are psychological in origin rather than physiological, but that this is not necessarily a reflection on parenting skills. It is interesting to note that the term is 'refrigerator mother' and not 'refrigerator father'. Whilst it could be argued that this is due to the possibility that mothers are more involved with the development of their child than many fathers, this could also be due to a possible misalignment of power. It is historically easier to blame certain categories of people for social and health problems on the strength of unequal power relationships and dynamics.

Brain trauma

Lorna Wing (1981) noted that some of the people she was diagnosing with autism and Asperger's syndrome also had a common history of problems during pregnancy and before, during and after birth. Some of these problems may have caused or contributed to 'brain damage' or 'dysfunction'. Wing's original findings have subsequently been confirmed by other studies. Cederlund and Gillberg (2004) suggest that problems throughout pregnancy were identified in as many as 31% of children with Asperger's syndrome and problems during and immediately after birth were identified in as many as 60% of children with developmental issues, including those with Asperger's. However, no single problem or condition during pregnancy has been associated with developmental delays or the later development of signs of Asperger's or autism. Neither was it known whether or not autism or Asperger's syndrome pre-existed within the developing foetus prior to any brain trauma or damage due to problems or health conditions during pregnancy and childbirth. Babies born pre-term to older mothers and who were smaller than they should be for their gestational age were also seen to be susceptible to the later development of autism and Asperger's.

Maternal consumption of alcohol and other recreational drugs during pregnancy give rise to health conditions in the unborn child including foetal alcohol syndrome. These could cause brain injuries in the foetus which could, in turn, affect how the baby's brain develops and could contribute to developmental problems, including autism and Asperger's syndrome.

It may well be correct to suggest that problems during pregnancy and in the perinatal period could contribute to the later development of autism and Asperger's syndrome due to brain trauma. However, caution must be exercised so as not to blame the parents for any subsequent developmental delays and disability in their children as they are probably already feeling guilty. Causing guilt through blame and accusation is not helpful and may serve only to further alienate and isolate an already potentially vulnerable family.

Brain areas affected

There are a number of possible areas of the brain that could be associated with autism and Asperger's syndrome. These have been identified through the use of brain imaging studies involving both individuals on the autism spectrum and 'neuro-typicals'. These studies can, according to Attwood (2006), identify the structures and systems that operate together to form the 'social brain' and whether any of these areas function differently in those with an ASC. The areas of the brain that appear to be implicated in Asperger's syndrome and autism are the frontal and temporal regions of the cortex; more specifically, the medial pre-frontal and orbito-frontal areas of the frontal lobes, the superior temporal sulcus, inferior basal temporal cortex and temporal poles of the temporal lobes. There is also evidence of dysfunction of the amygdala, the basal ganglia and the cerebellum (Frith 2004, Gowen and Miall 2005, Toal et al 2005).

According to Welchew et al (2005), it is suggested that there may be a weak connectivity between many if not all of these component brain areas. There is also some evidence (Gunter et al 2002) to suggest damage in the right hemisphere cortical area and an 'abnormality' in the dopamine system (Nieminen-von Wendt et al 2004).

Neurological research that examines brain function, according to Attwood (2006), demonstrates a consistency with the psychological, emotional and behavioural profile of Asperger's and autism. Such research also shows which areas of the human brain are 'wired differently' in people with an autism condition.

Environmental causes

Vaccines

Two theories link autism and vaccines. The first theory suggests that the MMR vaccine, which may cause intestinal problems, could also lead to the development of autism. The second theory suggests that a mercury-based preservative called ethylmercury, used in some vaccines, could be connected. Nearly all of the leading health organisations maintain that there is no relationship between vaccines and autism. Yet many parents are convinced that they (particularly the MMR vaccine) are a cause, and doubts about their safety linger in their minds. How did this controversy get started, and why is it still such a concern?

The scientific consensus is that no credible evidence links the MMR vaccine to autism, and that the vaccine's benefits greatly outweigh its risks. The controversy led to a sharp drop in vaccination rates in the UK and Ireland, which led to an increased incidence of measles and mumps, which in turn resulted in a small number of deaths and some severe and permanent disabilities in children.

Claims of a connection between the vaccine and autism were raised in a 1998 paper in the respected British medical journal *The Lancet* (Wakefield et al 1998). In 2009, *The Sunday Times* reported that Wakefield had manipulated patient data and misreported results in his article, creating the appearance of a link with autism (Deer 2009). A special court convened in the United States to review claims under the National Vaccine Injury Compensation Program ruled on February 12, 2009 that parents of autistic children are not entitled to compensation in their contention that certain vaccines caused autism in their children (CNN 2009). *The Lancet* (2010) fully retracted the 1998 paper on February 2, 2010.

Despite this, there are still a large number of families within the UK who have sought legal advice with a view to taking action against the manufacturers of the MMR. There appears to be anecdotal suggestions that nurses who support parents' rights to choose not to have their children vaccinated with the MMR vaccine are openly criticised by their nursing colleagues.

Mercury poisoning

For decades, ethylmercury (a form of mercury that is highly neurotoxic) was used extensively as a preservative and anti-bacteriological agent in medical products ranging from vaccines to topical ointments. It appears that in the US thimerosal (an ethylmercury compound used in vaccines) did not undergo adequate testing with regard to its safety.

A number of largely American research studies into the use of ethylmercury and thimerosal seem to demonstrate that there is a link between their use and the rise in the incidence of autism. At the same time that the incidence of autism was growing, the number of childhood vaccines containing thimerosal was also growing, increasing the amount of ethylmercury to which infants were exposed threefold.

Research by Geier and Geier (2003) has shown strong epidemiological evidence for a causal relationship between thimerosal and neurodevelopmental disorders in children. However, despite the growing body of research, drug safety authorities in America appeared to act remarkably slowly to advise the removal of ethylmercury/thimerosal from vaccines, taking around 18 years from the first warnings and signs of problems to act. The actions taken to remove thimerosal in 1999 were not sufficiently aggressive and the compound still remains in several vaccines. With the addition of the influenza vaccine now being recommended for infants, children are exposed to more of the compound today than ever before. For more information about the American use of mercury in vaccines visit www.safeminds.org.

Whilst the above relates to the US, a similar debate has been quietly raging within the UK around the use of mercury as a preservative in childhood vaccines. Indeed, during a recent workshop on autism held in Birmingham, a contributor who herself has autism suggested that the rancorous debate around the 'link' between the MMR vaccine and autism is false; the real debate should be around the use of mercury in vaccines and its possible link with autism, since the characteristics of mercury poisoning and both autism and Asperger's syndrome are almost identical.

Genetic causes

Evolution

A website, Scienceagogo.com, poses a number of interesting questions: What is the difference between a genetic abnormality and genetic evolution? Is the human body's adaptability responsible for many of the conditions that we call mental disorders? This website suggests that researchers concede that the scientific world is still in the dark about the causes of autism and Asperger's syndrome, but they also concede that autism and Asperger's are most likely genetically oriented. Is it possible that in certain conditions that we call 'disorders', we are witnessing evolution at work?

Another website, a-shade-of-grey.blogspot.com, suggests that genetic mutations are the drivers of evolution. They can be caused by copying errors during cell division, exposure to environmental factors (e.g. radiation, chemicals, viruses), or occur naturally during meiosis (the process of dividing a diploid cell, i.e. with two sets of chromosomes, into four haploid cells, e.g. sperm or ovum, each with one half of the chromosomes of the original cell). Most mutations have no significant effect, and the changes are reverted via DNA repair before they become permanent. Those that affect the organism become subject to the rules of natural variation (for beneficial and deleterious mutations) or genetic drift (neutral variations). Autism may be in part the result of regularly occurring genetic mutation.

Such ideas are not confined to occasional obscure websites; Attwood (2006) suggested that Asperger's syndrome and autism are the next stage in human development and evolution and Fitzgerald (2004) also appears to support this when he suggests that the debate could be argued to revolve around the idea of an autism spectrum *dis*order versus an autism spectrum *re*-order. Since autism and Asperger's syndrome may involve significant areas of the brain being connected and wired differently to those in the 'non-autistic' or 'neuro-typical' population, this amounts to an evolutionary 're-ordering' of the brain. It could be this evolutionary re-ordering that produces musical, artistic, mathematical or scientific geniuses.

Family traits

Much research into the possibility that autism, Asperger's syndrome and related conditions could be passed on from parent to child has been carried out over the years since Kanner and Asperger formulated and presented autism to the world in the 1940s. Asperger noticed that some of the children with whom he was working appeared to share some of the personality and behavioural characteristics of their parents, particularly their fathers. Asperger thought that such sharing of 'autism characteristics' was due to genetics, to inherited genes, rather than the environment in which the family lived (Attwood 2006). Hobson (1995) suggested that in monozygotic twins if one twin has an ASC or Asperger's syndrome, then the other twin is likely to have the same or similar condition.

Attwood (2006) also found that 20% of fathers and 5% of mothers of children with Asperger's had the syndrome themselves, although many of these parents had not had a formal diagnosis for themselves (Volkmar et al 1998). Including the wider family, such as uncles, aunts and cousins, almost 66% of children with Asperger's had a family relative with the same condition (Volkmar et al 1998). Attwood (2006) suggests that family members who exhibit characteristics of Asperger's syndrome or high functioning autism may have inherited the characteristics that could contribute towards having a successful career in the arts, mathematics, engineering, computing, physics and accountancy.

Genetic testing

Genetic testing is the use of a variety of tests on blood and other body fluids to determine the presence or otherwise of certain conditions within the individual's DNA. One such test is amniocentesis, which involves the withdrawal of amniotic fluid from the uterus, and is used to diagnose chromosomal conditions within the foetus. With the use of these tests during pregnancy, it is possible that around 100 separate health conditions within the foetus can be diagnosed. At the moment, there are no genetic tests available to determine the presence or otherwise of autism or Asperger's syndrome in the unborn child. Nevertheless, that is not to say that at some point in the future there will not be.

However, the following should be taken into account when debating the use of genetic testing for ASCs. Over 90% of those who know that their unborn child has Down's syndrome opt for an abortion (Ward 2001). Even relatively minor conditions such as cleft palate and hair lip are seen by some as grounds for abortion. The Abortion Act 1967 states:

> *it will not be unlawful... if there is substantial risk that if the child were born it would suffer from such physical or mental abnormalities as to be seriously handicapped.*

Genetic testing for autism and Asperger's raises the following questions:

- Will those parents who choose not to abort their foetus be discriminated against by medical, nursing, health, social and educational care professionals?
- Is there a link between genetic testing and eugenics?
- Do we as healthcare professionals and as part of society welcome and value diversity, even if that diversity comes in the shape of a disability?
- What does this say about the society in which we live?

As Fitzgerald (2004) somewhat bluntly suggested, genetic testing for autism and Asperger's syndrome could be seen as an example of 'castrate or conform', i.e. if parents do not conform to the underlying eugenics agenda allegedly underpinning genetic testing then the balance of the human stock could be threatened and the parents 'forced' to undergo an abortion.

Genetic counselling

Genetic counselling can stir up a hornets' nest of feelings and emotions. In a positive sense, genetic counselling is merely one way of providing accurate and unbiased information about a healthcare condition, in this case autism or Asperger's syndrome, to those who may be at risk of having a child with such a condition. As such, genetic counselling is a 'value neutral' term or process that

Box 4.1. Genetic counselling case studies

- A couple with a daughter with autism comes into your GP clinic. They tell you that they are considering having another child and ask what are the risks of having another son or daughter with autism or Asperger's syndrome.
- You meet a couple during an outpatient gynaecology clinic. You know this couple as they attend the same Catholic church as you. and you know that the wife has a brother who has Asperger's syndrome. They tell you that they are going to start a family and want to know what the possibility is of having a child with autism or Asperger's syndrome.
- A single mother who has a teenage daughter with high functioning autism asks you how she should present information to her daughter about the possibility of her having a child with an autism spectrum condition.
- A couple, one of whom has autism, approaches you during a routine health promotion session at your local health centre where you work. The non-autistic partner asks you for information and advice around the possibility of having a son or daughter with an autism spectrum condition.
- A young lady who has high functioning autism approaches you during an autism support group meeting that you are facilitating. She informs you that she and her partner would like to have a baby and asks for your advice.
- A young man whose parents both have Asperger's syndrome approaches you during a health screening session at your local health centre and asks about the possibility of him having a child with an autism spectrum condition.

is used to enable adults to decide whether or not to start or continue a family based on this information and their own particular set of circumstances and world view. Peate and Fearns (2006) suggest that whilst genetic testing and counselling may be able to determine the likelihood of having a child with a particular set of characteristics, it cannot be held responsible for how disability and personal characteristics are valued within society or within the family.

People with autism or Asperger's syndrome, their siblings or children may well want to know the possibility of themselves having a child with these conditions. These are legitimate issues that will have to be faced. Likewise, if a parent already has a child with an ASC, they may well want to know what the likelihood is of them having another similarly affected child. Some people may value having a child with a disability, whilst others may not. Consider the case studies in *Box 4.1*.

- How would you approach these different people?
- What information would you give them?
- Do you consider that each of the people in the case studies have the same information and advice needs? If yes, why? If not, why not?
- Do you consider that you would give the same information in the same way to each of the people in the case studies? If yes, why? If not, why not?

Conclusion

On the plus side, interest in and funding for autism research is on the rise, so new and better information about the possible causes of autism and Asperger's syndrome should be forthcoming over the next few years. However, as this chapter has tried to show, there is no one single cause but rather a wide range of possible 'suspects' that could be contributory, including no known cause and both environmental and genetic factors.

The link between autism spectrum disorders and environmental pollution such as radiation from mobile telephone transmitter masts and from domestic and industrial pollutants is tenuous. Further research to prove or disprove any such links will be both interesting and useful.

The reality is that ASCs are likely to be caused by a very complex and subtle interplay between genetics and the environment. To 'champion' one side over the other is too simplistic and may lead to inaccurate and inappropriate information, support and help being made available to people with the condition. The 'nurture versus nature' debate has been applied to a wide range of issues, such as intelligence, personality, learning disability, mental health and certain physical health conditions including cancers, diabetes, and hypertension. It could be that the discussion around the causes of autism and Asperger's syndrome is little more than a continuation of this ongoing and wide-reaching debate.

Some may argue that such debate is meaningless and pointless and the province of academics and they may well be right. However, it could also be argued that gaining a greater knowledge and understanding of the subject will help support those with an autism spectrum condition and their families.

Key points

- There is no single, known, proven cause of autism spectrum conditions.
- However, there are a number of contributory factors.
- Contributory factors include autism as an idiopathic condition, the now discredited 'refrigerator mother', vaccine damage, mercury poisoning and genetic inheritance.
- Whilst there are no genetic tests available to determine autism conditions *in utero*, this does not mean that at some point there won't be any.
- Caution needs to be exercised in the use of any future genetic testing due to the historical connection between genetics, genetic testing and eugenics.
- Likewise, although genetic counselling can be viewed as giving 'value neutral' information to parents, siblings and people with autism spectrum conditions, caution must be exercised to prevent such information promoting a eugenics agenda.

References

a-shade-of-grey.blogspot.com (2010) http://a-shade-of-grey.blogspot.com/2006/04/autism-genetics-and-evolution_19.html [Last accessed 29 April 2010)

Attwood T (2006) *The Complete Guide to Asperger's Syndrome*. Jessica Kingsley Publishers, London

Cederlund M, Gillberg C (2004) One hundred males with Asperger's syndrome: A clinical study of background and associated factors. *Developmental Medicine and Child Neurology* **46**: 652–661

CNN (2009) *Vaccine didn't cause autism, court rules*. Available from: http://www.cnn.com/2009/HEALTH/02/11/autism.vaccines/ [Last accessed: 04 May 2010]

Deer B (2009) MMR doctor Andrew Wakefield fixed data on autism. *Sunday Times*, **Feb 8**.

Fitzgerald M (2004) *Autism and Creativity*. Hove, UK, Brunner-Routledge

Frith U (2004) Emanuel Miller Lecture: Confusions and controversies about Asperger syndrome. *Journal of Child Psychology and Psychiatry* **45**: 672–86

Geier M, Geier D (2003) Thimerosal in childhood vaccines, neurodevelopment disorders, and heart disease in the United States. *Journal of American Physicians and Surgeons* **8**(1): 6–11

Gowen E, Miall C (2005) Behavioural aspects of cerebellar function in adults with Asperger syndrome. *Cerebellum* **4**: 279–89

Gunter H, Ghaziuddin M, Ellis H (2002) Asperger syndrome tests of right hemisphere functioning and interhemisphere communication. *Journal of Autism and Developmental Disorders* **32**: 263–81

Hobson RP (1995) *Autism and the Development of Mind*. Lawrence Erlbaum Associates, Hove, UK

Kanner L (1943) Autistic disturbances of affective contact. Nervous Child 2: 217–50. Reprinted in Kanner L (1968) Autistic disturbances of affective contact. *Acta Paedopsychiatrica* **35**(4): 100–36

Kanner L (1949) Problems of nosology and psychodynamics in early childhood autism. *American Journal of Orthopsychiatry* **19**(3): 416–26

Kanner L (1960) *The child is father*. Time 25 July. Available from: http://www.time.com/time/magazine/article/0,9171,826528,00.html. [Last accessed 11 April 2010]

Lancet (2010) Retraction—Ileal-lymphoid-nodular hyperplasia, non-specific colitis, and pervasive developmental disorder in children. *Lancet* **375**: 9713; 445

Nieminen-von Wendt T, Metsahonkala I, Kulomaki T, Aalto S, Autti T, Vanhala et al (2004) Increased pre-synaptic dopamine function in Asperger syndrome. *Classical Neuroscience and Neuropathology* **15**: 757–60

Peate I, Fearns D (2006) *Caring for People With Learning Disabilities*. John Wiley, Chichester

Scienceagogo.com (2010) http://www.scienceagogo.com/news/autism_evolution.shtml [Last accessed 26 April 2010]

Toal F, Murphy D, Murphy R (2005) Autistic spectrum disorders: Lessons from neuroimaging. *British Journal of Psychiatry* **187**: 395–7

Volkmar F, Klin A, Pauls D (1998) Nosological and genetic aspects of Asperger syndrome. *Journal of Autism and Developmental Disorders* **28**: 457–63

Wakefield A, Murch S, Anthony A et al. (1998) Ileal-lymphoid-nodular hyperplasia, non-specific colitis, and pervasive developmental disorder in children. *Lancet* **351**(9103): 637–41

Ward I (2001) *Considered Choices? The new genetics, prenatal testing and people with learning disabilities*. BILD Publications, Kidderminster

Welchew D, Ashwin C, Berkouk K, Salvador R, Suckling J, Baron-Cohen S, Bullmore R (2005) Functional disconnectivity of the medial temporal lobe in Asperger's syndrome. *Biological Psychiatry* **37**: 991–8

Wing L (1981) Asperger's syndrome: A clinical account. *Psychological Medicine* **11**: 115–30

CHAPTER 5

Diagnostic issues

By the end of this chapter the reader will have acquired a basic knowledge and understanding of the following issues:

- The meaning of the term 'diagnosis'.
- The reasons why some people will want to seek a diagnosis.
- How to seek a diagnosis.
- The criteria used to reach a diagnosis.
- Diagnosis or a label?
- Whether or not to disclose a diagnosis.

What is a diagnosis?

The diagnosis of any condition, is, according to the 1997 edition of *Bailliere's Nurses Dictionary,* 'a determination or an identification of the nature of a disease reached at through the identification and study of signs and symptoms'. As far as this short definition goes, it is simple, fair and accurate enough. However, whilst the 'study of signs and symptoms' should not cause a problem, the word 'disease' may well do. To take one simple example: pregnancy. Pregnancy has many clear signs and symptoms and thus can be clearly determined, diagnosed and identified as a human life condition that may or may not require specific healthcare input. However, is pregnancy a disease? If it is not, can pregnancy ever be truly 'diagnosed'?

Again, according to *Bailliere's Nurses Dictionary* a disease has a definite pathological process. The word 'process' could be argued to imply that in autism and Asperger's syndrome there is a clear pathway from causation to signs and symptoms to cessation. Whilst, again, 'causation and signs and symptoms' should not pose a major intellectual problem, cessation does as this implies that there is a cure for autism and Asperger's syndrome. This is actually not the case, although that is not to say that at some future point there will not be.

When one uses the language of diagnosis and disease in relation to autism and Asperger's syndrome a number of issues are raised. The diagnosis of autism can be based on the occurrence and severity of the behaviours mentioned in *Chapter 2*. However, three other issues are implicit in the word 'disease': prognosis, curability and infectiousness, and these can cause problems as all arguably stem from a medical rather than a social model of disability. Use of a medical model can affect the understanding of the nature of the autistic condition, the person affected, the support offered by healthcare professionals and issues around power. Such problems may not be constructive for either the person with an autism spectrum condition (ASC) or the healthcare professional. This debate around the use of language will be covered in more depth in *Chapter 21*.

Why seek a diagnosis?

> *We sought a diagnosis for our son so that we could access the support he needed to help us manage his behaviour. We did not wish to label him.*
>
> Parent 'A'

There can be a wide number of reasons why someone may seek a diagnosis of autism or Asperger's syndrome. Some of these reasons may be personal to the individual seeking a diagnosis. Understanding of the self and behaviour by both the individual and others features largely amongst these reasons according to Attwood (2006). A formal diagnosis will allow for that 'eureka' moment of understanding: 'So that is why I behave as I do, that is why I am how I am. I'm not mad after all!'. Self-knowledge and understanding are powerful drivers in anyone's life, particularly when there are issues of why a person is how he or she is in terms of behaviour and life experiences.

A formal diagnosis allows for a validation of the person and his or her life experience and gives credibility to that person. Thus, someone with an ASC may not feel validated without such a diagnosis. This raises the question of whether a formal diagnosis should act as a gateway to a person being or feeling validated. Is it right that the only way a person can feel validated is through engaging in the power structure and relationship implied by the diagnostic procedure and outcome? However, with a sense of validation often comes a sense of coming home, a sense of belonging, whereas before receiving a diagnosis a person may have spent years as an emotional and spiritual 'nomad', not really fitting in or belonging anywhere or with anyone. Therefore, a diagnosis of autism may bring about a sense of peace and rest. Often those with an ASC may have been aware that they have spent years 'marching to the sound of a different drum'; with a formal diagnosis comes an understanding of why. A diagnosis allows people with an ASC to 'plan' the next stage of their life journey with a bit more self-knowledge and confidence: they may know where they want to go, why, how they are going to get there, and with whom.

A diagnosis may bring about recognition and understanding by others of the problems and difficulties associated with autism and Asperger's syndrome. As a result of this recognition and understanding, strategies of support and help can be offered to those with an ASC and their families by health, education and social care professionals. For example, teachers of children and young people with an ASC may be able to provide 'tailor made' learning strategies to enable them to progress in their academic studies without adversely affecting other pupils or students. Such help and support may be of huge benefit to families, including spouses and partners as well as siblings and parents, as problems associated with communication and interaction can often be minimised and corrected. Having a child with an ASC may motivate one or both parents to seek a diagnosis for themselves, and the 'neuro-typical' partner, who may have spent years working alone trying to understand and help their ASC partner, may be able to access appropriate support.

How to seek a diagnosis

There are a number of ways in which a person can seek and receive a diagnosis. These may differ depending on whether the person seeking the diagnosis is a child or an adult. The reasons a diagnosis is sought will be different for healthcare professionals, such as nurses; parents of young children or adolescents; teachers; and adults who suspect that they may themselves have an autism condition. For example, a teacher or parent may notice that the pupil, student, son or daughter may be exhibiting certain patterns of behaviour, such as sensory sensitivity to certain noises, smells, tastes or touch, or their social communication and interaction may be interfering with their development. Again, a diagnosis of autism or Asperger's syndrome in another family member, or an increased exposure to knowledge about autism conditions through the media, may prompt a thoughtful questioning of whether a child or young adult may be affected. In adults, ongoing problems with employment and relationships may lead them to question whether they may have an autism condition.

The most appropriate care professional to approach in order to seek a diagnosis varies depending on whether it is a child or an adult who is the subject of the potential referral. For a child who is at school, a referral may be made by the teaching staff to the local educational psychologist who will make an assessment. If concerns are raised by the parents of a child or young person regarding the child's behaviour then the care professional to consult would be the family's GP who would make the appropriate referral to a specially trained psychologist or psychiatrist. Likewise, if an adult seeks a diagnosis the usual first port of call would be the GP. GPs are unlikely to possess the necessary knowledge and ability to perform the diagnostic tests with the level of accuracy needed to arrive at a diagnosis and would probably make an appropriate referral. If a nurse or healthcare assistant notices behaviour suggestive of autism or Asperger's syndrome in a hospital inpatient, a discussion could be held with the hospital's clinical psychologist or psychiatrist for advice and support.

However, in all of this, three points need to be borne in mind. The first is that, in adults with a possible autism condition, there are few psychologists or psychiatrists with the specific, in-depth knowledge, skills and abilities to be able to make a formal diagnosis with any degree of accuracy. However, the number of suitably experienced and qualified clinicians is increasing. Second, since diagnostic tests carry a significant cost implication, if carried out properly, funding may not be available to make 'out of geographic area' referrals. Although money is now supposed to follow the patient, the reality is that this rarely happens. Those who hold the purse strings may deny an 'out of county' choice of diagnostician on the grounds of cost and maintain that there may be clinicians available locally who could diagnose. In some cases, this may well be true, but not in all.

In all cases where a patient or service user is suspected of having an autism condition, their consent must be gained before making a referral for diagnosis. Not to do so could be construed as an invasion of the individual's privacy, and possibly even amount to emotional or psychological assault. Where the person is a child then consent must be obtained from the child's parents.

For details of the pathway to my own diagnosis see my discussions with Zoe and Jo in *Chapter 6.*

Diagnostic methods

A wide range of diagnostic tools is available in order to gain a diagnosis of autism or Asperger's syndrome. There are, for example, different diagnostic tools for use with children and adults, males and females and even different tools for diagnosing the same condition in the same gender and age group. Different clinicians favour different diagnostic tools which can lead to different diagnostic decisions being arrived at when presented with exactly the same set of signs, behaviour and experiences. The use of different diagnostic tools could also lead to inaccuracies in the reporting of prevalence rates for autism and Asperger's syndrome within the UK population, thereby influencing the debate about prevalence.

The various diagnostic tools for Asperger's syndrome include the following:

- Australian Scale for Asperger's Syndrome (Garnett and Attwood 1998).
- Asperger Syndrome Diagnostic Interview (Gillberg et al 2001).
- Asperger Syndrome Diagnostic Scale (Myles et al 2001).
- Autism Spectrum Screening Questionnaire (Elhers et al 1999).
- Childhood Asperger Syndrome Test (Scott et al 2002, Williams et al 2005).
- Gilliam Asperger Disorder Scale (Gilliam 2002).
- Krug Asperger's Disorder Index (Krug and Arick 2002).

The following may be of use in diagnosing adults with Asperger's syndrome:

- Autism Spectrum Quotient (Baron-Cohen et al 2001a, Woodbury Smith et al 2005).
- Empathy Quotient (Baron-Cohen and Wheelwright 2004).
- Reading the Mind in the Eyes Test (Baron-Cohen et al 2001b).
- Reading the Mind in the Voice Test (Rutherford et al 2002).
- Friendship Questionnaire (Baron-Cohen and Wheelwright 2003).
- Autism Spectrum Disorders in Adults Screening Questionnaire (Nylander and Gillberg 2001).

Two diagnostic tools are used specifically for children with autism:

- Autism Diagnostic Interview – Revised (Lord et al 1994).
- Autism Diagnostic Observation Schedule – Generic (Lord et al 2000).

The diagnostic criteria for Asperger's disorder according to Gillberg (1991) and DSM-IV (American Psychiatric Association 2000) are shown in *Boxes 5.1 and 5.2.* Although only excerpts are given in the boxes, it can be seen that there are both similarities and subtle differences between the two. These differences may give different diagnostic results with consequences for the person seeking a diagnosis.

It is recommended, if not crucial, that the formal diagnosis of autism or Asperger's syndrome in children is made by a clinician who has extensive experience with, or specialises in, ASCs, such as a paediatric neurologist, a developmental paediatrician, a child psychologist or child psychiatrist. It is also vital that the diagnosis of autism or Asperger's syndrome in adults is carried out by a clinician such as a psychiatrist or psychologist who is highly experienced, skilled in and knowledgeable about autism in adults. The way that autism and Asperger's syndrome become manifest or express themselves is subtly different in

Box 5.1. Extract from Gillberg's diagnostic criteria (Gillberg 1991)

Social impairment: the person will present with at least two of the following:

- Difficulties interacting with peers and other people.
- Indifference to the contact offered by peers and other people.
- Difficulties interpreting social cues.
- Socially and emotionally inappropriate behaviour.

Narrow interests (at least one of the following):

- Exclusion of other activities.
- Repetitive adherence to specific interests or routines.
- Activities engaged in more by rote than with real understanding and meaning.

Compulsive need for introducing routines and interests (at least one of the following):

- Which affects every aspect of the individual's everyday life.
- Which affects others.

Box 5.2. DSM-IV diagnostic criteria

A total of six (or more) items from (1), (2), and (3), with at least two from (1), and one each from (2) and (3), with onset prior to age 3 years:

(1) Qualitative impairment in social interaction (at least two of the following):
- Marked impairment in the use of multiple non-verbal behaviours such as eye-to-eye gaze, facial expression, body posture and gestures to regulate social interactions.
- Failure to develop peer relationships appropriate to developmental level.
- A lack of spontaneous seeking to share enjoyment, interests or achievements with other people (e.g. by a lack of showing, bringing or pointing out objects of interest to other people).
- Lack of social or emotional reciprocity (note: this could include the following as examples: not actively participating in simple social play or games, preferring solitary activities, or involving others in activities only as tools or 'mechanical' aids).

(2) Qualitative impairments in communication as manifested by at least one of the following:

- Delay in, or total lack of, the development of spoken language (not accompanied by an attempt to compensate through alternative modes of communication such as gesture or mime).
- In individuals with adequate speech, marked impairment in the ability to initiate or sustain a conversation with others.
- Stereotyped and repetitive use of language or idiosyncratic language
- Lack of varied, spontaneous make-believe play or social imitative play appropriate to developmental level.

3. Restricted repetitive and stereotyped patterns of behaviour, interests and activities (at least one of the following):
   - Encompassing pre-occupation with one or more stereotyped and restricted patterns of interests that is abnormal either in intensity or focus.
   - Apparently inflexible adherence to specific, non-functional routines or rituals
   - Stereotyped and repetitive motor mannerisms (e.g. hand or finger flapping or twisting or complex whole body movements).
   - Persistent preoccupation with parts of objects.

(4) The disturbance causes clinically significant impairment in social, occupational, or other important areas of functioning.

(5) There is no clinically significant general delay in language (e.g. single words used by age two years, communicative phrases used by age three years).

(6) There is no clinically significant delay in cognitive development or in the development of age-appropriate self-help skills, adaptive behaviour (other than in social interaction), and curiosity about the environment in childhood.

(7) Criteria are not met for another specific pervasive developmental disorder, Rett's or schizophrenia.

children and adults, possibly because adults are more able than children to 'hide' the more obvious signs of autism. Thus, the diagnostic tools used for children with an ASC will be different to those used for adults.

When using any diagnostic tool it is imperative that you approach and treat the individual as a unique human being: a 'one size fits all' approach should not be used; this only serves to dehumanise all those concerned in the diagnostic procedure. Secondly, diagnosis of a person must not be based on a tick chart mentality but should be lingered over. It should consist of a variety of assessment techniques including observation, thorough and in-depth history taking, talking to the family, including parents, siblings and spouses/partners, as well as carrying out batteries of tests.

Thirdly, regardless of the test used, it is vital it is used with thought, intelligence and care as the outcome of the diagnostic procedure may have far reaching implications for the individual being investigated and his or her family. Lastly, regardless of the outcome of the diagnostic procedure, it is imperative for appropriate counselling and support to be offered to the person and his or her family. They must not be left in limbo as this is unfair, potentially harmful and unprofessional.

Changes in diagnostic criteria

In February 2010, the American Psychiatric Association (APA) released a draft of possible revisions to the Diagnostic and Statistical Manual of Mental Disorders (DSM). The APA plans to revise the category of Pervasive Developmental Disorder, simplifying the criteria and removing the distinctive divisions. With this revision, there will no longer be a diagnosis of Asperger's syndrome. All individuals who meet the criteria will be given a diagnosis of Autism Spectrum Disorder. The reasoning for these changes is to create a more consistent diagnosis. A spectrum-type diagnosis may solve the problems of inconsistency and will also eliminate the need to diagnose an individual based on the severity of the condition.

There are a number of advantages and disadvantages to the proposed changes. The advantages include:

- More services could be available for all levels of ability. Many services require a diagnosis of classic autism which excludes mildly affected individuals.
- All related health problems could be recognised and treated. People with autism spectrum disorder often suffer anxiety, gastrointestinal problems, seizures and sensory integration dysfunction, along with autism.

The disadvantages include:

- Some people feel that milder cases of autism spectrum disorder, those normally diagnosed as pervasive developmental disorder not otherwise specified (PDD-NOS) or Asperger's syndrome, are more likely to be missed or not to qualify for the new autism spectrum disorder diagnosis.
- Some people believe that the less affected individuals will not want the stigma of autism placed on them. Asperger's syndrome carries a more neutral connotation than autism.
- To people affected by Asperger's, the diagnosis is part of who they are, and changing that to autism may cause anxiety.

- Many people with Asperger's are comfortable with, and even embracing of, their diagnosis. It can even give a sense of identity and pride. To take this away and just 'lump' people in the much broader autistic spectrum category could be damaging.

A diagnosis or a label?

> *We sought a diagnosis for our son so that we could access the support needed to help us manage his behaviour, we did not wish to label him.*
>
> Parent 'A'

One of the reasons why a person may not wish to pursue a diagnosis of autism or Asperger's syndrome is that he or she may not want to be burdened with a label. The question here is does a diagnosis have to become a label? If it does, does the label have to be negative?

On the one hand, having a diagnostic label could lead to the person being treated as part of a homogenous group devoid of individuality. In this way having a label of autism or Asperger's could lead to a 'one size fits all' approach to support, treatment and care that is based on a stereotyped and false understanding of what autism is and how to approach a person with autism or Asperger's syndrome. This could lead to poor care. A label could also lead to stigma, discrimination and isolation due to the devaluing power structures inherent in the labelling process.

On the other hand, Lawson (2008) positively welcomes her label of Asperger's syndrome and uses it to inform other people about Asperger's and autism. Lawson suggests that a diagnosis as label defines who she is. This is interesting as she does not say that it defines what she is but who she is. Lawson further suggests that when food shopping, we buy according to what is printed on the food label. In the same way, human 'labelling' means that 'what you see is what you get'. This, Lawson believes, can only be positive. However, she also suggests that individuals who are autistic and those who are 'neuro-typical' should welcome and celebrate their differences. This debate continues in *Chapter 21*.

To disclose or not to disclose

There are many reasons why, having received a diagnosis of autism or Asperger's syndrome, people may wish to disclose or not disclose this diagnosis. The decision can be highly personal and may be arrived at through a great deal of 'soul searching'.

A major reason that people give for disclosing their autism diagnosis is to elicit information, support and understanding from those around them. Such support and understanding could be from friends, family, teachers/lecturers or employers. It may be necessary to disclose the diagnosis in order to access services and support from autism-specific organisations or to gain entrance to and acceptance by the autism sub-culture or 'tribe'. Finally, some people may disclose their diagnosis so as to enable teaching or healthcare staff to access information that would be vital to the provision and delivery of appropriate support packages. However, should it be necessary to disclose a diagnosis and risk the negative reactions of those around simply to obtain appropriate support? Should the provision and delivery of appropriate support and appropriately tailored care be conditional upon disclosure? Would it be ethical and professional for care staff to withhold appropriate information or care if an autism diagnosis was not disclosed?

This leads on to possible reasons why some people who are diagnosed with an ASC do not disclose their diagnosis. First of all, a person's choice to disclose or not to disclose *must* be respected; he or she *must not* be bullied or coerced into disclosing his or her diagnosis. Such bullying is inappropriate and unprofessional.

Some people, both children and adults, with an ASC feel that by disclosing their diagnosis they are giving bullies the opportunity to pick on them. Others feel that they will be ridiculed and ostracised for being different, or that they will be discriminated against by teachers, lecturers or potential or actual employers (see *Box 5.3*). Some people who are recently diagnosed may feel that disclosing their condition will lead to a lower expectation of their abilities on the part of friends, families, teachers, lecturers and employers.

Whatever the person with an ASC chooses to do, whether it be to disclose or not, an uncertainty regarding when, how, why, what and to whom the disclosure is to be made will often be encountered and careful and wise counsel will likely be needed.

On a lighter note, one adult who had received a diagnosis of Asperger's syndrome had a 'coming out' party to celebrate whilst another had a tee-shirt specially designed to celebrate her diagnosis. Both welcomed and embraced their autism status in a public manner. The next chapter covers some of the same territory as this chapter but from a highly personal perspective.

Box 5.3. Disclosure: Case example

A middle-aged healthcare worker, 'B', disclosed to a potential employer his recently acquired Asperger's diagnosis during a job interview. The person who interviewed him informed his new manager of his diagnosis without gaining his consent. This manager informed her deputy of B's diagnosis, again without his consent. 'B' felt his trust had been violated and that he was coerced into disclosing his diagnosis and status to one of his new colleagues who then compounded B's social and communication vulnerability by encouraging him to engage in conversations that were inappropriate and less than professional.

A subsequent disciplinary hearing led to B's dismissal. B felt that he had been discriminated against by his employer who cited as a reason for his dismissal that he posed a threat to the well-being of the service users and the staff team. The disciplinary panel chair also stated that the employing organisation did not have the resources needed to support him. This from an organisation that works with service users with autism.

Key points

- The reasons why people want to seek a diagnosis of autism spectrum conditions are varied and complex.
- Likewise, people will have different views as to whether or not to disclose that they have autism or Asperger's. These differing views *must* be respected.
- There are a number of possible routes to take and care professionals to consult in order to obtain a diagnosis.
- These care professionals include specialist nurses, psychologists, psychiatrists, GP's and teachers.
- There are a number of different tools that can be used to diagnose autism spectrum conditions in both children and adults.
- These tools focus on subtly different aspects of the 'triad of autism impairments'.

References

American Psychiatric Association (2000) *Diagnostic and Statistical Manual of Mental Disorders, 4th edition*. American Psychiatric Association, Washington, DC

Attwood T (2006) *The Complete Guide to Asperger's Syndrome*. Jessica Kingsley Publishers, London

Baron-Cohen S, Wheelwright S (2003) The Friendship Questionnaire: An investigation of adults with Asperger syndrome or high functioning autism and normal sex differences. *Journal of Autism and Developmental Disorders* **33**: 509–18

Baron-Cohen S, Wheelwright S (2004) The empathy quotient: An investigation of adults with Asperger syndrome or high functioning autism and normal sex differences. *Journal of Autism and Developmental Disorders* **34**: 163–75

Baron-Cohen S, Wheelwright S, Hill J, Raste Y, Plumb I (2001a) The 'Reading the Mind in the Eyes' Test, revised version: A study with normal adults with Asperger syndrome or high functioning autism. *Journal of Child Psychology and Psychiatry* **42**: 241–51

Baron-Cohen S, Wheelwright S, Skinner R, Martin J, Clubley E (2001b) The autism Spectrum Quotient (AQ): Evidence from Asperger syndrome/high functioning autism, males and females, scientists and mathematicians. *Journal of Autism and Developmental Disorders* **31**: 5–17

Elhers S, Gillberg C, Wing L (1999) A screening questionnaire for Asperger's syndrome and other high-functioning autism spectrum disorders in school age children. *Journal of Autism and Developmental Disorders* **29**: 129–41

Garnett M, Attwood T (1998) *The Australian Scale for Asperger's syndrome. In T Attwood: Asperger's Syndrome: A Guide for Parents and Professionals*. Jessica Kingsley Publishers, London

Gillberg C (1991) Clinical and neurobiological aspects of Asperger syndrome in six family studies. In U. Frith (ed) *Autism and Asperger Syndrome*. Cambridge University Press, Cambridge

Gillberg C, Gillberg C, Rastam M, Wentz E (2001) The Asperger Syndrome (and high-functioning autism) Diagnostic Interview: A preliminary study of a new structured clinical interview. *Autism* **5**: 57–66

Gilliam J (2002) *GLADS. Examiners Manual*. PRO-ED, Austin, TX

Krug D, Arick J (2002) *Krug Asperger's Disorder Index*. PRO-ED, Austin, TX

Lawson W (2008) *Concepts of Normality*. Jessica Kingsley Publishers, London

Lord C, Risi S, Lambrecht L, Cook E, Levanthal B, Dilavore F, Pickles A,Rutter M (2000) The Autism Diagnostic Observation Schedule – Generic: A standard measure of social and communication deficits associated with the spectrum of autism. *Journal of Autism and Developmental Disorders* **30**: 205–23

Lord C, Rutter M, Le Couteur (1994) Autism Diagnostic Interview – Revised: A revised version of a diagnostic interview for caregivers of individuals with possible pervasive developmental disorders. *Journal of Autism and Developmental Disorders* **24**: 659–85

Myles B, Bock S, Simpson B (2001) *Asperger Syndrome Diagnostic Scale Examination Manual*. PRO-ED, Austin, TX

Nylander L, Gillberg C (2001) Screening for autism spectrum disorders in adult psychiatric out-patients. *Acta Psychiatria Scandinavica* **103**: 428–34

Rutherford M, Baron-Cohen S, Wheelwright S (2002) Reading the Mind in the Voice: A study with normal adults and adults with Asperger syndrome and high functioning autism. *Journal of Autism and Developmental Disorders* **32**: 189–94

Scott F, Baron-Cohen S, Bolton P, Brayne C (2002) The CAST (Childhood Asperger Syndrome Test): Preliminary development of a UK screen for mainstream primary-school-age children. *Autism* **6**: 9–31

Williams J, Scott F, Stott C, Allison C, Bolton P, Baron-Cohen S, Brayne C (2005) The CAST (Childhood Asperger Syndrome Test): Test accuracy. *Autism* **9**: 45–68

Woodbury-Smith M, Robinson J, Wheelwright S, Baron-Cohen S (2005) Screening adults for Asperger Syndrome using the AQ: A preliminary study of its diagnostic validity in clinical practice. *Journal of Autism and Developmental Disorders* **35**: 331–5

CHAPTER 6

Diagnosis: A personal journey

This chapter discusses a diagnosis of Asperger's syndrome/high functioning autism from a personal perspective through conversations between the author and two friends about diary entries written by the author during 2008.

Zoe: Hi. I'm Zoe and I'm a healthcare assistant within a learning disability service and have known Chris for around 14 years as both a colleague and a friend. I am rather intrigued by the notion of this conversation and rather flattered to be asked to take part in it. So, Chris, can you tell me how and why you thought that you may have autism?

Chris: Well, around the mid-90s I began work on a learning disability residential unit that focused specifically on autism. During my time at this home I decided to commence a Masters degree in autism as I believed that the service users deserved to have staff with an in-depth knowledge of the condition. I was awarded my Master of Education degree in December 2001.

Zoe: Did you start to think at this point that you may have autism?

Chris: Well, actually no! It took a few years for a growing awareness that I may have autism to sneak up on me. Around 2004 I was reviewing books for a number of nursing journals. One of these books was *High Functioning Autism and Creativity* by Michael Fitzgerald of Dublin University. As I read the first two chapters of Fitzgerald's book the penny dropped and aspects of my own life started to fall into place like jigsaw pieces, and finally made sense.

Zoe: What do you mean, 'the penny dropped'?

Chris: Without going into too much personal detail, I finally realised why I had issues in a whole host of areas since early childhood. These include my relationships and interactions with family, colleagues and friends, why I had problems with 'multi-tasking', why I had the occasional problem when dealing with events and incidents that disrupted my established routines. I had always been a 'loner', preferring my own company to that of others and I never really felt as though I fitted in or belonged anywhere and I began to understand why.

Zoe: How did this growing awareness translate into a diagnosis?

Chris: Having completed my review of the Fitzgerald book, I asked my GP to refer me for a diagnosis and was sent to our local psychiatric hospital. What was funny about this diagnostic process was that it took place at the same hospital I was working at on an agency basis as a registered nurse.

Zoe: That was weird! How did you deal with this?

Chris: Beyond accepting the irony and even weirdness of the situation, I just got on with it. Anyway, after a series of sessions with a clinical psychologist who administered a whole battery of diagnostic tests, he informed me that I did not match the criteria for autism or Asperger's and was discharged.

Zoe: How did that make you feel?

Chris: Surprisingly, disappointed, even gutted. You see, I had so accepted the possibility that I may have an ASD [autism spectrum disorder] that the judgement of the clinical psychologist left me rather deflated and empty. I felt that I had not truly been listened to, heard, understood or validated.

Zoe: Did the psychologist suggest or offer an alternative reason for your observations and did he offer you any support or guidance after his judgement?

Chris: No and no. That hurt at the time and even now it still rankles. Such a lack of support and guidance on the part of the psychologist was possibly both unwise and even unprofessional.

Zoe: What did you do next? I'm assuming that you did not, could not, let it go.

Chris: Well, my sessions with this psychologist took place throughout 2005 and, yes, you are right, I could not let it go. I tried, however, to put the idea, the feeling that I did have autism or Asperger's on the back burner for the next two and a half years and got on with life. The possibility that I may have an ASD resurfaced on a number of occasions throughout this time, however, and around the end of 2007 I felt that I had to try and obtain a second opinion. I contacted a former colleague who was a consultant psychiatrist but he declined to see me on the grounds that he was no longer taking on private diagnostic work. I contacted Autism West Midlands and the National Autistic Society for advice and I also searched the internet for potential clinicians with expertise in diagnosing adults with autism and/or Asperger's. I spoke to my GP again and explained that I wanted a second opinion and suggested a clinician who may have the expertise needed to diagnose accurately. He stated that he had to obtain permission from the local PCT as there were financial issues to take into account, the clinician in question being based at Leicester.

Zoe: Was the PCT helpful or sympathetic?

Chris: Not exactly, no! I was rather brusquely informed by the PCT to go away and choose a clinician within the area.

Zoe: I thought that in today's healthcare market, the money followed the patient. I thought that the patient as consumer was 'king' and that he or she could choose where they were treated, even if where they chose was outside of the PCT's geographical and thus funding area.

Chris: So did I. Apparently, the rhetoric of consumer choice is just that: rhetoric. Consumer choice does not exist in reality. The reality was that the PCT as 'purse string holder' was 'king' and dictated where I could be diagnosed. The PCT also made it clear that any psychiatrist had the necessary knowledge and skills needed to arrive at a correct diagnosis, regardless of what that diagnosis may be.

Zoe: Is that true?

Chris: At this point, I would like to swear but it would be unprintable! The short answer is *no*! I would hazard a guess that those medical doctors who wanted to pursue a career in psychiatry would have had some training around autism. However, I would also hazard a guess that such autism input in psychiatric training would have been fairly basic and certainly not of a sufficient depth to accurately diagnose autism in adults. Remember that diagnostic tools used with adults are not the same as those used with children.

Zoe: I know. So, what else did you do, what else could you do?

Chris: Well, I did have the support of my GP who admitted to me that he knew very little about the subject and that because of my professional, personal and academic backgrounds I probably knew more about autism and Asperger's than he did. I attended an autism social event around December 2007 during which the name of a particular local psychiatrist was mentioned in the course of a general conversation between myself and the event host. During February and March 2008 I held long debates with myself over the pros and cons of seeking a diagnosis.

Zoe: Yes, I looked at these [see *Boxes 6.1 and 6.2*]. There are a number of issues that I wanted to discuss with you regarding these pros and cons. I must admit, many do appear to be somewhat pompous. Fear of the reactions of others and cowardice I can understand as they are linked. However, whilst fear of others' reactions is legitimate, that fear does not make you a coward, at least not in my eyes.

Chris: Maybe not, yet surely to be a coward involves not doing something out of fear?

Zoe: Not necessarily. Not to do something out of fear could be a sign of both a

Box 6.1. Diary entry: 9th February 2008
Reasons against seeking a diagnosis

- Cowardice.
- Fear of the reactions, my own and others, if I am diagnosed with an ASD/Autism/Asperger's.
- Fear and disappointment if I do not receive a diagnosis of ASD/ autism/ Asperger's.
- Loss of 'outsider' status.

Box 6.2. Diary entry: 9th February 2008
Reasons for seeking a diagnosis

- To legitimise my personal 'life story', experiences and events.
- To legitimise my own personality, characteristics, how I behave, how I feel, how I think.
- To legitimise my often publicly and privately repeated claim to have and be Asperger's.
- Insofar as I have always felt to be an 'outsider' and that those with autism/ASD/Asperger's are generally 'outsiders' and 'misfits', would I lose any outsider status I may have if I don't seek a diagnosis?
- Being reasonably well-educated and articulate I could use my diagnosis to advocate for others who may be less articulate than me.
- To use a diagnosis to advocate, campaign and agitate for change in how those with autism/ASD/Asperger's are understood, approached and treated, to agitate, campaign and advocate for better services.

healthy survival instinct and a desire not to be hurt by either the outcomes or people's reactions to them. Fear is a normal reaction to the unknown, not a sign of cowardice. What did you mean by your fear of not receiving a diagnosis?

Chris: Having already been through a previous diagnostic assessment, I was afraid that any belief that I had in myself and my life experiences would be invalidated if I was to go through another diagnostic assessment that proved either inconclusive or that I did not have an ASD. This would cause me much pain and it was this that I was afraid of.

Zoe: What did you mean by 'loss of outsider status', and isn't this a tiny bit pretentious?

Chris: Well, yes it is rather pretentious, for which I apologise. However, by 'outsider' I meant that as a 'non- or self-diagnosed autistic' I could not access any autism-specific services. Indeed, when I contacted Autism West Midlands for assistance I was informed that unless I had a formal diagnosis they could not offer me any services or support as they were not mandated or funded to provide such support to those who were 'undiagnosed' or 'self-diagnosed'. This was in direct contrast to the letter that I had earlier received from my PCT which stated that such support and services were available.

Zoe: So, someone was being less than honest and even lying to you?

Chris: So it would appear! Anyway, not having a 'formal diagnosis' allowed me to a certain extent to be a sort of representative to and for others in a similar position to myself and to do so from outside of the 'autism establishment'. I felt that if I was to receive a formal diagnosis then I could no longer represent others who had not received a diagnosis.

Zoe: In your 'reasons for seeking a diagnosis' [*Box 6.2*] you again highlight the perceived legitimacy that you felt regarding yourself and your life experiences. Can you explain this to me?

Chris: If I did not seek a diagnosis then the validity of my perceptions and interpretations of my life experiences would be called into question. In a sense, I was damned if I did seek a diagnosis and damned if I didn't. Either way, how I perceived and saw myself could be damaged if not destroyed if I made the wrong decision. To seek and receive a diagnosis would allow me to accept, to confirm what I had always felt: that I was an 'outsider'. There would be a valid reason for me feeling that I did not 'fit in', either at work or socially.

Zoe: You also mention that one of the reasons for seeking a diagnosis is that you could use your diagnosis to advocate on behalf of others. Can you explain why you believe that you have a right to do so, which is what I think you are implying?

Chris: First of all, I don't have a right to advocate for anyone except for myself. I have a right to be in control and assert that control in relation to myself. I apologise if I inadvertently gave the impression that I would set myself up as some sort of autism 'guru'. Having said that, it could be suggested that 'autism gurus' do exist in the guise of academics who have little personal experience of what it is really like to be autistic, to be Asperger's. Historically, change has always been achieved through someone or a small group of people who had the guts and the anger to make change happen. The disability advocacy and gay rights movements are examples of this. I see no problem in using a diagnosis to enable me to legitimately engage in the political and ideological battle around autism.

Zoe: All right, you can get down from your soap box now, Chris!

Chris: Sorry!

Zoe: Your diary entries for the 5th and 13th October 2008 I can understand, as

Box 6.3. Diary entry: 5th October 2008

Meeting with RBF (psychiatrist): Having 'psyched myself up' about the meeting, she was late and I was getting nervous and agitated. She had already cancelled the previous meeting a fortnight ago and verbally re-arranged, promising to follow up this re-arrangement with an appointment letter, which never arrived. When she eventually did arrive, she appeared not to be aware of the possible negative effects this communication lapse may have on me. She asked me a lot of questions about my past and present, particularly around my 'mental state' (depression). Before she left, I asked RBF if she thought that I had Asperger's syndrome to which she replied, 'Yes'.

Box 6.4. Diary entry 13th October 2008

Letter from RBF arrived. I was less than happy with the negative slant that she had put on my 'mental state/behaviour', suggesting that I had 'attention seeking tendencies'.

you speak of the need for predictability and your frustration when RBF cancelled on you and did not confirm the verbally re-arranged meeting with you.

Chris: Thanks, Zoe! Yes, the need for predictability is a major issue for those with an ASD. Likewise, RBF did not forewarn me that she was looking at me as someone who was 'attention seeking'. That hurt and I felt it was unnecessary, particularly as, coming from a learning disability/mental health nursing background, I was aware of the possible implications of labelling someone as 'attention seeking'.

Chris: I would like to briefly introduce Jo at this stage of the conversation. Welcome Jo.

Jo: I used to work in the same building as Chris for a while. I have experienced mental health problems and periods within psychiatric units myself on an 'informal basis'.

Chris: You may remember that a while ago, during a training workshop on the Mental Capacity Act that we attended, I mentioned that there was a possibility that I may be Asperger's and that I was seeking a diagnosis. If I remember correctly, you were surprised that I was seeking this diagnosis. Could you explain why?

Box 6.5. Diary entry: 15th October 2008

Attended a training course at work on the Mental Capacity Act (2006). Talked to colleague who had enduring mental health problems about diagnosis. She was surprised that I was seeking a diagnosis of ASD. I replied that a diagnosis would validate me, my life and experiences. Her stance was that a diagnosis leads to labelling, a labelling which, in turn, leads to discrimination.

Jo: Well, I always link diagnosis with a label. Once diagnosed, you are labelled, and labelled as deviant. At least, that has always been my experience. When I was diagnosed and labelled as having mental health problems, and several times since, I felt that the medical and nursing professions discriminated against me. I lost my human dignity, my human rights and my human autonomy, not because of my mental health problems but because of the way that care professionals labelled and thus treated me as a result of me experiencing mental health issues. I have also observed such negative consequences of labelling many times in other people who have had similar mental health problems to myself. One has only to look at the often sub-standard nursing and medical care that people with a learning disability, for example, receive in acute general hospitals because of care professionals' labelling and lack of understanding of learning disabilities. Before anyone denies this is the case, read the Mencap report *Death by Indifference*. Will you as an 'emerging Asperger's' fair any better?

Chris: I am aware that, since the debate around the negative and possible positive aspects of labelling has been around for decades and will be around long after we've gone, this dichotomy will probably never be truly resolved. However, I still believe that receiving a diagnosis of Asperger's or autism will validate who I am and that such a diagnosis will allow me to access and receive services and resources that I would not be able to otherwise.

Zoe: Beyond the obvious reason of finance or rather the lack of it, why should services be denied you simply because you choose not to seek and obtain a diagnosis? Surely there are as many people out there who are undiagnosed autistic or Asperger's, and undiagnosed for whatever reason, as there are those who have been diagnosed, and who are in need of help and support but don't get it. Surely it is wrong and unjust to deny these people support because they have not been formally diagnosed; to make diagnosis a condition of support being offered. Surely this is an example of power and control exercised by those in authority against the relatively powerless and vulnerable.

Chris: Which is one of the reasons why I am seeking a diagnosis, to give me a platform from which I can legitimately raise these and other issues. Anyway, although this may sound like a 'cop out', these issues are very unlikely to be resolved within this current dialogue so I am not going to try!

Zoe: Now that you have received your diagnosis, what do you mean by

Box 6.6. Diary entry: 22nd November 2008

Second session with RBF during which Asperger's syndrome/high functioning autism was confirmed. My use of the word 'journey' as describing the diagnosis experience was questioned by RBF who believed that having acquired a diagnosis, my journey had ended rather than begun or had at least reached a 'milestone'.

'journey'?

Chris: I believe that a diagnosis is not a static, 'one off', incident but is, by its nature dynamic and reaches both into the past and into the future.

Zoe: That's a bit heavy! What do you mean by that?

Chris: A diagnosis, any diagnosis, has a history, it has a past. There is a glimmer and then a growing possibility and awareness that, in my case, I could have autism. There is the growing dialogue both within the individual and with others as to what this condition is and what the diagnosis could mean. It has a present, the diagnostic process itself, with all that follows from that in terms of the procedure itself and the debate around 'do I/ don't I have' autism or Asperger's and the consequences of the diagnosis or non-diagnosis. It has a future in the way of a coming to terms and living with both the diagnosis and the condition (or not, as the case may be). This is what I meant by journey: the diagnosis has a beginning, a dynamic middle and, at some far distant point, an end with the paths between these points being winding and even spinning off at unknown tangents and going in unknown directions.

Zoe: Disclosure! What do you mean by 'issues around disclosure'?

Box 6.7. Diary entry: 7th November 2008

Attended a three-day training course at work on HIV/AIDS which raised questions and issues around disclosure and how disclosure could affect me at work, with my family and with my friends.

Jo: This is partly what I meant by labelling. If you, Chris, do not have any issues with a labelling diagnosis, then you should not have any issues with disclosure!

Chris: Put like that, you are right Jo, I shouldn't. However, being human I should be allowed a certain amount of anxiety as to who gets to know, how, when and why and any reactions, both positive and negative, that others may have regarding any disclosure. Will I be in control of any disclosure, will I be seen as any less of a person, will I be discriminated against by current or future employers or colleagues, will I lose any friends as a result of my diagnosis?

Jo: Sorry Chris, but we can't answer that. Only time will tell. All we can say is to have a little bit of faith in other people.

Zoe: Why did you have this concern as to whom to disclose to?

Chris: Any disclosure of this nature could be likened to a gay or lesbian person 'coming out'. There is the possibility of people accepting me as being

Box 6.8. Diary entry: 1st December 2008
Who do I tell?

Having received the diagnosis, there is the issue of to whom do I disclose my autism, when, how and why. Those I believe should possibly know include:

- Family
- Friends
- My church
- RCN
- Work

autistic. However, there is also the possibility of being rejected by people who may not understand. There is the possibility of having to face ridicule due to people's ignorance. Conversely, there is a possibility of being wrapped up in 'well-meaning cotton wool' by those who become over-protective towards me.

Jo: Indeed, many nurses, teachers and social workers who develop mental or physical health problems either before they start their professional training, during their training or after qualifying, face similar dilemmas over disclosure for fear of losing their jobs at the hands of uncaring or unsympathetic employers. There is also the issue of being seen as 'deviant' and having to swap sides in the 'us and them' power structure that still exists.

Zoe: The issue of what help you would need is fairly straightforward. You

Box 6.9. Diary entry: 1st December 2008
What help do I need? I don't know – what help is there?

- Possible help in relating to and helping my son who also has Asperger's.
- Possible help in long-term, secure, meaningful and well-paid employment.
- Possible help in coming to terms with and accepting my past, present and future.
- Possible help with problems in social interaction.
- Possible help with problems in social communication.
- Possible help with assertiveness.

can only really answer this over time and with both experience and hindsight with some issues being resolved and new issues coming to light as time progresses and as you develop. I notice that you have not included possible help with any mental health issues that you may have or experience. Are there any reasons for this?

Chris: No, not really. I probably forgot to include mental health issues in the diary that I was keeping at the time. As you point out, the list of possible support needs, which is by no means inclusive, will change over time and it is right that it should do so.

Zoe: We now come to the final issue that you have recorded in your diary,

Box 6.10. Diary entry: 1st December 2008
Implications of receiving a diagnosis on my immediate, mid and long-term future

- Being able to access services offered by the NAS and Autism West Midlands.
- Being able to be involved actively within the NAS and Autism West Midlands.
- Being able to legitimately write and lecture on the subject of autism from a personal perspective.
- However, a diagnosis may negatively affect my employment as a nurse and how I function as a nurse.

that of 'implications of receiving a diagnosis'. Again, most of the issues you've recorded are fairly straightforward and we have touched on them throughout the course of this conversation. I notice with interest that you have recorded both receiving and being involved in services. Would you mind expanding on that?

Chris: I had hoped to have been involved in the autism movement and battle as a possible Trustee of Autism West Midlands and had actually applied to become a Trustee, but after having gone through the application process, the existing Trustees decided that I did not have the right skill set that they were looking for.

Jo: Could that have been because you are Asperger's/high functioning autism and that the existing Trustees felt uncomfortable having a 'service user' on the Board of Trustees as an equal to themselves? Could it be that people with autism and Asperger's are still very much the 'done to' rather than the 'doers' and that to have a person with autism on the board upsets the 'status quo'?

Chris: In all honesty, I don't know. I hope not! However, I do intend to use any teaching, lecturing, nurse activist and writing opportunities that may come my way to raise and campaign for the issues of autism and Asperger's syndrome and for those with Asperger's and autism if and when appropriate.

Chris: At this point, I would like to draw this conversation to an end. I am aware that some of what has been said may come across as rather pompous and pretentious...

Zoe: You can say that again!

Chris: Thank you! However, this has not been my intention. What I would like to say, finally, is a huge 'thank you' for your kind, energetic and thought-provoking questioning, observations and contributions.

CHAPTER 7

Children with autism and autism spectrum conditions

Introduction

According to recent British statistics, as many as 1 in 58 children are somewhere on the autism spectrum (Baron-Cohen et al 2007). When one thinks about autism, the image is often of a child. Indeed, in some circles, autism is looked upon as a childhood condition. Although part of the definition of an autism spectrum condition (ASC) focuses on it being life-long, it generally starts to manifest itself in very young children and even in babies. However, it may not be recognised and the person can go through childhood, adolescence and adulthood without being assessed and diagnosed. It is now acknowledged that ASC has a large genetic component. In other words, autism, or at least autistic traits, often run in families and can be found in parents, siblings, aunts and uncles.

This chapter discusses ASCs in children from birth to the end of their primary school education at age 11 years and covers the following areas:

- Obtaining a diagnosis.
- Diagnosis day.
- Benefits available following a diagnosis
- Multi-disciplinary working.
- Behaviour management.
- Respite services.
- Finding the right school and educational services.
- Social activities and making friends.

Obtaining a diagnosis

Is your child able to talk to or play with only one other person or child at a time?

The above question may be asked by a therapist working with young children who are suspected to be on the autism spectrum. Normal developmental milestones include the ability to do certain things at certain times (physical abilities such as walking; communication abilities such as talking; and social abilities such as play and sharing), in a particular progression and over a particular time period (Lawson 2008). In children with an ASC, many of these developmental milestones are not met, particularly in the areas of communication, social interaction and imagination. By the time the child attends nursery or starts primary school, these issues are likely to be picked up by parents or nursery or school staff. Parents will often compare the development of their child with his or her siblings or the children of friends and will become concerned if their child does not reach the recognised milestones. Their first course of action is likely to be to raise these concerns with their health visitor, practice nurse or GP who, unless fully aware of ASCs, may not be able to recognise the signs of autism and may treat the parents as being over-anxious and not take their concerns seriously. However, a more appropriate and helpful response would be know to whom to refer the parents and their child for help, advice and a diagnosis and to know of the various diagnostic tools that are available for children. These include:

- Asperger Syndrome Diagnostic Interview (Gillberg et al 2001).
- Asperger Syndrome Diagnostic Scale (Myles et al 2001).
- Autism Spectrum Screening Questionnaire (Elhers et al 1999).
- Childhood Asperger Syndrome Test (Scott et al 2002).

However, caution must be exercised as there may be problems with all of these tools regarding validity, reliability, specificity and sensitivity (Howlin 2000).

Diagnosis day

> *And at some point, despite the false starts and hopes, you say the words out loud, 'I think there's something wrong'. If you are lucky, the person you say it to listens, asks questions, refers you in the right direction. If you are not, you will say these words a hundred, a thousand times before anyone takes you seriously.*
>
> Cerebra (2010: 20)

Diagnosis day comes and goes in a blur. Parents probably will not be able to take in and remember much of what is said to them, only that it was 'diagnosis day', the day in which their fears and concerns were validated. Some parents will start searching for a cure for their child's autism or Asperger's but they will not find one.

As the months pass, some parents will start the various therapies or diets that have been suggested to them. Many parents will lose contact with friends and family members, causing isolation and great emotional and spiritual pain whilst others will make new friends within the autism support community. Parents' expectations for their autistic child will change. Over time, parents and their children will learn to live again, both within and outside of this strange world called 'autism'.

The role of the nurse and healthcare assistant is to listen, understand, inform and support the family as a unit in whatever way is necessary whilst recognising that each individual family member may have different support needs.

Benefits available following a diagnosis

There are a number of benefits associated with a child receiving a diagnosis. These include:

- A sense of self-realisation, self-understanding and self-acceptance for the child and his or her parents: 'So that's what I've got! I'm not mentally ill after all', 'It's not me being a bad parent'.
- Access to social service support for both the child and his or her family, such as respite care and travel training.
- Access to voluntary sector support such as the National Autistic Society (NAS), regional autism support organisations, such as Autism West Midlands (AWM), and local support groups.
- Access to autism-specific, general disability and carer workshops and training courses.
- Access to welfare benefits such as the Disability Living Allowance (DLA) and Carer's Allowance.
- Access to autism-specific educational support, such as educational psychologists, statementing and classroom support.
- Enabling school staff to understand the child and put in place appropriate support structures.

However, such support can come at a price: There may be a sense of a loss of control by the family, with the transference of control from the family to external care professionals.

Multi-disciplinary working

> *It is the bane of our lives when nurses, doctors, speech and language therapists, teachers and psychologists do not talk to each other.*
>
> Parent 'A'
>
> *Instead of one care professional coming out to see us to carry out a single assessment that could be shared with other members of the multi-disciplinary team, each care profession sends someone to ask us the same questions over and over again. We wouldn't mind so much, but they don't actually listen to us.*
>
> Parent 'B'
>
> *Sometimes, it can be like Piccadilly Circus in our house, what with the large numbers of care professionals coming to assess us and our lad. I've lost control of the process of obtaining help and services for him.*
>
> Parent 'C'

Multidisciplinary teams are groups of professionals from diverse health and social care disciplines and organisations who come together to provide comprehensive assessment and health, education and social care planning and implementation. These teams normally include health visitors, specialist nurses, communication therapists, GPs, dieticians, and psychologists, amongst others. Such teams *must* include the parents of the child with an ASC and, where appropriate, the child him or herself; it is not appropriate to side-line the views, wants or needs of parents or children in assessing or planning services. Multi-disciplinary teams work best when each individual member, including the parents, siblings (when and where appropriate) and children acknowledge and respect the knowledge, skills and abilities of all other members whilst being able to calmly assert their own knowledge, skills and position. Multi-disciplinary teams work well when each member of the team communicates openly and honestly with each other.

Behaviour management

There is no such thing as a cure for autism or its behavioural manifestations. That is not to say that at some point in the future there may not be. However, there are a number of behaviour management tools and strategies that can be used to help deal with and lessen the impact of the more negative behaviours associated with ASCs in young children. Behaviour, here, is meant any action that can be seen or heard, such as tearing of clothes, shouting, screaming, hitting, biting, scratching of self or smearing faeces.

In order to promote 'positive behaviour', you need to be certain as to:

- What the 'negative behaviour' is that needs to be changed.
- What the desired behaviour is.
- How long or well the child should perform the wanted behaviour.
- Under what circumstances he or she will perform this behaviour.
- What reward, if any, should be offered as a result of the changed behaviour.

Some forms of neuroleptic medications may be useful in amending behaviour but such drugs need to be used very carefully, particularly in young children, and some may not be indicated or licensed for use in curbing certain autistic-type behaviour.

A casein, lactose and gluten free diet may be useful in managing, controlling or lessening the effects of 'negative behaviour' (Jackson 2002).

There are ethical and moral issues around the use of drugs and behaviour modification techniques that aim to change behaviour of which care professionals and parents should be aware. Some of these issues may focus on social and political control and what is 'normal' within society.

Respite

Respite programmes provide planned short-term, temporary and time-limited breaks for families and other unpaid caregivers in order to allow them to recharge their batteries physically, emotionally and mentally. The aim of respite care is to support and maintain the primary caregiving relationship. Good respite care should also provide a positive experience for the person receiving care. Without respite, families can suffer economically and emotionally, and caregivers may face serious health and social risks as a result of stress associated with continuous caregiving.

There are several ways of providing respite care:

- In-home respite where the respite provider comes to the family home in order to allow caregivers the chance to engage in activities outside of the home. Relatives or friends 'babysitting' for the family could provide this type of respite.
- The provision of day care services.
- Specialised residential care facilities where the person being cared for goes for a short break, usually on a planned basis.

All of these can be provided either on an on-going and planned basis or on an emergency basis in order to prevent family breakdown. One example of respite care in the Birmingham area is the Norman Laud Centre, a voluntary sector organisation that provides residential support for children with disabilities ranging from a day or overnight stay through to a weekend or longer if needed. Funding for such respite care can sometimes be difficult to obtain, although it may be funded by local authorities or grant-making charities. Many local authorities and NHS trusts provide their own respite care services.

Finding a school

Finding the right school for a child who is on the autism spectrum can be extremely problematic.

- Should the child be sent to a 'special' or 'mainstream' school? There is a long-running debate as to which is better for the young child with an ASC.
- Is the special school's set-up resourced and able to meet the specific needs of young primary school aged children who have an ASC? Some may not be. How far is the school from the family home; will it be accessible?
- Is the local State primary school able to provide appropriate support, resources and education for the child with an ASC?
- Should the child be assessed for a 'statement of special educational needs'?
- If the child is already in a mainstream school, will he or she be able to stay within that school?
- Should the child be placed in a private, fee-paying, school?
- Should a small autism specialist school be established with collaboration with other parents of autistic children?
- Should the child be educated at home?

There are advantages and disadvantages to each option. In the case of Bill (a 10-year-old diagnosed with Asperger's syndrome three years ago), his parents had many long arguments regarding some of these issues and decided to keep Bill in his primary school because he liked the school and had made some friends there. They felt it would be unfair to uproot him and place him within a specialist educational setting. However, many parents will come to a different decision and it is not unusual for the parents of a child with an ASC to disagree between themselves. Care professionals working with the family must maintain their neutrality and not take sides. Any personal views regarding mainstream versus special educational schools must be acknowledged but must not be allowed to influence the care professional's advice in any way. The role of the care professional is to provide accurate and accessible information and to act as advocate.

Social activities

Children who have an ASC have exactly the same rights as any other child to access and engage in social activities. By social activities is meant playing in the local park, going to the cinema, meeting friends in cafes, using the local swimming pool, accessing sports facilities and joining clubs and organisations, such as the Scouts and Guides, etc. An ASC must not be used as an excuse to deny children such social activities. Carefully exposing children with an ASC to and helping them experience ordinary child-centred social activities can teach valuable social communication and interaction skills, as well as greater social understanding and acceptance on the part of children who do not have an ASC and their parents.

However, exposure to and experiencing of ordinary social and leisure activities can be hindered by unhelpful attitudes and practices on the part of 'neuro-typicals'. Bill has experienced social clubs for young children where those with an ASC have been excluded as a result of their behaviour and it appears to him that some social clubs and organisations observe inclusion as merely a 'paper exercise' and where children with an ASC have been accepted there has been more than a 'whiff' of tokenism. However, Bill has been welcomed with open arms in some social settings. This, he suggests, has had a huge and positive impact on his sense of self-worth and self-esteem and he would like health and social care professionals such as nurses to build links between themselves and leisure organisations like the Scouts and Guides in order to foster and promote genuine social inclusion. Lawson (2008: 96) suggests that many children with an ASC find fitting in within a social context difficult as a result of not knowing or understanding social rules and that they are ostracised as a result.

There are a number of books available on social skills training, including Wrobel (2003), Foley (2003) Harpur et al (2006) and Cotugno (2009). These can be used with both adolescents and younger children in order to help them gain the social skills that would make accessing leisure environments easier.

In relation to social skills, nurses or healthcare assistants can:

- Provide accessible and accurate information, suggestions and guidance

to parents and siblings of young children with an ASC either directly or through autism and Asperger's support groups.
- Provide accessible and accurate information, suggestions and guidance to young children with an ASC.
- Facilitate and initially lead social skills sessions for children and their parents. These could be in separate sessions.

Conclusion

Possibly, of all the issues covered in this chapter, the most important for both the child and his or her parents is diagnosis, as arguably all the other issues spring from this. The key roles of the nurse and healthcare assistant are, firstly, to provide whatever support the family needs, either directly or within a multi-disciplinary context, and secondly, to provide accurate and accessible information to the child and parents in formats that are appropriate for the child, the parents and any siblings as each will have different information needs.

Key points

- Parents and/or nursery/crèche staff will often raise concerns when normal developmental milestones are not achieved.
- A number of diagnostic tools are available that can be used to diagnose ASCs in children.
- There are a number of advantages and disadvantages to seeking and acquiring a diagnosis.
- There can be a variety of issues and difficulties that children with an ASC are likely to experience, including access to multi-disciplinary assessments and support, behaviour management, an appropriate school, respite care and leisure and social activities.
- Children with an ASC and their parents are likely to need assistance from health and social care teams in accessing support in order to overcome these issues.

References

Baron-Cohen S, Scott F, Stott C (2007) *One in 58 children will be somewhere on the autistic spectrum*. Unpublished study. Autism Research Centre (ARC), Cambridge

Cerebra (2010) The visible and the invisible. *Newsbeat* Summer: 20

Cotugno A (2009) *Group Interventions for Children with Autism Spectrum Disorders*. Jessica Kingsley Publishers, London

Elhers S, Gilberg C, Wing L (1999)A screening questionnaire for Asperger syndrome and other high-functioning autism spectrum disorders in school age children. *Journal of Autism and Developmental Disorders* **29**: 128–41

Foley D (2003) Starting from scratch: Being innovative in finding interventions for your adolescent with Asperger syndrome. In Willey LH (ed) *Asperger Syndrome in Adolescence*. Jessica Kingsley Publishers, London

Gillberg C, Gillberg C, Rastam M, Wentz E (2001) The Asperger Syndrome (and high-functioning autism) Diagnostic Interviews (ASDI): A preliminary study of a new structured clinical interview. *Autism* **5**: 57: 66

Harpur J, Lawlor M, Fitzgerald M (2006) *Succeeding with Interventions for Asperger Syndrome Adolescents*. Jessica Kingsley Publishers, London

Howlin P (2000) Assessment instruments for Asperger syndrome. *Child Psychology and Psychiatry Review* **5**: 120–9

Jackson L (2002) *Freaks, Geeks and Asperger Syndrome*. Jessica Kingsley Publishers, London

Lawson W (2008) *Concepts of Normality: The autistic and typical spectrum*. Jessica Kingsley Publishers, London

Myles B, Bock S, Simpson R (2001) *Asperger Syndrome Diagnostic Scale Examiner's Manual*. PRO-ED, Austin, TX

Scott E, Baron-Cohen S, Bolton P, Brayne C (2002) The CAST (Childhood Asperger Syndrome Test) preliminary development of a UK screen for mainstream primary -school-age children. *Autism* **6**: 9–31

Wrobel M (2003) *Taking Care of Myself*. Future Horizons, Arlington, TX

CHAPTER 8

Adolescents with autism and autism spectrum conditions

Introduction

In many ways, the period of life known as adolescence can be one of the most difficult and trying in any person's life. Just ask a parent! The previous chapter focused on the needs of children from birth up to the age of 11 years with an autism spectrum condition (ASC). This chapter focuses on the needs of adolescents, that is, those aged 11 to 21 years. The following issues that may affect or have an impact upon young people with an ASC are highlighted:

- Diagnosis.
- Disclosure.
- Transition from primary to secondary school.
- Puberty.
- Social skills.
- Bullying.
- Sexuality and relationships.
- Transition from school to college, university or work.

By the end of the chapter, the reader will have a basic awareness of:

- The impact of the above issues on the lives of those with an ASC.
- The role of the health and social care professional in supporting the young person with an ASC.

Definition and meaning of adolescence

Adolescence can be one of the most difficult and trying but also one of the most exhilarating periods in a young person's life. However, what exactly is adolescence? What does it mean?

According to Weller (1997: 10), adolescence is the period between puberty and maturity which in males is between 14 and 25 years of age and in females between 12 and 21 years of age. Such a definition is fine as far as it goes. However, there is no distinction made between physical, emotional, psychological or mental maturity. Sometimes physical maturity may lead on to psycho-emotional maturity and sometimes it is the other way round. Again, if one takes the onset of puberty as the start of adolescence then a much earlier age of 11 and even 10 may be more accurate, particularly in girls. It is not unusual for puberty to begin and in some cases be complete in the last year or two of primary school. The upper age limit can also be problematic: when does adolescence end and adulthood begin? Can a person be both an adult and an adolescent at the same time? If 'maturity' is taken as the end of adolescence, such an end is very much a moveable feast as different people mature at different times and there are many levels of maturity. Many people can display marked maturity in some areas of life whilst displaying marked immaturity in other areas.

Adolescence, teenage years or youth, to give it other names, can be a time of rebellion, of questioning and challenging and of growing social, economic and political independence.

Diagnosis

By the time children have left primary school and entered secondary school it is likely that they may have already received a diagnosis of an autism spectrum condition (ASC). However, many may not have. For a list of appropriate diagnostic tools that can be used, please refer to *Chapter 5*. Due to the complexity of the condition, those with Asperger's syndrome are often diagnosed much later in life than those with 'classic autism' (Harpur et al 2006). According to Attwood (2006), if a person is not diagnosed with an ASC until their teen years that person has already missed the opportunity to benefit from early interventions. However, once a diagnosis is made the adolescent can benefit from support whilst at school or college.

Sally, sister of Bill who we met in *Chapter 7*, was not diagnosed until she was 12 and in her second year at secondary school (year 8). This came about because Bill, her younger brother, had just been diagnosed with classic autism and many of Sally's own behavioural traits were similar to Bill's. After extensive diagnostic assessments and tests, Sally was diagnosed as high functioning autism/Asperger's syndrome. Sally was helped and supported during and after the diagnosis by her GP, practice nurse and the autism specialist who diagnosed her, all of whom provided accurate information to her and her family in ways that could be understood.

Disclosure

Running alongside either an existing or a new ASC diagnosis is the often thorny issue of whether or not to disclose this diagnosis and how such disclosure is to be managed.

Sally suggests that the first people who should be told are the young person him or herself and the parents and siblings. Such disclosure needs to be handled sensitively with accurate and accessible information being given at a time and in a manner that is most helpful to the newly diagnosed person. Sally says that it would not be appropriate just to tell her and her parents that she has an ASC and then be shown the door. This, she says, has happened to other young people and their parents with disastrous results. The next group of people that the newly diagnosed person may want to disclose to is the wider family of grandparents, aunts, uncles and cousins. The young person will need support and advice as to whether and how to disclose their autism diagnosis to wider circles of school and college teachers/ lecturers and friends. A useful rule of thumb would be to suggest disclosing only to those who need to know. It may be helpful for the young person and their family to join a support group for young people with an ASC and/or their parents.

Transition from primary to secondary school

Transitions from one environment to another can be traumatic at any age. However, the transition from primary to secondary school can be very difficult for the young person with an ASC to manage.

Friendships that have been made at primary school may come to an end as different secondary schools will be attended. Young people may have to start again when making friends and for those with an ASC learning and understanding the social rules and codes which govern these more mature friendships and relationships may make this problematic.

The move from a relatively small school to one that is three to four times the size, possibly on two or three different sites, can create problems in knowing what to do and where to go. The small number of staff at Sally's primary school meant that she and her teachers got to know and understand each other well. However, at secondary school she had to work with about 12 different teachers and this was intimidating and threatening. Sally felt lost and lonely within such a big school. There can also be issues around statements of special educational needs which may have to be assessed or re-assessed and updated in order for the adolescent to receive the appropriate educational support.

A number of measures to help the young student can be put in place.

- A longer amount of time could be spent visiting the new school prior to starting. This would allow the student to become acclimatised to the new environment.
- A peer mentoring or 'buddy' system could be implemented which would help the transfer to go smoothly and the new student to find his or her way around the school and timetable. Such a peer mentor or 'buddy' would need to be appropriately prepared and recognised in order to carry out the role.
- The young person with an ASC could be allowed to enter the classroom before and leave after everyone else. This could eliminate any anxiety or behavioural issues associated with having to mix with large numbers of other people whilst moving between classrooms.
- A 'safe haven', such as the Special Educational Needs Coordinator's office or the office of the student/pupil support staff, could be made available for the young person with an ASC to go to if his or her anxiety levels should become an issue.

Puberty

According to Wainscott and Corbett (1997) because of the lack of imagination of most adolescents with an ASC, physical changes such as menstruation, deepening of the voice, breast development and growth of pubic hair are accepted in a 'matter of fact' way. However, Attwood (2006) suggests that adolescents with an ASC may need advice on puberty and how this will affect their bodies and mood, and how to manage certain aspects of puberty such as menstruation, sexuality and relationships.

There are a number of resources available to help young adolescents come to terms with their changing bodies and moods. These include:

- Henault's *Asperger's Syndrome and Sexuality from Adolescence Through Adulthood* (2005). This useful text explains puberty and sexuality specifically for those with an ASC.
- Henault (2003) has also contributed a chapter on puberty and the sexuality of teenagers with Asperger's syndrome in Lianne Willey's book (Willey 2003). Whilst Hainault's focus is on those with Asperger's, what she says in terms of understanding sexuality and physical and emotional development, and the advice she gives for parents has relevance to all those on the autism spectrum.

Having said that, the content of her chapter may need to be modified and adapted to meet the needs of those who also have a learning disability.
- Wrobel's (2003) handbook contains very useful teaching sessions and material that covers most, if not all, issues connected with puberty. These include personal hygiene (washing, bathing, showering), health, modesty, growth, menstruation, touching, personal safety and masturbation. These broad areas are then broken down into smaller, more specific and manageable issues including being naked, where the person can be naked, wearing a bra, shaving, how to manage periods, and stranger awareness.

Social skills

Adolescence is a time to spend less time with parents and siblings and more with friends in social settings such as cafes and shopping malls. This is normal and to be expected. However, many adolescents with an ASC experience difficulties with the social skills needed to 'hang out' with friends. They may find the following difficult:

- Issues of self-esteem.
- Entering into contact with another person.
- Social manners.
- Initiating a conversation.
- Turn taking in conversations.
- Voicing opinions and defending points of view.
- Sharing an interest.
- Listening skills.
- Appropriate eye contact.
- Learning to decode the intention of others through understanding subtle facial expressions and body language.

The goal of social skills training according to Henault (2003) is to refine and increase the individual's repertoire of appropriate behaviours.

One way to instil and improve social skills acquisition and use is through social skills training or learning groups. The groups need to be small with no more than six students at a time (Foley 2003) and need to be well structured with clearly defined rules. There appears to be an increasing interest in social skills learning in schools and youth clubs, many of which host and run such groups. One of the roles of a nurse or healthcare assistant working with adolescents who have an ASC may be to help facilitate such social skills groups within an educational or a healthcare environment. Cotugno (2009) provides much useful information in terms of setting up and running social skills groups.

Bullying

Those with an ASC can be as, and possibly more, prone to bullying as anyone else and bullying can occur across all ages, socio-economic backgrounds, gender and ethnic cultures. Those with an ASC can also be bullies themselves. Both Attwood (2006) and Jackson (2002) focus on bullying and its impact on people with an ASC. Bullying can take many forms such as:

- Verbal, including name calling, shouting, teasing, ridiculing and gossiping.
- Physical, including pushing, shoving and kicking or any act of physical aggression.
- Emotional, including isolation, belittling a person, making fun of someone, spreading rumours about a person and gossiping.

Bullying can occur in school or college, in the workplace, in the street, by telephone or text message and via email or social networking sites. Some behaviour may be bullying in nature and intent whilst some is harmless banter. However, one person's banter may be another person's bullying and it is with this 'grey area' that people with an ASC can experience real problems as they may not realise and understand the difference between the two.

Jackson (2002) suggests that when working with a person with an ASC the following needs to be taken into account:

- Ask specific questions and use specific words about bullying rather than posing the question in a general way or using ambiguous words.
- Reinforce the fact that bullying is never the fault of the person being bullied.
- The person with an ASC may not realise they are being bullied.
- Bullies should not be confronted.
- Teachers, lecturers or employers should be spoken to in private.

It may be useful to incorporate bullying awareness and how to deal with bullies in social skills sessions and groups.

Sexuality and relationships

Attwood (2006) suggests that teenagers with an ASC may be keen to understand and experience the same social, relationship and sexual worlds as their 'neuro-typical' peers but may not have access to appropriate, accurate and reliable information on sexual relationships. Same-age peers may see the naivety of the young person with an ASC as a chance to have fun at their expense. The combination of social and sexual naivety and poor information could increase the chances of abuse in an already vulnerable group. Attwood (2006) further suggests using trusted friends and family members for sources of appropriate information regarding relationships and sexuality.

Jackson (2002) suggests that ASC and dating do not mix due to the very complex social interactions that are involved. However, he does make a number of helpful suggestions in his chapter entitled 'The dating game' with relation to the 'do's and don'ts' of dating and forming of relationships, many of which include:

- Personal hygiene.
- Being yourself.
- Communication.
- The use of physical space, touch and intimacy.

These issues could be discussed within a social skills group.

Transition from school to college, university or work

In the same way that transition from primary to secondary school can be seen as a milestone, so, too, can the transition from school to either college, university or employment. All these are adult environments and the young adult with an ASC will have to learn a completely new set of social rules to cope with them. Liaison between the school and the college, university or employer is strongly advised (Attwood 2006). Some universities will have a support group specifically for students with an ASC which may be helpful.

The general experience of those with an ASC (Attwood 2006) is that finding and keeping an appropriate job or career is not as easy as it is for 'neuro-typical' people with the same qualifications. It may be helpful to assist the person with an ASC to compile a *curriculum vitae* which can be presented together with a portfolio of school, college or personal work and achievement to prospective employers. It may also be useful to practise job or college interviews and this could form a number of sessions within a social skills group for older adolescents. Likewise, the person with an ASC may need assistance in knowing whether to accept or decline an employment offer since not all offers of employment may be suitable. The local Youth Connexions Employment Team would be invaluable here.

Engagement in work experience forms a crucial aspect of a young person's portfolio of work. Care must be exercised to ensure that the form of work chosen is realistic, reflects a real work environment and is tailored to the strengths of the student with an ASC. Again, the local Youth Connexions Employment Team may prove useful in advising and setting up appropriate work experiences.

Finally, once in employment the person with an ASC may need on-going support and guidance from his or her employer and colleagues in relation to job and interpersonal skills expectations.

Conclusion

The period of life known as adolescence throws up many issues and challenges. Those with an ASC may find navigating round these issues and challenges even more difficult than their 'neuro-typical' peers. Due to the nature of these issues, the bulk of this chapter will mostly be of use to those nursing and care staff who work within secondary schools, colleges and universities. However, parents may be able to play a role in ensuring appropriate help and support for adolescents with an ASC through becoming school governors which will allow for a greater insight into and influence of the education and support of those with an ASC.

Key points

- Having received a diagnosis of an autism spectrum condition (ASC), either at primary or secondary school, many young people may find that when and to whom to disclose the diagnosis can cause problems.
- Young people with an ASC may experience bullying as a result of disclosing their autism.
- Other issues that the young person will have to deal with include puberty, transition from primary to secondary school and secondary school to college, university or work, social skills, personal hygiene, sexuality and relationships. This is in common with all other adolescents.
- Young people with an ASC and their parents are likely to need substantial support in order for adolescence to be safely navigated and enjoyed. One way that nurses can help is to facilitate social skills training.

References

Attwood T (2006) *The Complete Guide to Asperger's Syndrome*. Jessica Kingsley Publishers, London

Cotugno A (2009) *Group Interventions for Children with Autism Spectrum Disorders*. Jessica Kingsley Publishers, London

Foley D (2003) Starting from scratch: Being innovative in finding interventions for your adolescent with Asperger syndrome. In Willey LH (ed) *Asperger Syndrome in Adolescence*. Jessica Kingsley Publishers, London

Harpur J, Lawlor M, Fitzgerald M (2006) *Succeeding with Interventions for Asperger Syndrome Adolescents*. Jessica Kingsley Publishers, London

Henault I (2003) The sexuality of adolescents with Asperger syndrome. In Willey LH (ed) *Asperger Syndrome in Adolescence*. Jessica Kingsley Publishers, London

Henault I (2005) *Asperger's Syndrome and Sexuality From Adolescence Through Adulthood*. Jessica Kingsley Publishers, London

Jackson L (2002) *Freaks, Geeks and Asperger Syndrome*. Jessica Kingsley Publishers, London

Wainscott G, Corbett J (1997) Health care of adults with autism. In Morgan H (ed) *Adults with Autism*. Cambridge University Press, Cambridge

Weller B (1997) *Bailliere's Nurses Dictionary*. Bailliere Tindall, London

Willey LH (ed) (2003) *Asperger Syndrome in Adolescence*. Jessica Kingsley Publishers, London

Wrobel M (2003) *Taking Care of Myself*. Future Horizons, Arlington, Texas

CHAPTER 9

Less able adults with autism spectrum conditions

Introduction

> *The aggregate costs for adults amount to £25 billion each year. Of this total, 59% is accounted for by services, 36% by lost employment for the individual with ASD [autism spectrum disorders] and the remainder by family expenses.*
>
> Knapp et al (2007: 2)

The previous two chapters focused on young children (those aged 3–11) and adolescents and young adults (those aged 11–22) who have an autism spectrum condition (ASC). This chapter focuses on the needs, experiences and issues affecting 'less able' adults with an ASC. There are significant numbers of people with an ASC who are either unable to live independently or who need significant input and support from health and social care professionals in many areas of living including residential, daily occupation and healthcare. Some, due to the severity of their ASC and any associated mental health condition and/or learning disability may be unable to live independently.

By the end of this chapter, you will have gained a basic knowledge and understanding of how the following issues will impact upon the lives of those with an ASC who are less able to live independently:

- The various types of residential care and support that are available.
- Daily activities including employment.
- Day care services and day care models.
- Healthcare issues, both acute and on-going.
- Overshadowing – where a person's autism or Asperger's is subsumed into, and thus hidden by, an associated mental health condition or learning disability.

In each of these areas and issues affecting the lives of the less able adult with an ASC, the role of the nurse and healthcare assistant will be highlighted.

Residential care and support

There are many forms of residential care and support that can be offered to and accessed by less able adults.

Many of the early 20th century learning disability hospitals, such as Monyhull and Brooklands Hospitals in Birmingham and South Ockendon Hospital in Essex, have either closed or 'downsized'. They offer specialised residential services and support for specific groups of service users. These include those who have forensic issues and those who have severe autism and concurrent learning disabilities. By forensic issues is meant those who have committed serious criminal acts, such as arson, sexual assault and murder. Many of these larger residential units are structured on 'campus' or 'village' lines where many of the services that residents need in their daily life are found on site. Whilst many of these residential units for adults with an ASC are designed and staffed specifically to meet the needs of this user group, unfortunately some will not and those with an ASC may well be housed together with non-ASC service users.

National and regional autism organisations also run large residential units for those with an ASC along similar lines. One such example is Gorse Farm, a large residential unit run by Autism West Midlands. Gorse Farm combines residential units with an occupational centre and a small horticultural centre, all based on the specific care and support needs of adults with an ASC.

There are many small residential homes run by national and regional autism organisations. These are similar to ordinary family homes and, whilst being an integral part of the local community, provide specific support and care packages for adults with an ASC by specially trained staff.

There are many small residential homes that are owned and run by either 'not for profit' or commercial organisations. Some of these homes offer specific support and environments for less able autistic adults but in others less able adults with an ASC may be 'lumped together' and treated the same as other adults with a learning disability.

An increasing number of less able adults with an ASC are being offered and are choosing the opportunity to live 'semi-independently' in their own homes with significant daily support by specially trained care and support staff.

The role of the nurse and healthcare assistant or support worker is to be able to provide appropriate and accurate information regarding the types of residential units that are available for less able adults. The service user and his or her family must be supported throughout the often long and difficult process of accessing and understanding this information and choosing a suitable residential and care support package.

Daily activities and occupation

Traditionally 'occupation' for those with severe autism and/or learning disabilities revolved around day centres. Some of these day centres were provided within the large mental handicap/learning disability hospitals and incorporated occupational therapy and industrial therapy. On-site industrial therapy units were staffed by a combination of nurses, healthcare assistants and technical instructors who had experience and skills in the manufacturing sector and sought to provide basic and simple 'employment' opportunities for the residents. Some of these industrial therapy units were 'stand-alone' (such as the unit at South Ockendon Hospital in southwest Essex during the 1980s) whilst others formed part of a traditional day centre.

Many of the large hospitals had small horticultural units where the residents were taught how to grow fruit, herbs and vegetables and run small vegetable gardens, allotments or smallholdings. However, very few if any of these units were designed or planned around the needs of those with autism; those with autism would were seen as having a 'mental handicap' or mental illness and were treated accordingly. Again, most local authority social service departments ran very similar forms of occupational day services within the community; these were called adult training centres.

During the past two decades, there has been a growth in small independent day care services. Some of these services are owned and run by not for profit organisations. The quality of service provision in these independent day care services is variable and ranges from very good to very poor. Again, very few were set up specifically for those with severe autism. However, a small number of voluntary, not for profit organisations, including the National Autistic Society and Autism West Midlands, have set up and run high quality day care provision that is centred on the specific needs of those with severe autism.

An increasing number of further education colleges provide services for those with severe and profound autism and learning disabilities. Much of this provision has centred on literacy, numeracy and vocational skills. However, a number of possible shortcomings have been found with such provision:

- The curriculum is too narrow.
- Few courses are set up to meet the specific needs of severely autistic adults due to an emphasis on the provision of nationally accredited courses.
- Only specialist courses and classes are provided, which further isolates service users.

- There is a lack of systematic evaluation of the value of such courses in the lives of adults with autism.

Although in past years employment opportunities tended to be a paper exercise rather than real work for real pay, there are an increasing number of supported employment schemes available where real employment is found for adults with severe autism in line with their skills, abilities, strengths and interests (Martin et al 1999).

The role of the nurse is to be aware of what occupational services and providers are available for adults with severe autism, to be aware of when and to whom to refer the service user, to provide accessible information to adults with severe autism and, when appropriate, their families, and to act as a service user advocate.

Day centres

While the previous section covered occupation for adults with severe autism, including that provided at day centres, it is worth revisiting the role and forms of day centres that were and are available.

As mentioned above, traditional day centres, be they NHS or local authority run, were fairly large, self-contained units sometimes located within large learning disability hospitals and sometimes within the local community. The services they provided included much of the following:

- Social and leisure facilities where the service user spent time and interacted and communicated with other people with a learning disability or other condition, many of whom lived within the hospital or small community home.
- Basic and simple vocational manufacturing, retail or gardening activities.
- Adult basic education such as literacy and numeracy.

Little real attempt was made to provide an individualised care package based on the assessed needs of each service user. Indeed, to have done so would have been hugely expensive and complex. The disadvantage was that the service user had to fit into existing service provision; a 'one size fits all' approach to day services both for those with a learning disability in general and for those with autism in particular.

During the 1990s, the function and role of day centres began to change and adapt to the needs of service users. Differing models of service provision such as satellite centres and drop-in centres were investigated (McIntosh 2002).

One of the functions of day centres is to act as a form of unofficial respite care for families and informal carers. The gradual closure of day centres as a result of changing care philosophies, directions and priorities caused problems to families of those with severe and profound autism as day care facilities became scarcer and more difficult to access. As well as changes in day care provision, there was a radically different way of funding these services. This change in funding included the provision of personal budgets, where service users are allocated a specific sum of money which they then use to purchase day care services that specifically meet their needs. This could include, but is not limited to, traditional day centres, where such exist. Thus, in order to compete for the 'autistic pound', for want of a better term, day care services and service providers now offer more autism friendly and autism-specific services.

The role of the nurse is to be aware of changes in day centre and day care provision and to provide accurate and accessible information and support to those with an ASC who are 'less able' and to act as their advocate should this be needed.

Health

Adults with severe autism are as likely as anyone else to experience physical and psychological health problems (Barber 2001). These could include:

- Developing various cancers.
- Having or developing circulatory and heart problems.
- Having strokes.
- Having or developing problems with hearing and sight loss.
- Infections warranting antibiotic treatment.
- Problems with the reproductive system.
- Visits to A & E, with and without the need for X-rays.
- Visits to outpatients.
- Development of diabetes requiring access to a whole host of healthcare professionals such as community nurses, diabetes specialist nurses, dieticians and renal nurses.
- Dental problems requiring visits to a local dental surgery.
- Health problems that require admittance to the local general hospital's medical or surgical wards.

There are a number of ways that the nurse and other healthcare professional can assist less able adults with severe autism. They should:

- *Assess the patient*: It is vital that a full, thorough and holistic assessment of patients is carried out which includes their strengths and abilities as well as their presenting health or medical condition and needs. Such an assessment needs to be acted upon.
- *Read the person's case notes*: This may sound obvious, but case notes are often either misread or not read at all with much vital information being missed, and poor quality care being offered as a result.
- *Read the person's personal 'passbook'*: This will contain details of the patient's routines, likes, dislikes, strengths, abilities, needs, etc.
- *Listen to the person*: Close and attentive listening and observation of how and what the patient is communicating is vital for the correct and appropriate care, therapy and treatment to be offered, even if the patient has minimal or no verbal communication skills.
- *Listen to the person's carers*: The patient's carers, be they care home staff or the patient's family, will know the patient better than you and will have much to tell you about the patient; listen to them and include them in the care of the patient.
- *Communicate*: Again, this may sound obvious, but communication is key to all interactions, treatments, therapies and care offered by the nurse. Thus, it is vital to be imaginative and learn and understand how the patient prefers or is able to communicate, and incorporate this understanding in your work with each individual.
- *Appointment times*: Try to offer appointment times that are appropriate and realistic to the needs and routines of the patient. Try to avoid busy times when there are lots of people 'milling around'. Try to offer specific rather than general appointment times (a 9.00 appointment time should mean 9.00 and not 9.45).
- *Pre-admittance visits*: Such visits could be useful in allaying and decreasing fear, uncertainty and anxiety as they will mean the patient will be admitted to a familiar environment with familiar people around him or her. This could result in a decrease in 'difficult behaviour' on the part of the patient.

Diagnostic overshadowing

According to Jones et al (2008) the term 'diagnostic overshadowing' was first used in 1982 to refer to 'the tendency for clinicians to attribute symptoms or behaviours of a person with learning disability to their underlying cognitive deficits, and hence to under-diagnose the presence of co-morbid psychopathology', such as autism or mental health problem.

It is possible that autism is hard to recognise in people with learning disabilities since, it is argued, severe autism and severe learning disabilities share many behaviours and characteristics. Overshadowing, where the symptoms of autism in people with learning disabilities are overlooked and autism is attributed to being part of 'having a learning disability', may contribute to this. In other words, a person with severe autism and a learning disability will be treated as being predominantly learning disabled and their autism will be seen as part of, and not separate from, their learning disability. Diagnostic overshadowing may contribute to the difficulties that many mental health and learning disability care professionals commonly experience in identifying autism in people with intellectual disabilities.

The role of the nurse in this situation is primarily to approach and treat the person with severe autism as a person first and foremost. This may sound strange, but there is a tendency for people to be treated as if they were no more than a medical condition. The nurse must also be very clear as to the differences between learning disability, mental health problem and autism and where these conditions do and do not overlap. With this in mind, the nurse must devise appropriate care plans that recognise and address the various elements, conditions and needs of the person with severe autism without confusing the conditions.

Conclusion

This chapter has focused on the health, day care, leisure and residential needs of less able adults with an ASC. Throughout the chapter it has been stressed that nurses and other healthcare professionals are likely to meet and work with people with an ASC, be they more or less able, in a wide range of work environments. However, in all of these settings the needs of the nurse are the same:

- To become aware of the residential, occupational, social and healthcare needs of those with an ASC.
- To acquire a wide range of appropriate residential, occupational, social and health information.
- To present that information in ways and formats and at times that those adults who are less able can access, even though the person may have no literacy or verbal abilities.
- To act as advocate on behalf of a person who may not be able or have the skills to speak up for themselves even if that involves becoming aware of and involved in the politics of disability.

Key points

- There is a large overlap between the needs of and services provided for those who have a learning disability and those with an ASC who are less able.
- The forms of residential services available for those who are 'less able' include specialist campus or village, specialist community-based housing and non-specialist community-based housing. Some of these are run by autism societies whilst others are not.
- Work and occupation opportunities include the 'traditional' day care centre, paid work, college, occupational therapies and autism-specific day care facilities. The quality of these, however, varies.
- Adults with severe autism are as likely as anyone else to experience physical and psychological health problems and are also likely to encounter problems in having their healthcare needs assessed and met.
- Diagnostic overshadowing can often cause problems when assessing and providing healthcare services for those who are less able.

References

Barber C (2001) The training needs of registered nurses engaged in work with people with an autistic spectrum disorder. *Good Autism Practice* **2**(2): 86–96

Jones S, Howard L, Thornicroft G (2008) 'Diagnostic overshadowing': Worse physical health care for people with mental illness. *Acta Psychiatrica Scandinavica* **118**: 169–71

Knapp M, Romeo R, Beecham J (2007) *The Economic Consequences of Autism in the UK*. Mental Health Foundation, London

Martin N, Johnston G, Stevens P (1999) Adults with intellectual disabilities and challenging behaviour in supported employment: Initial findings. *Journal of Applied Research in Intellectual Disabilities* **12**: 149–56.

McIntosh B (2002) *The Strategies for Change Project: Modernising Day Services – Lessons Learnt in the Changing Days Programme*. King's Fund Centre, London

CHAPTER 10

Mental health issues and autism spectrum conditions

Introduction

Being autistic or having autism or an autism spectrum condition (ASC) is not the same as having a mental illness or psychiatric condition even though the psychiatrist who first used the term 'autism' (Eugene Bleuler) also called it 'infantile schizophrenia'. However, some of the key healthcare professionals involved in the diagnosis of ASC and in post-diagnosis care and intervention are likely to come from a mental health background. Anecdotally, it is becoming more widely recognised that those who have an ASC are more likely to experience episodes of mental ill health than those who do not. Despite this, one mental health nurse who qualified in 2002 admitted that she knew very little about ASCs and that she did not recall having any lecture or teaching session on autism during her pre-registration training.

By the end of this chapter you will:

- Be able briefly to define what is meant by mental ill health/illness.
- Be aware of the more common forms of mental illness or mental health problems.
- Be aware of the prevalence of certain forms of mental health problem amongst those with an ASC as compared to those who do not have an ASC.
- Be aware of the various forms of therapy or treatment that are available to those with an ASC who experience a mental health problem.

What is mental health?

Mental health and mental illness could be argued to have a number of definitions and meanings. Mental disorder is:

> *A term defined by the Mental Health Act (1983) to cover all forms of mental illness and disability including mental impairment and psychopathic disorder.*
>
> Weller (1997: 365)

Mental hygiene is

The science that deals with the development of healthy mental and emotional reactions.

Weller (1997: 365)

Mental illness is

...not defined (by the Mental Health Act 1983) and is therefore left open to interpretation. This is, however, established through common practice and case law (previous legal cases involving the Act which have set precedents) as meaning the opinion of psychiatrists backed up by the official classification of mental illness.

Parsons (2003: 501)

A term used to describe a number of disorders of the mind that affect the emotions, perceptions, reasoning or memory of the individual.

Weller (1997: 365)

Close scrutiny of these definitions raises a number of issues:

- Parsons (2003) suggests that mental illness has no definition as such and that its meaning is left open to interpretation. Such a position could imply that mental illness is whatever the psychiatrist, psychologist or mental health nurse says it is.
- Weller's (1997) use of the terms 'mental disorder' and 'mental hygiene' as definition categories suggests that mental health is often seen and couched in negative terms and language. To suggest, for example, that a person's mental state is somehow 'unhygienic' is to infer the idea of 'dirtiness'.
- The use of certain, often negative, language to define a person's mental state is to allow the 'non-mentally ill' to control and subjugate those who experience mental health problems or difficulties.
- It could further be suggested that this is why some mental health professionals have allied themselves with mental health service users and survivor groups. Such an alliance has immersed the participants in the struggle for social, economic and political justice regarding how those who experience a mental health difficulty are viewed and treated by society in general and the nursing and medical professions in particular.

Mental health conditions

A small number of mental health problems are described below. Those described are by no means exclusive or clear-cut in terms of presentation or experience. Often, the symptoms relating to these various conditions may be subtle and may also indicate the existence or lived experience of more than one mental health condition.

Depression

> *A morbid and long-lasting sadness or melancholy which may, or may not, be a symptom of an underlying psychiatric problem.*
>
> Weller (1997: 120)

Causes could be numerous and may include:

- The loss of a job.
- Being a victim of a crime.
- The loss of a family member though death (bereavement) or the loss of a partner through separation or divorce.

Symptoms may include:

- Depressed mood for most of the day.
- Decreased interest or pleasure in daily activities.
- Insomnia, significant weight gain or loss.
- Feelings of worthlessness.
- Diminished ability to think, concentrate or make decisions.
- Thoughts of death, dying, self-harm or suicide.

Bipolar disorder

This condition, which used to be known as 'manic depression', is characterised by a dramatic fluctuation between the two extreme poles of severe mania and severe depression. The person could experience a single or multiple episodes of such severe and extreme mood swings. Bipolar conditions are chronic and recurrent and consist of two forms:

- *Bipolar 1* is typified by the occurrence of one or more manic episodes, or mixed episodes, and often one or more major depressive episodes. It is distinguished by a distinct period of abnormally and persistently elevated, expansive or irritable mood, lasting at least one week (or any duration if hospitalisation is necessary).
- *Bipolar 2* has the same symptoms as bipolar 1 except that the people do not have mania requiring hospitalisation.

(American Psychiatric Association 2000)

Anxiety disorders

Anxiety can be a chronic state of physical and mental tension (Weller 1997). However, Muir-Cochrane (2003) suggests that anxiety is a normal part of what it is to be human; that it is a normal human experience. Certain memories, experiences or anticipated events and unwarranted worrying can either cause or trigger anxiety states. Physical and behavioural symptoms of anxiety may include:

- Shortness of breath.
- Dizziness.
- Choking sensation.
- Palpitations.
- Sweating and dry mouth.
- Elevated blood pressure.
- Fear, apprehension, sense of impending doom, terror or dread.
- Altered sleep patterns.
- Irritability.
- Motor tension.
- Panic.

> *'Normal anxiety', when experienced in the extreme, is sometimes seen as 'anxiety disorder'.*

Muir-Cochrane (2003: 215)

Schizophrenia

According to Keen (2003) schizophrenia refers to a complex and controversial group of conditions. Major symptoms include:

- Delusional thinking and perceptions.
- Auditory hallucination or 'thought echo'.
- Broadcasting, withdrawal or insertion of thoughts into a person's head.
- Thought disorder, 'word salad', loosened associations.
- Obsessive preoccupation with fantasy and esoteric ideas (Barker 2003 calls this 'autism').
- Showing less interest, enthusiasm or emotion than usual.
- Inappropriate behaviour.

Borderline personality disorder (BPD)

BPD is a collection of personality traits that underpin certain groups of behaviours and is a pervasive pattern of instability of interpersonal relationships, self-image, and marked impulsivity. Diagnostic criteria for BPD (Parsons 2003) include the following:

- Frantic efforts to avoid real or imagined abandonment.
- A pattern of unstable and intense interpersonal relationships.
- Marked and persistently unstable self-image or sense of self.
- Potentially self-damaging impulsivity.
- Recurrent suicidal behaviour.
- Chronic feelings of emptiness.
- Inappropriate, intense anger or inability to control anger.
- Short-lived stress-related paranoid thoughts.

Addictions

There are a number of definitions of the word 'addiction'. It is now narrowly defined as 'uncontrolled, compulsive use despite harm'; if there is no harm to the patient or another party, there is no addiction. Addiction is a persistent, compulsive dependence on a behaviour or substance. The term has been partially replaced by the word dependence for substance abuse. Addiction has been extended, however, to include mood-altering behaviours or activities (process addiction), for example, gambling, shopping, eating, and sexual activity). There is a growing recognition that many addicts, such as polydrug abusers, are addicted to more than one substance or process.

Attention deficit hyperactivity disorder (ADHD)

ADHD is characterised by the presence of a set of chronic and impairing behaviour patterns that display abnormal levels of inattention, hyperactivity, or their combination. DSM-IV (American Psychiatric Association 2004) criteria for ADHD are either A or B as follows:

A. Six or more of the following symptoms of inattention present for at least 6 months to a point that is disruptive and inappropriate for developmental level:

Inattention

- Often does not give close attention to details or makes careless mistakes in schoolwork, work, or other activities.
- Often has trouble keeping attention on tasks or play activities.
- Often does not seem to listen when spoken to directly.
- Often does not follow instructions and fails to finish schoolwork, chores, or duties in the workplace (not due to oppositional behaviour or failure to understand instructions).
- Often has trouble organising activities.
- Often avoids, dislikes, or does not want to do things that take a lot of mental effort for a long period of time (such as schoolwork or homework).
- Often loses things needed for tasks and activities (e.g. toys, school assignments, pencils, books, or tools).
- Is often easily distracted.
- Is often forgetful in daily activities.

B. Six or more of the following symptoms of hyperactivity-impulsivity present for at least 6 months to an extent that is disruptive and inappropriate for developmental level:

Hyperactivity

- Often fidgets with hands or feet or squirms in seat.
- Often gets up from seat when remaining in seat is expected.
- Often runs about or climbs when and where it is not appropriate (adolescents or adults may feel very restless).
- Often has trouble playing or enjoying leisure activities quietly.
- Is often 'on the go' or often acts as if 'driven by a motor'.
- Often talks excessively.

Impulsivity

- Often blurts out answers before questions have been finished.
- Often has trouble waiting one's turn.
- Often interrupts or intrudes on others (e.g. butts into conversations or games).

Obsessive/compulsive disorder (OCD)

An obsession is a persistent, intrusive and unwanted thought or emotion that the person cannot ignore. A compulsion is a behavioural manifestation of an obsessive thought. Behavioural manifestations could include the uncontrollable, repetitive performance of a seemingly purposeful act or ritual such as the constant washing of hands or checking that lights are turned off or the front door closed and locked.

Dementia

Dementia is a global and progressive atrophy of brain cells leading to a gradual and irreversible decline in all areas of cognitive functioning, including memory, intellect, social judgement, personality, social skills/behaviour and physical skills. Whilst dementia is usually associated with old age, it is not unheard of for symptoms to appear at any age.

Prevalence of mental health conditions and ASC

Having briefly identified some of the forms of mental health problems that people may experience, what is their prevalence amongst those with an ASC? *Table 10.1* shows the percentage of those with an ASC who are likely to experience mental health problems, compared with the percentage of the UK population (currently around 60 million) who experience the same problems.

Treatment

Three main forms of treatment are available to help manage the symptoms of the various mental health problems and difficulties described above. Whether these forms of treatment can be seen as 'cures' for these conditions is open to debate. These three forms of treatment are:

Table 10.1. Prevalence of mental health conditions

Mental healthcare condition	*Total population (60 million) Number (%) with this condition*	*Population with an ASC (0.3–1 million) Number (%) with this condition*
Depression	1 680 000 (2.8%)	20 100–67 000 (6.7%*)
Anxiety disorder	4 800 000–7 200 000 (8–12%)	841 000 (84.1%*)
Schizophrenia	250 000**(1%)	3000–10 000 (1%*)
Obsessive/compulsive disorders	720 000 (1.2%)	27 000–90 000 (9%*)
*NAS (2010); **Keen (2003)		

- Pharmacotherapy.
- Physical therapies.
- Psychological therapies.

Pharmacotherapy

A wide range of medication is available to help people with a mental health problem manage or treat their condition and symptoms. These include:

- Antidepressants: used to treat depression. Includes amitriptyline, fluoxetine, doxepin, imipramine, mianserin, phenelzine, citalopram and paroxetine amongst many others. Parsons (2003) suggests that selective serotonin reuptake inhibitors (SSRIs), such as fluoxetine, can have a role in the management and treatment of BPD.
- Anxiolytics: sometimes referred to as 'minor tranquilliser'. Used to manage and treat anxiety states such as OCD, severe panic attacks and generalised anxiety disorder (previously known as neurosis). Anxiolytics include diazepam and lorazepam.
- Anti-convulsants: can be used to stabilise mood swings either alone or in conjunction with lithium carbonate. Such anti-convulsants include carbamazepine, sodium valproate and lamotrigine.
- Stimulants: Ritalin (methylphenidate) and amphetamine can be used to manage and treat ADHD.
- Anti-psychotics/neuroleptics: sometimes referred to as 'major tranquilliser'.

Used to treat various forms of psychosis, such as schizophrenia, bipolar disorder and BPD. Chlorpromazine, haloperidol, benperidol, thioridazine, clozapine and olanzapine are some of the better known anti-psychotics. These medicines are not curative but they do help people to manage many of the symptoms of psychosis.

Physical therapies

Two main types of physical therapy are used to manage and treat certain mental health conditions:

- Occupational therapy: this could include any form of occupation such as that provided at a day-care centre, industrial therapy, voluntary work or paid employment.
- Medical therapies, such as electro-convulsive therapy (ECT): ECT, which is used to treat severe depression, involves the passage of an electric current across the brain of an anaesthetised patient. However, there appears to be very little quality research into the value or efficacy of ECT (Bray 2003).

Psychological therapies

These could include a combination of:

- Behaviour management: through acknowledging, praising or rewarding 'good behaviour' and setting in place behavioural boundaries. Behaviour management has also previously been known as positive and negative reinforcement.
- Counselling: aims to help people talk through the reasons for their behaviour and its consequences.
- Psychotherapy: this is an umbrella term that includes cognitive behavioural therapy, problem solving therapy, manual-assisted cognitive therapy, interpersonal therapy and cognitive analytic therapy.
- Social skills training: teaches people how to manage their relationships better by reading the hidden signals of communication. It teaches them to understand what impact their behaviour has on other people, so they can change it.
- Complementary or holistic therapies: some people may use acupuncture, acupressure, hypnosis, relaxation, guided imagery and even prayer and

spiritual support as holistic and non-invasive forms of therapy and symptom management.

- Education: schools may play a crucial part in the management of a child's ASC. Additional in-class support may be available through the school's special needs department. Behavioural techniques may be used but, most importantly, the school will develop strategies to improve the child's academic achievement, which will have beneficial effects on his or her self-esteem and, consequently, behaviour and engagement in lessons.

For more information regarding the forms of therapy and treatment available see the MIND website and Barker (2003).

Discussion

> *The AS [autism spectrum] neurosystem is often joined by a variety of 'kissing cousins' including OCD, ADHD and anxiety.*
>
> Willey (2003: 182)

Table 10.1, which shows the prevalence of many of the major mental health conditions in people with an ASC, suggests two issues: there is a higher prevalence of certain mental health conditions in those with an ASC than in the general population, and that, consequently, there may be a link between ASC and these mental health conditions. Indeed, the National Autistic Society (2010) suggests that people with an ASC are vulnerable to mental health problems, particularly in late adolescence and early adulthood, with an incidence possibly as high as 65%. (Two-thirds of all those with an ASC will experience some form of mental health problem.) The reason for this is far from clear. With regard to anxiety and depression, one possible reason suggested by both the National Autistic Society (2010) and Willey (2003) is that anxiety, OCD and depression, for example, are caused by problems with sensory issues, social interactions and communication experienced by those with an ASC.

However, care must be taken not to confuse 'autistic behaviour' with a mental health condition (known as 'shadowing'). As mentioned at the start of this chapter, autism and mental health conditions are not the same. It is therefore not appropriate to suggest that a person's mental health condition is caused by or is a part of their autism and not to offer suitable treatment. It is also inappropriate to consider ASCs as a mental illness or mental health condition and treat them accordingly.

There is a long history of viewing life's ups and downs as pathogenic, that anything that deviates from a 'happy norm' is wrong and that there is a 'pill for every ill'. Mild stress, mild insomnia, sadness at the death of a friend or family member, mild euphoria brought on by one's football team winning the FA cup are all fertile ground for medicinal, psycho-pharmaceutical treatment. Television advertisements for 'sleeping aids' are an example of the pathologising of mild insomnia. Care should be taken to prevent the creeping demonisation of common life experiences and to think critically whether such life experiences require to be medicated. Indeed, Clarke (1999) appears to accept this position by recommending drugs are used only to manage the mental health or behavioural needs of those with an ASC.

This is not to say, however, that some people with an ASC may not have an extreme reaction to a life event such as unemployment, school transition, bullying, separation, divorce, death or bereavement. Neither is it to say that such a reaction does not require nursing or medical intervention. However, as some may have such an extreme experience and some may not, each person presenting with behaviour that is 'out of the ordinary' for them must be assessed on an individual basis.

Support for those with a dual diagnosis of ASC and a mental health condition will include pharmacotherapy, community mental health teams, behaviour management, counselling, psychotherapy, social skills training, holistic and complementary therapies and, in extreme cases, hospital in-patient care.

Many, if not most, of the psychological therapies rely on human interaction, communication and imagination, all areas of difficulty for those who have an ASC. Therefore, it is likely that any therapeutic and treatment approaches that rely heavily on the use of communication, interaction and imagination may have to be modified in order to make them useful for those who have an ASC.

Conclusion

In a recent survey into the mental health needs of young people with an ASC carried out by the National Autistic Society (2010), the following was highlighted:

- Mental health services failed to improve the mental health of two thirds of children with autism.
- 43% of parents whose children are currently registered with mental health services said their child's mental health had got worse because of non-existent services.

- Parents are twice as likely to say that services have improved their child's mental health when an autism specialist is involved in their treatment.
- Over half of parents do not think that mental health services know how to communicate with their child.

Sadly, it is likely that the above findings will also reflect the experience of adults with an ASC.

However, much good work is being led by nurses in the mental health services. This work will be supported and given real teeth by the Autism Act, the Autism Strategy and the Autism Guidelines (Department of Health 2009, 2010). It is essential that the opportunities offered by the Act, Strategy and Guidelines are incorporate into clinical practice.

Key points

- Mental illness can be defined as a number of disorders of the mind.
- Despite many of those with an ASC also having a mental health issue, such a dual diagnosis is not well understood by nurses.
- Those with an ASC are as likely as anyone else, if not more so, to develop various mental health conditions including depression, bipolar disorder, anxiety, schizophrenia, borderline personality disorder, ADHD, addictions, OCD and dementia.
- Treatments could include pharmacotherapy, physical therapies and psychological therapies either as 'stand-alone' therapies or in combination.
- Care must be taken not to demonise common life experiences by treating them as mental aberrations.

References

American Psychiatric Association (2000) *Diagnostic and Statistical Manual IV-TR*. American Psychiatric Association, Washington, DC

Barker P (2003) *Psychiatric and Mental Health Nursing: The Craft of Caring*. Arnold Publishers, London

Bray J (2003) The nurses role in the administration of ECT. In Barker P (ed) *Psychiatric and Mental Health Nursing: The Craft of Caring*. Arnold Publishers, London

Clarke D (1999) Psychiatric and behavioural problems and pharmacological treatments.

In Morgan H (ed) *Adults with Autism*. Cambridge University Press, Cambridge

Department of Health (2009) *Autism Act*. The Stationary Office, London. Available from:www.opsi.gov.uk/acts/acts2009/pdf/ukpga_20090015_en.pdf [Last accessed 25 June 2009]

Department of Health (2010) *Fulfilling and Rewarding Lives: The Strategy for Adults with Autism in England*. Available from: http://www.dh.gov.uk/prod_consum_dh/groups/dh_digitalassets/@dh/@en/@ps/documents/digitalasset/dh_113405.pdf [Last accessed 1 June 2010]

Keen T (2003) The person with schizophrenia. In Barker P (ed) *Psychiatric and Mental Health Nursing: The Craft of Caring*. Arnold Publishers, London

MIND website: http://www.mind.org.uk/help/information_and_advice?signpost

Muir-Cochrane E (2003) The person who experiences anxiety In Barker P (ed) *Psychiatric and Mental Health Nursing: The Craft of Caring*. Arnold Publishers, London

National Autistic Society (2010) Available from: http://www.autism.org.uk/working-with/health/mental-health-and-asperger-syndrome.aspx

Parsons S (2003) Psychiatric legislation: An international; perspective. In Barker P (ed) *Psychiatric and Mental Health Nursing: The Craft of Caring*. Arnold Publishers, London

Weller B (1997) *Bailliere's Nurses' Dictionary* (22nd edn). Bailliere Tindall, London

Willey LH (2003) *Asperger Syndrome in Adolescence*. Jessica Kingsley Publishers, London

CHAPTER 11

Autism and the criminal justice system

Introduction

> *There is a popular misconception that if a person commits a crime it is due to those with an AS [autism spectrum] being more prone to criminality...and that the opinion that AS people are more likely to commit crime is based on the assumption that [they] are incapable of recognising that this will hurt other people.*
>
> Jackson (2002: 183)

> *There is no evidence of an association between ASD [autism spectrum disorder] and criminal offending... Those with an ASD are more at risk as victims of crime rather than as offenders.*
>
> National Autistic Society (2010: 1)

It is likely that, at some point, most, if not all, of us will have some contact with the criminal justice system (CJS) either as victims of crime, as witnesses of crime or as perpetrators of crime. Those with an autism spectrum condition (ASC) are just as likely to come into contact with the CJS as anyone else. However, due to their condition, they are perhaps more vulnerable than anyone else when confronted with the law.

This chapter focuses on discussing what is meant by the term CJS and then highlighting the experience of those with an ASC as victims, witnesses or perpetrators of crime and the role of the nurse and other healthcare professional in relation to those with an ASC.

By the end of this chapter you will have gained a basic understanding of:

- The components of the CJS.
- Those with an ASC as crime victims.
- Those with an ASC as witnesses of crime.
- Those with an ASC as crime perpetrators.
- The training needs of those who work in the CJS.

What is the criminal justice system?

The aims of the CJS are to:

- Reduce crime and the fear of crime by:
  - Reducing the level of actual crime and disorder.
  - Reducing the adverse impact of crime and disorder on people's lives.
  - Reducing the economic costs of crime.
- Dispense justice fairly, which it does through:
  - Ensuring just processes and just and effective outcomes.
  - Dealing with cases throughout the criminal justice process with appropriate speed.
  - Meeting the needs of victims, witnesses and jurors within the system.
  - Respecting the rights of defendants and treating them fairly.
  - Promoting confidence in the CJS.

(McConville and Wilson 2002: 7)

In order to meet these aims, the CJS has a number of component parts:

- *The police*: The first contact an offender has with the CJS is usually with the police (or law enforcement officer) who investigate a suspected wrong-doing and make an arrest. When warranted, law enforcement agencies or police officers are empowered to use force and other forms of legal coercion to effect public and social order and safety.
- *The Crown Prosecution Service:* This service is responsible for prosecuting people in England and Wales charged with a criminal offence.
- *The Criminal Defence Service:* This service is responsible for defending people in England and Wales charged with a criminal offence.
- *The Courts Service*: This service, which is an executive agency of the Department for Constitutional Affairs, provides administrative support to a number of courts and tribunals, including Magistrates Courts, which deal with most 'low-level' crime, the High Court, the Crown Court and County Courts.
- *The National Probation Service:* This service is a criminal justice agency that works with offenders. The aim of the service is to reduce reoffending and to protect the public. The probation service is sometimes used as an alternative to a prison or custodial sentence by the courts.

- *The Youth Justice Board for England and Wales:* This is a non-departmental public body. The aim of the Youth Justice Board is to prevent offending by children and young people.
- *Victim Support*: This service helps residents cope with the effects of crime by providing confidential support and information to victims of crime and to witnesses attending local courts.
- *Her Majesty's Prison Service:* The Prison Service serves the public by keeping in custody those committed by the courts.
- *The Criminal Case Review Commission:* This is an independent body responsible for investigating suspected miscarriages of criminal justice in England, Wales and Northern Ireland.

Victims of crime

An individual with an ASC is as likely as anyone else to become a victim of crime, including theft, burglary, assault (verbal, physical and sexual) and harassment. It could be that because of their enhanced vulnerability due to issues around social immaturity, problems with communication, lack of understanding and inability to read correctly situations and people, those with an ASC are at increased risk of becoming victims of crime. Indeed, Mencap (2010) reported an incidence of physical assault of a person with an ASC.

> *It is outrageous that these crimes have gone virtually unpunished. Such a violent and brutal attack deserves a sentence that reflects the seriousness of the crime. This sends the message that the police and the courts do not take disability hate crime seriously.*
>
> Mark Goldring, Chief Executive of Mencap (Mencap 2010)

The National Autistic Society (2010) has made a number of suggestions that could be of help to those with an ASC who have become victims of crime.

- A scheme that uses intermediaries (knowledgeable volunteers) to help vulnerable victims in their contact with the various branches of the CJS is being rolled out across the country.
- Those with an ASC sometimes require and are offered specialist, tailor-made counselling services during and after accessing the CJS.
- People with an ASC should carry an 'autism alert' card to inform key people within the local CJS that the person has an ASC.

However, caution must be exercised with this third suggestion. Many people may not be aware that they have an ASC because they remain undiagnosed; others may not be aware of or willing to carry such a card due to the social stigma associated with autism.

> *In the criminal justice system, police officers, probation services and courts may all be unaware of the communication challenges posed – leading to overly heavy-handed responses to incidents.*
>
> (Department of Health 2010)

It will be helpful to remember the following when working with and supporting those who have an ASC who are victims of crime:

- Keep unpredictable sensory stimuli to a minimum.
- Use clear, accurate, unambiguous and concise language.
- When questioning the victim, allow time for him or her to respond.
- Address people by name so that they know that they are being talked to.
- Be aware of 'autistic behaviour and characteristics' such as hand flapping, and sensory and anxiety issues.

Witnesses of crime

Just as with those with an ASC are as likely to be victims of crime as anyone else, so they are as likely to be witnesses of crime. However, there are a number of issues that need to be borne in mind when working with this group.

- The image of a police officer that many with an ASC may have is one of a person in a police uniform. Therefore, a person with an ASC may not be able to understand the concept of a 'plain clothes officer' or recognise the authority of such an officer.
- When supporting a crime witness who has an autism spectrum condition, be aware of how communication, imagination, social relationships, personal space and sensory issues may impact upon that person's understanding of what he or she has seen and how this is to be reported to the police.
- Be aware of 'autistic' type behaviour, such as hand flapping, in the witness and, wherever possible, do not try to stop this behaviour as to do so will only serve to increase the witness's anxiety.

- When asking questions of the witness, try to couch the questions in clear, unambiguous and precise language.
- Whenever possible use short closed questions rather than open questions that could be misinterpreted.
- Allow time for the person to respond.
- Address witnesses by name so they know that they are being addressed.
- Use of an 'autism aware' card carried by the witness may be useful in alerting scene of crime or interview officers to the needs of the witness.
- When supporting a witness at a police station, it may be useful to seek the advice of a psychiatrist or psychologist, preferably from outside the CJS, who is familiar with and understands ASC.
- The National Autistic Society (2010) guide to the CJS includes many useful resources that could be used when working with or supporting crime witnesses who have an ASC, including Victim Support, the Crown Prosecution Service and the Intermediaries Registration Board.
- At all times, those with an ASC must be reassured that, as witnesses, they have done nothing wrong and that it is not them that are being accused of a crime.
- Those with an ASC who have witnessed a crime may benefit from post-incident de-briefing and counselling to allow them mentally and emotionally to 'unload'.

Perpetrators of crime

> *There is no evidence of an association between ASD and criminal offending.*
>
> National Autistic Society (2010: 1)

Although the National Autistic Society and Attwood (2006) suggest that those with an ASC are no more likely than the general population to commit crime, Attwood (2006) goes on to report that there have been numerous published examples of those with an ASC committing serious crimes. Attwood (2006) also suggests that media coverage of crime will sometimes refer to the perpetrator's ASC diagnosis, the result being that criminal propensity and ASC are linked in the public's mind. However, Jackson (2002) suggests that such linking is a misconception based on the assumption that those with an ASC are unable to understand the effects that their behaviour may have on others. Crimes committed by those with an ASC are similar to those committed by anyone else and range from homicide to public nuisance, such as fighting and shouting due to an acute and heightened sense of injustice or simply not knowing the rules of social engagement, via theft, aggression and violence.

According to Attwood (2006) there are a number of possible reasons why those with an ASC engage in minor crime, such as public order offences. These reasons include 'social immaturity' which may make adolescents with an ASC more vulnerable to being 'set up' to commit crimes or engage in antisocial behaviour by their peers, and social isolation. In many instances, Attwood (2006) further asserts that prison or some other forms of custodial sentence may not act as a deterrent to those with an ASC.

There are a number of discrete stages in the process of involvement with the CJS:

- Confrontation by the police and being arrested.
- Being taken to the police station.
- Being interviewed.
- Appearing before the courts (magistrates' or judges').
- Being sentenced.
- Carrying out that sentence.
- Post-sentence.

Case example

Joe is a 35-year-old man with Asperger's syndrome/high functioning autism. He has just been arrested after being involved in a post-football match fight with a small group of rival football supporters, a fight that he instigated due to what he considers to be the unjust outcome of the match (his team lost). This fight resulted in the potentially serious injury of another person. This is not Joe's first offence, however, and he is well known to the local police due to his antisocial behaviour. This scenario presents a wide range of issues for the various branches of the CJS.

- *At the scene of the incident:* it would be helpful if the flashing lights and car siren were to be switched off. Not to do so would heighten Joe's sensory overload which, in turn, would heighten his anxiety levels and aggressive mood (National Autistic Society 2010). The police officer involved has arrested Joe before and knows he has an ASC and that communication must be simple and specific.
- *At the police station:* the custody officer will have a duty to ask if Joe has a 'special educational need'. It is essential that Joe's family and carers

talk to the custody officer about ASC since, according to the National Autistic Society (2010), custody officers rarely have any knowledge of the condition. The custody officer has a common law duty of care for Joe's welfare whilst Joe is at the police station and to ignore Joe's condition could be to place the officer in breach of this care. A registered medical officer (usually a local GP) will assess Joe and decide whether he is fit to be interviewed. An 'approved social worker' may be called in if it is thought that Joe may need a psychiatric assessment. However, neither the medical officer nor social worker may have much knowledge about ASC.

- *Being interviewed:* it would be good practice here to seek the input of an 'appropriate adult' to safeguard Joe's rights whilst Joe is in custody. Issues around communication come to the fore and it is vital that the interviewing officer communicates appropriately with Joe. By that is meant asking direct and closed rather than indirect or open questions, being aware of Joe answering by repeating the question, giving Joe time to process the question and answer, not using irony or sarcasm, addressing Joe by name, being aware of eye contact and being aware of sensory issues. It may also be helpful to access the support of an 'ASC specialist'.
- *Appearing before the courts:* a magistrate, judge or jury can determine whether Joe is mentally fit to stand trial. A magistrate or judge will determine whether to proceed under criminal or mental health law (National Autistic Society 2010). Again, communication is vitally important. It is also helpful if the judge and barristers remove their wigs and other symbols of office as Joe may find these confusing and even threatening.
- *Being sentenced:* Attwood (2006) suggests that a custodial sentence in prison or young offenders institute (borstal) is unlikely to act as a deterrent for those who are deliberately malicious, violent or antisocial. It is questionable whether Joe is malicious or just does not understand the rules governing social behaviour. However, that is not to say that a custodial sentence may not be appropriate or necessary for certain crimes. Again, the magistrate or judge may need to take into account whether Joe is likely to self-harm or attempt suicide if given a custodial sentence.
- *Carrying out the sentence:* due to a possible combination of factors including:
  - a lack of understanding of the criminal justice process,
  - what is expected of Joe,
  - heightened anxiety and depression,
  - disruption to Joe's daily and even hourly routine,

- a lack of understanding of issues around ASC on the part of prison or probation personnel,
- being vulnerable to bullying and assaults by other prison inmates or probation service users (if Joe was to receive a custodial or probation sentence),
- being vulnerable to possible self-harm and attempts at suicide.

Joe may need extra support in order to both survive and learn from the experience of serving the sentence. Therefore, suitable and appropriate on-going professional development in aspects of autism such as communication, sensory issues, social interaction and social skills may be needed by prison and probation staff so that they can more easily support Joe. Again, it may be useful for those care professionals involved in supporting Joe to access the support and advice of a care professional who has an expertise in ASC.

- *Post-sentence:* once the sentence, be it custodial or non-custodial, has been completed, Joe may need assistance and support psychologically and emotionally to process and make sense of his experience of the CJS. He may need help to re-adjust to his 'previous life'. To this end, Joe may benefit from counselling and 'de-briefing'. This would need to be carried out by a skilled care professional with experience of providing such support to those with an ASC. Joe could be offered social skills training either individually or as part of a small group. The social skills group could be used to help Joe to realise, understand and accept the inappropriateness of his behaviour, and the harm and distress that he could cause to others. More appropriate behaviour could be presented and modelled in a manner that Joe could understand, accept and assimilate.

Conclusion

Whilst there may not be a link between having an ASC and involvement in crime, either as a victim, witness or perpetrator, there are still significant numbers of people with an ASC who are involved in the legal system. It could be suggested that there is a need for a better understanding of autism through training, and for developing techniques for communication and intervention in criminal justice settings (Welsh Assembly 2006, Bishop 2008, Benton and Sharp 2009). Nurses and other healthcare professionals may be involved in a wide number of different settings:

- Prison nurses.
- Expert witnesses.
- Advocates or 'appropriate adults'.
- Facilitators of social and life skill courses so that those with an ASC do not come into contact with the CJS as crime perpetrators.
- Designers, facilitators and leaders of training courses for CJS professionals such as the police, lawyers, and probation and prison staff.

Finally, in order to support appropriately Joe and other people with an ASC who come into contact with the CJS, there is a need for on-going and robust professional development for nurses and other healthcare professionals in all aspects of the criminal justice system.

Key points

- Those with an ASC are just as likely to come into contact with the criminal justice system as anyone else, either as victims, witnesses or perpetrators of crime.
- Whether as victim, witness or perpetrator of a crime, the support needs of those with an ASC are likely to be very similar. These include:
  - Keeping unpredictable sensory stimuli to a minimum.
  - Using clear, accurate, unambiguous and concise language.
  - When questioning the victim, allowing time for him or her to respond.
  - Addressing individuals by name so that they know they are being talked to.
  - Being aware of 'autistic behaviour and characteristics' such as hand flapping and sensory and anxiety issues.

References

Attwood T (2006) *The Complete Guide to Asperger's Syndrome*. Jessica Kingsley Publishers, London

Benton C, Sharp M (2009), West Midlands Forum on the Criminal Justice System and the Autistic Spectrum. *Good Autism Practice* 10: 1

Bishop D (2008) An examination of the links between autistic spectrum disorders and offending behaviour in young people. *Internet Journal of Criminology*. Available from: http://www.internetjournalofcriminology.com/Bishop%20%20Autistic%20 Spectrum%20Disorders%20and%20Offending%20Behaviour%20in%20Young%20

People.pdf [Last accessed 07 April 2011]

Department of Health (2010 *The Autism Strategy: Fulfilling and Rewarding Lives*. HMSO, London

Jackson L (2002) *Freaks, Geeks and Asperger Syndrome*. Jessica Kingsley Publishers, London

McConville M, Wilson G (eds) (2002) *The Handbook of the Criminal Justice Process*. Oxford University Press, Oxford

Mencap (2010) *Mencap responds to the sentencing of three men found guilty of attacking a teenager with autism*. Available from: http://www.mencap.org.uk/news.asp?id=19483&pageno=2&year=2010&menuId=91 [Last accessed 11 March 2011]

National Autistic Society (2010) *Criminal Justice Systems and ASDs*. NAS, London. Available from: http://www.autism.org.uk/working-with/criminal-justice/criminal-justice-system-and-asds.aspx [last accessed 08 March 2011]

Welsh Assembly Government (2006) *Identifying and Supporting People with Autistic Spectrum Disorders within the Youth Justice System in Wrexham and Flintshire*. Available from: http://wales.gov.uk/topics/housingandcommunity/research/safety/autisticjustice/?lang=en [Last accessed 07 April 2011]

CHAPTER 12

Nursing interventions: Past, present and future

Introduction

The history of autism spectrum conditions (ASCs) goes hand-in-hand with the development of nursing knowledge, understanding and interventions for those with an ASC. Both ASCs and nursing knowledge have gone through specific, even similar changes. It is important to highlight these historical developments since an awareness and understanding of the past will help prevent mistakes being made in the future.

This chapter highlights the changes in nursing knowledge, understanding and interventions over the last century, and speculates on what care might look like in the future. It is divided into the following eras:

- 20th century up to 1960.
- 1960–1980.
- 1980–2000.
- 2000–2015.
- 2015 onwards.

The first three eras up to 2000 cover much of the same territory as *Chapter 3*, the fourth covers current knowledge and interventions and the fifth looks to the future. Knowledge and interventions will be discussed separately in order to prevent a mere recording of these changes, and to put them into context.

By the end of this chapter, the reader will be able to:

- Chart the changes and progress that have been made in nursing knowledge and understanding of ASCs.
- Chart the changes and progress that have been made in nursing interventions for those with an ASC and their families.
- Predict how future knowledge and services are going to look.
- Debate these changes and predictions from an informed standpoint.

Nursing interventions: Past

20th century up to 1960

Nursing had no specific input for those with an ASC during the period up to 1960 because in the UK the condition was not recognised as being a separate neurological condition requiring specialist nursing input. Although autism was first identified as a neurological condition by Blueler in 1912 and later by Kanner and Asperger in 1943 and 1944, respectively, specialist nursing intervention was virtually non-existent. Many of those with an ASC were considered 'normal' and would not have come to the attention of the mental subnormality (as it was then known) or psychiatric service; those affected would have received medical and nursing services in the same way as anyone else within society. Those who were considered to have a 'mental subnormality', a major psychiatric problem or whose 'moral and/or social behaviour' was 'questionable' (prostitutes or women bearing illegitimate children, for example) would likely have spent several years as mentally subnormal or psychiatric in-patients and have received nursing intervention and care along with other in-patients.

However, the eugenics movement was making its mark both here in the UK and elsewhere so it is not impossible that nurses were complicit in eugenics programmes that involved people with an ASC. This could have included segregation, sterilisation and, in Germany in the 1940s, experimentation.

1960–1980

The two decades from 1960 to 1980 were marked by debates around the validity and value of institutional care as a model for living for those with learning disabilities and psychiatric problems, including those with an ASC. Such issues were still being debated in some circles in the opening years of the 21st century and have yet to disappear entirely.

In the early 1960s a group of parents realised that they and their autistic children were receiving very little help and intervention from care professionals. The Autistic Children's Aid Society of North London (ACASNL) was founded on 23 January 1962 by parents of autistic children living in the area, with the assistance of a member from the Spastics Society (later Scope). The current name of the National Autistic Society was adopted by the ACASNL in 1975 when the charity extended its interest to the whole of the UK.

However, despite the existence of the ACASNL and possibly other similar fledgling support and pressure groups within the UK in the 1960s and 1970s, specific nursing support and interventions for both those with an ASC and their families were virtually non-existent outside of mental health and learning disability services. Student nurses did not have any input in their training about autism since it was largely unknown outside of specialist psychiatry.

The late 1960s also saw the idea, which emerged from the work of Bruno Bettelheim, that autism was a result of either bad or absent parenting. It is possible that nurses and doctors, due to their lack of knowledge and understanding about ASC, followed Bettelheim's lead and were engaged in and promoted the theory that parents were to blame for their child's autistic behaviour. This was likely to be the case not only in the UK but also throughout the world. For example, Caiseal Mor (an Australian who has an ASC) recorded in his autobiography (Mor 2007) the sexual abuse and anal rape that he experienced at the hands of his mother. This rape, which involved the forcible insertion of a kitchen rolling pin into his rectum, was suggested to his mother and sanctioned by his family's GP at the time on the grounds that pain would cure autism. Caiseal was only five years old at the time of this pain 'therapy/treatment'.

Poor and inappropriate nursing and medical care for those with a learning disability, including those with an ASC, who lived in many of the long stay institutions such as Ely and South Ockendon Hospitals came under the spotlight in various Government reports in the early to mid-1970s. These reports paved the way for the Jay report (DHSS 1979) which, amongst other recommendations, suggested the ending of learning disability nurse training and specialism, a suggestion that is still being debated.

At the same time as these reports, Wolfensberger's theory of 'normalisation' and its attendant 'social role valorisation' (see *Chapter 3*) was having an impact on the lives of those with an ASC who lived in the old mental subnormality institutions. Nurses began to realise and understand that those with a learning disability, including those with an ASC, had a right to the same positive and life-affirming opportunities and experiences as anyone else and that nursing and residential care and support should be delivered accordingly. Thus nurses were involved at all levels of care assessment, planning, implementation and evaluation in order to improve the lives and experiences of their service users. Such input included behaviour modification programmes, amongst many other interventions. Such programmes were designed to modify, change and eliminate 'autistic behaviour' in the individual so as to enable them to fit more easily into 'normal society'.

1980–2000

It could be suggested that nurses' awareness, understanding and interventions really took shape during the last two decades of the 20th century, as a result of a number of events including:

- Publications by academic care professionals, including Lorna Wing, Uta Frith, Tony Attwood and Simon Baron-Cohen.
- Publications by those with an ASC, including Donna Williams and Temple Grandin.
- An emerging user and self-advocacy movement.
- An emerging social model of care which challenged the existing medical model of care.

However, even in the mid- to late 1980s autism, Asperger's syndrome and other ASCs did not feature in the training courses and curricula of many student nurses. Knowledge and understanding about ASCs would have been gained during post-qualification clinical practice as a result of working with those with an ASC. Because of this, nursing interventions would have been limited to either 'drug therapy', such as the administration of antipsychotics or anxiolytics, or the administration of behaviour modification techniques. Indeed, in one residential unit in the West Midlands, it was thought that some service users' behaviour was partially caused by lithium carbonate; because some of the residents were bipolar, all were prescribed the drug. Despite this particular residential unit being designated an 'autism unit', none of the staff had any specific training in autism and, where Wing's 'triad of impairment' (Wing, 1999) was used by staff, it was used without question. Likewise, it was possible that the behaviour modification techniques used by nurses working with those with an ASC would have been used without critical thought of the causes of 'autistic behaviour' and thus their appropriateness and value.

Nursing interventions: Present (2000–2015)

There are a number of schools of thought in relation to current nursing and medical interventions. Some have emerged out of the views of individuals and groups of those with an ASC and their families, many of whom are increasingly informed and active in disability politics and awareness. Behaviour modification techniques and medication are still being used to manage 'autistic behaviour' but are being used with more thought and appropriateness. Such use of antipsychotic and antidepressant medication and behaviour modification techniques will probably remain an important aspect of nursing and medical intervention for some but by no means all of those on the autism spectrum for some time to come.

One current school of thought is that autism is 'treatable'. The website of the Autism Research Institute (ARI) in the US (http://www.autism.com/) makes it clear that their aim is to research into and provide 'treatment' for autism. Indeed, with the 'alarming increase in autism diagnoses', the ARI encourages medical professionals to learn about treatments, and to offer them to patients. Autistic children and their families need medical and professional help, and ARI recommends its Defeat Autism Now! approach as a foundational treatment. It is questionable or even undesirable to assume that autism can be 'treated'. However, certain aspects of autism and Asperger's may be amenable to interventions, such as diet, sensory modification, communication and behavioural modification programmes and even certain prescribed medication such as Ritalin and melatonin. Some of these interventions are seen as 'treatments' by the ARI. However, beware, the ARI website also proposes not only that autism is treatable but also that people can recover from autism, however, they cannot.

As a result of increased self-advocacy on the part of both those with an ASC and their families, there is now a plethora of support groups. Some of these are targeted at and run by those with an ASC whilst others have been targeted at and run by parents, partners, siblings and even children of those with an ASC. Not all of these support groups are facilitated by nurses or other care professionals. One form of nurse intervention would be to allow support groups to meet in health service facilities such as health centres with the addition of offering basic administrative support and simple refreshments. The National Autistic Society (NAS) facilitates support groups for those with an ASC and their families in various parts of the UK, supporting the self-advocacy of both stakeholders. This is in line with the aspirations and demands of the autism 'user movement' that has been emerging over the past few years.

Many parents, nurses, psychiatrists, speech and language therapists and psychologists have been actively involved in the vital area of life skills training with both pre-teen and teenagers with an ASC. Such life skills training can include work and interventions in many of the following areas:

- Bullying.
- Communication.
- Social interactions.

- Relationships.
- Sexuality.
- Personal hygiene.
- Eating and diet.

Many of these issues increase in importance as the person with an ASC becomes a teenager in the same way as their non-ASC peers. The pressure to 'fit in' with normal adolescent activities will be greatly accentuated in the person with an ASC. Indeed, there is a growing library of resources that focus on such life skills (see Wrobel 2003, Harpur et al 2006, Painter 2006, Larkey 2007, Attwood 2007, Cotugno 2009).

Sensory issues are major areas of nurse intervention, as will be seen in *Chapter 15*. These areas include diagnosing sensory issues, developing an individual's sensory profile and developing, implementing and evaluating sensory interventions. Both Larkey (2007) and Wrobel (2003) provide useful copyright-free sensory activities that can be photocopied and used with both individuals and groups of people with an ASC.

A number of recent reports and legislation will have a direct impact on the nursing care of those with an ASC. These include:

- The Disability Discrimination Act (1995, amended in 2005) seeks to make illegal discrimination against those with a disability.
- *Valuing People* and *Valuing People Now* (Department of Health, 2001 and 2008, respectively) introduced person-centred care and services and health action plans into the lives of those with a learning disability, including many of those with an ASC.
- *I Exist,* published by the National Autistic Society (2008) highlights the aspirations, desires and needs of adults with an ASC.

These will provide a contextual basis and framework for the provision of nursing, medical and social care for those with an ASC, particularly the introduction of person-centred care which includes personal budgets and health action plans. Many nurses are already engaging with these issues, seeing those with an ASC as equal partners in service planning and delivery and working alongside those with an ASC and their families to this end.

I Exist, the Autism Act of 2009, the Autism Strategy (Department of Health 2010) and the Autism Guidelines (2010) will have huge implications for nursing practice for the foreseeable future. Indeed, five out of the six recommended Autism Guidelines (awareness training, developing a clear and consistent diagnostic pathway, improving access to services and support, supporting adults with an ASC into work, and working with other care agencies in order to develop relevant services) will have a direct impact on both current and future nursing services. The exact details of how these Guidelines will translate into service provision will differ due to geographical location, level of pre-existing knowledge, understanding, services and need, and available funding.

Nursing interventions: Future (2015+)

Autism spectrum conditions are like an onion: peel away one layer of skin and another appears. However as knowledge about and understanding of ASC improves, deepens, expands and changes over time so will nursing strategies and interventions. Although it is almost impossible to speculate about the future of nursing interventions over the next 20 to 30 years with any degree of certainty or accuracy, the following may be worth investigating:

- *Pre- and antenatal diagnosis of an ASC.* At present, there are no tests available that can detect or predict the likelihood of a child having an ASC. Please note, pre- and antenatal testing is not the same as genetic counselling, where prospective parents are advised of the possible likelihood that any child they may have will be on the autism spectrum based on the incidence of ASCs in their family. However, that does not mean that discussions and research are not currently taking place with a view to developing such genetic testing. Possible links between antenatal testing and the subsequent offering of termination of pregnancy need to be carefully thought through.
- *A search for a 'cure' for autism and a means to enable 'recovery' from autism.* At the moment, any such 'cure' or 'recovery' is a pipe dream. Anecdotally, when parents of newly diagnosed children are asked what they should be told, they say, very emphatically, 'There is no such thing as a cure for or recovery from autism so don't waste your time, effort, money or hopes in looking for one.' However, the search for a 'cure' and subsequent 'recovery' continues, as can be seen by looking at the ARI website. However, what the ARI understand as a 'cure' may well be little more than improvements obtained in a person's 'autistic behaviour' due to the input of specific diet regimes, such as gluten and lactose free diets; occupational therapy; behavioural therapies; communication strategies; or medication.

Nurses may well be asked if there are or will be any cures for autism. If so, be honest and careful about the answer that is given.

- *Greater collaboration between all stakeholders and care professionals.* There needs to be an end to the Berlin Wall of poor or non-communication, poor or non-cooperation and 'professional protectionism' between service providers. This will mean that those with an ASC and their families will be empowered and treated as equals by all other stakeholders.
- *People with an ASC flexing their individual and collective service and political muscles.* This will include those with an ASC negotiating with service providers about what services they need.
- *More accurate use of diagnostic criteria and tools in older adults as well as young children.* This will be in line with the ideas and aspirations underpinning the Autism Act, Autism Strategy and Autism Guidelines. The current lack of appropriately qualified and experienced clinicians who can accurately and competently diagnose adults will be consigned to history. Nurses will, increasingly, be involved in administering and evaluating such diagnostic tools.
- *More in-depth work on communication strategies, social skills programmes and sensory profiles.* These will be ignored or side-lined to the peril of both service providers and service users.

Discussion

Although there have been occasions when nurses have been trailblazers in the care of those with an ASC, close scrutiny reveals that they have often followed where others have led. Such leadership may have come in the form of political and social ideology, for example. This chapter gives examples of the possible consequences of following rather than leading.

However, times have changed. Those with an ASC are 'in the ascendency'; more politically aware, more vocal, more savvy. Many are demanding a piece of the social, economic and political action. Nurses need to be empowered to be able to contribute to and work within this new and exciting world. The basic tools of such empowerment are there, tools such as the Autism Act, the Autism Strategy and the Autism Guidelines. Nurses need to have the will to change such tools into reality, working alongside those with an ASC in order to change the world for the better. Such ownership and empowerment are implicit within much of the Autism Guidelines. However, there is a nagging doubt that any such ownership and empowerment is an exercise in rhetoric rather than reality, and, as such, nurses will always play a supporting rather than a leading role in autism interventions.

Conclusion

The history of nursing interventions in the lives of those with an ASC has been tentatively sketched out in this chapter. Despite the difficulty in making predictions, the future for nurse interventions for people with an ASC looks bright. Nurses need to take the lead and come out of the shadows cast by politicians and other care professionals. Nurses will be key in making improvements happen.

Key points

- The history of nursing interventions mirrors the development of society's understanding of autism spectrum conditions.
- In the first half of the 20th century, nursing interventions were very closely related to the care of those with a learning disability. Much of the care delivered was heavily institutionalised and largely followed a eugenics agenda.
- The third quarter of the 20th century saw debates around the institutional care of those with an ASC and other forms of learning disability.
- The last quarter of the last century saw a growth in self-advocacy which helped to influence nursing interventions.
- The first few years of the 21st century saw debates around the medical and social models of care, whether autism is treatable and the Autism Act and Strategy.
- It will be up to those with an ASC, working with health and social care professionals and politicians, to shape nursing interventions for the coming decades.

References

Attwood T (2007) *The Complete Guide to Asperger's Syndrome*. Jessica Kingsley Publishers, London

Cotugno A (2009) *Group Interventions for Children with Autism Spectrum Disorders*. Jessica Kingsley Publishers, London

Department of Health (2001) *Valuing People: A New Strategy for Learning Disabilities for the 21st Century*. The Stationary Office, London

Department of Health (2006) *Valuing People Now*. The Stationary Office, London

Department of Health (2009) *Autism Act*. HMSO, London. Available from: www.opsi.

gov.uk/acts/acts2009/pdf/ukpga_20090015_en.pdf [Last accessed 25 June 2009]

Department of Health (2010) *Fulfilling and Rewarding Lives: The Strategy for Adults with Autism in England*. Available from: http://www.dh.gov.uk/prod_consum_dh/groups/dh_digitalassets/@dh/@en/@ps/documents/digitalasset/dh_113405.pdf [Last accessed 1 June 2010]

DHSS (1979) *Report of the Committee of Enquiry into Mental Handicap Nursing and Care*. (Cmnd.7468) HMSO, London

Harpur J, Lawlor M, Fitzgerald M (2006) *Succeeding with Interventions for Asperger Syndrome Adolescents*. Jessica Kingsley Publishers, London

Larkey S (2007) *Practical Sensory Programmes for Students with Autism Spectrum Disorders and Other Special Needs*. Jessica Kingsley Publishers, London

Mor C (2007) *A Blessing and a Curse*. Jessica Kingsley Publishers, London

National Autistic Society (2008) *I Exist: The Message from Adults with Autism*. Available from: http://www.autism.org.uk/iexist [Last accessed 15 June 2010]

Painter K (2006) *Social Skills Groups for Children and Adolescents with Asperger's Syndrome*. Jessica Kingsley Publishers, London

Wing L (1999) *The Autistic Spectrum*. Constable, London

Wrobel M (2003) *Taking Care of Myself*. Future Horizons, Arlington, TX

CHAPTER 13

Person-centred planning

Introduction

This chapter is on person-centred planning (PCP), 'person-centred' being the latest in-vogue term, used widely in the health and social care professions. Sometimes PCP is used incorrectly and neither it nor its implications are always fully understood; it is just followed blindly as the latest care fad. However, is this a fair way of approaching and using PCP? What does being 'person-centred' mean, anyway? Surely, health and social care professionals should always be 'person-centred', regardless of the clinical setting or who is providing care.

During this chapter you will consider and gain some understanding of the following issues:

- The meaning of person-centred approach and care.
- The history of person-centred care.
- The application of PCP for those on the autism spectrum.
- Person-centred assessment tools.
- Person-centred care delivery tools.
- Disadvantages of using a person-centred approach.

What does 'person-centred' mean?

There are a number of ways of looking at or defining what is meant by 'person-centred'. These include:

- Person-centred approach.
- Person-centred planning.
- Person-centred assessment.
- Person-centred care.
- Person-centred treatment.

Whilst these may seem to be similar, and in some ways they are, there are a number of differences.

Box 13.1. Case example: Steve

Steve is a fully mobile and capable young lady in her mid-20s living at home with her parents. She attended mainstream primary and secondary schools and college. Although she was diagnosed with Asperger's syndrome in her early teens, her parents had felt for many years before this that she may have been on the autism spectrum and fought to get her assessed, statemented and educated within mainstream schools. Her interests include cooking, anime (a type of Japanese animation), all things 'Goth', socialising with her mates and a taste in music that includes 'screamo' with its associated 'moshing'. Due to her Asperger's syndrome, her parents are concerned that Steve's long-term future in terms of employment, independent living and social relationships is very unclear.

Person-centred approach

> *For people using services, it is not the planning that matters quite as much as the presence of person-centred thinking.*

It could be suggested that the 'person-centred approach' as applied to Steve (*Box 13.1*) is an umbrella term in that it encompasses person-centred assessment, person-centred planning, person-centred implementation and person-centred evaluation. Common to all these is the subscription to an ethos, attitude and way of working that puts the service user at the heart of everything that is said and done on behalf of that person. This means that nursing, care and support staff hold person-centred values and a belief that people such as Steve must have control in areas such as who supports them, what they do with their day, being listened to and making decisions about their lives. Person-centred approaches will ensure that individualised care is at the very heart of mental health, learning disability, physical disability and sensory disability services. It is a framework for co-ordinating and delivering services, support and treatment and it requires a transfer of power from service provider to service user (Jukes 2009).

It could be argued, however, that for those with autism and Asperger's syndrome, as for any service user group, it is not the care and service planning that matters quite as much as the presence of person-centred thinking. This means that all care staff hold person-centred values, and a belief that service users must have control in all areas of their life.

Person-centred planning

Person-centred planning has five major features. In the case of Steve (*Box 13.1*) this means:

- Steve is at the centre of the planning process.
- Steve's family and friends are equal partners in planning care.
- The resultant care plan shows what is important to Steve now and for the future and what support she may need.
- The resultant care plan helps Steve to be part of a community of her choosing and helps the community to welcome her.
- The resultant care plan puts into action what Steve wants for her life and keeps on listening; the plan remains 'live' and will change to meet Steve's changing needs throughout her life.

Person-centred planning can be carried out by a number of people including self-advocates, families, PCP facilitators or brokers such as health and social care staff including nurses.

Person-centred care

The term person-centred care is not used consistently by all health and social care professionals, as each will have their own take and understanding of what it actually means, both in theory and practice. This can lead to problems in reaching a common understanding of the issues surrounding person-centred care.

Person-centred care is more commonly used when working with people with dementia than when working with those with autism, a mental health condition or a learning disability. Having said that, person-centred care is any care that is delivered around the needs of the service user rather than the needs of the service provider.

Person-centred assessment and treatment

Person-centred assessment and treatment puts the individual person or service user at its centre. The person controls the assessment and treatment or therapy processes.

Where does the person-centred approach come from?

Person-centred approaches grew out of user, self-advocate and survivor movements originating in the 1970s; American theorists, such as O'Brien in the 1990s; and reports and Government White Papers, such as *Valuing People* (Department of Health 2001), *Valuing People Now* (Department of Health 2006), *I Exist* (National Autistic Society 2008) and *Death by Indifference* (Mencap 2008).

Service user movement

The organised service user movement arose in the late 1960s and early 1970s against a backdrop of gay liberation and black civil rights movements and involved those with a learning disability and those with a mental health issue. Some of these people still received support from services whilst others, particularly those who saw themselves as service survivors, may not have done so. Many were no longer prepared to accept the labels and restrictions that psychiatry placed on them and questioned received wisdom. What developed was a backlash against the dominant 'medical' or 'illness' model of psychiatry. The 'anti-psychiatry' movement was supported by the writing and thinking of several well-known clinicians and academics of the time, most notably RD Laing (Mind 2010). People with an autism spectrum condition probably would not have been recognised as a separate user group, as they would be some 40 years later. Many would have been under the auspices of the learning disability and/or mental health services and so may have been active within user/survivor groups.

O'Brien's 'Five Accomplishments'

John O'Brien's Five Essential Service Accomplishments were devised in the 1990s and were aimed at focusing and guiding staff who work with people with a learning disability (Advocacy Resources UK 2010). Each accomplishment supports what was considered to be a vital aspect of human experience which, due to common practice at the time, was often limited for people with severe disabilities. Each accomplishment recognises the interdependence that exists between individuals, and challenges and strengthens the relationship between people with disabilities and other community members. The aim was to ensure that learning disability services focused on community participation which would help people with severe disabilities to form and maintain the variety of ties and connections that constitute 'ordinary' community life. The five accomplishments are:

- *Community presence:* The right to take part in community life and to live and spend leisure time with other members of the community.
- *Relationships:* The right to experience valued relationships with non-disabled people.
- *Choice:* The right to make choices, both large and small, in one's life. This include choices about where to live and with whom to live as well as what one does.
- *Competence:* The right to learn new skills and participate in meaningful activities with whatever assistance is required.
- *Respect:* The right to be valued and not treated as a second-class citizen.

Valuing People

The *Valuing People* Government White Paper was primarily set out as a five-year action plan from 2001 (About Learning Disabilities 2010) with the intention of improving services and support for those with a learning disability and their families and carers from birth through to old age. The basic goal of this published initiative reinforces four main beliefs of the UK Government at the time:

- That people with learning disabilities should have equal legal and civil rights to other people.
- That people with learning disabilities should be given the chance and the means to lead more independent lives.
- That people with learning disabilities should have more choice and be able to express and achieve their preferences.
- That people with learning disabilities should be included in mainstream society.

The Government hoped to achieve these goals by improving and modernising transport, education, health and care services, and providing people with learning disabilities more choice for housing arrangements, and greater support for finding employment and making their own choices. The Government set aside money in the form of the Learning Disability Development Fund to help finance the changes that they deemed necessary.

The UK Government believed that by making it easier for people with learning disabilities to be active, seen and heard within their local communities, they would not be ostracised or marginalised. The hope was that society's attitudes and, on some level, indifference about the issues facing learning disabled people would also change.

Thus it can be seen that through the growth in user and self-advocacy movements and changing philosophies of care there was a growing recognition that those with a learning disability deserved and had a right to a better life than they had had previously. It could be argued that person-centred care is the next stage in this recognition.

How the person-centred approach enhances the lives of those with an ASC

This is one of the central questions for this chapter: how do person-centred approaches enhance Steve's life? Indeed, does a person-centred approach enhance Steve's life?

Person-centred approaches *must*, if they are to have value and work, be based around the *individual* and are, therefore, likely to be ideal for those with autism and Asperger's syndrome. The key words here being '*must*' (not 'should') and '*individual*'. One size does not fit all. When working with a person with autism or Asperger's syndrome, planning tools may need to be adapted and terminology changed so they can be understood by that person. It is essential that people's preferred ways of communicating are taken into account so that they can play a full part in the planning process.

What would this mean for Steve and her parents? First of all, they must be listened to and understood. Steve's parents have spent years fighting health, social and education systems in order to provide the quality of life and range of services that they felt Steve was entitled to and deserved. One of the issues that has become obvious to them is the inability and/or refusal of healthcare, social care and education professionals actually to sit down and listen, to admit humbly that they did not even know all the questions, let alone the answers or where to find them. The same applies to interprofessional communication when professionals from different organisational backgrounds appear not to communicate appropriately with each other.

Secondly, be honest with Steve and her parents as to which services can be offered as part of a person-centred care package. Do not promise the Earth. Deliberately and wilfully misleading Steve and her parents as to what services and resources they can access and use is unprofessional and will only serve to exacerbate the anger, resentment and bitterness that have so far characterised much of the interaction between the various care professionals and Steve and her parents. Even being unintentionally misleading can have disastrous results. So be clear as to what can be offered and why. In an era where the money follows the service user, be honest and admit that some services and resources may not be offered due to cost, availability or staffing constraints.

Thirdly, if person-centred approaches to the care of Steve are to work, all aspects of Steve's life must be looked at including relationships, sexuality, spirituality/religious affiliation and the following:

- Where Steve wants to live.
- Who she wants to live with.
- Whether she wants to return to college and if so where and which courses does she want to take.
- Whether she wants to obtain a paid job and if so what and where.
- Access to transport and travel training.
- Social and leisure activities.
- Access to local shops.
- Money management.
- Personal hygiene.
- Health prevention and access to health and social care.

These areas are not exclusive but are likely to form much of the issues surrounding Steve. Although Steve is an articulate adult and knows what she wants, there are likely to be many people with an ASC who are not as articulate. They may be a child or elderly adult or have a learning disability so any assessment and planning tools used will have to be adapted to meet their individual needs and circumstances.

Person-centred planning

Person-centred planning is a broad term that describes a concept developed from the work of John O'Brien and Beth Mount from the US and Marsha Forest, Judith Snow and Jack Pearpoint from Toronto, Canada. All person-centred planning approaches share three basic features:

- Everyday events and activities in which the individual participates should be the focus of planning.
- Family and connections within the community are more important than the services currently available.
- Planning must be done with the individual with the disability and a group of people who knows the individual well and is committed to helping the individual achieve his or her goals.

System-centred approach

The system-centred approach differs from person-centred planning in many ways. In Personal Futures Planning the focus is on the gifts, abilities, dreams and desires of the person while the system-centred approach focuses on the person's deficits and weaknesses. System-centred approaches are usually controlled by care professionals such as nurses, doctors, social workers and teachers and usually include placement along a pre-established continuum with services that may be inflexible and not readily adapted to meet the specific needs of the individual. In contrast, the person-centred approach plans for an active, rewarding community life experience based on the person's interests and strengths. Decisions are made and outcomes controlled by the individual with disabilities and those people closest to him or her. While the system-centred approach concentrates on developing plans and programmes, the person-centred process strives to implement positive and possible plans to enrich the individual's future.

Whilst there are many ways to provide person-centred care plans with and for Steve, what is important is that the plan is meaningful for and understood by her. Some planning methods that could be useful to Steve, her parents and care staff could include any of the following.

Person-centred assessment tools

Making Action Plans (MAPS)

MAPS was developed by Judith Snow, Jack Pearpoint and Marsha Forest and is available from: http://edg.usablewebsites.org/files/MAPS.pdf. MAPS are very visual graphic plans that look at a person's history and aspirations for the future. MAPS is a tool that assists the person with learning disabilities, his or her family and friends in gathering information that can be used to generate a plan of action and care. There are seven key questions that are part of the MAPS process, which include:

- What is the person's history?
- What is his or her dream?
- What is his or her nightmare?
- Who is the person?

- What are the person's gifts or strengths?
- What are the person's needs?
- What is the best plan of action to obtain the dream and avoid the nightmare?

Planning Alternative Tomorrows with Hope (PATH)

PATH was developed by Jack Pearpoint, Marsha Forest and John O'Brien and is available from: http://edg.usablewebsites.org/files/MAPS.pdf. PATH looks at a person's 'North Star' (dream for the future) and puts it into action, reviewing the plan in one to two years' time. PATH is an extension of the MAPS process; it makes use of the important information gathered during the MAP assessment and develops a more definitive plan of action. PATH addresses both long and short-term planning. Through the eight-step process the dream is defined and a series of positive and possible goals is devised. Once the dream and goals are agreed upon, action plans are developed and appropriate people are asked to volunteer to be of support to the service user.

Personal Futures Planning (PFP)

PFP was developed by Beth Mount and John O'Brien and is available from: http://edg.usablewebsites.org/files/MAPS.pdf. PFP is a graphic plan that maps a person's life now and changes for the future. It is useful for community mapping.

Essential Lifestyle Planning (ELP)

Essential Lifestyle Planning was developed by Michael Smull and Susan Burke-Harrison (1992). This is a very detailed plan and was developed for people with high and complex support needs. It includes, amongst others, sections on communication and health action plans. ELP is an approach to person-centred planning intended to change the way we plan, design, and deliver supports for people with intellectual and developmental disabilities who are being cared for in the community.

According to Smull and Burke-Harrison (1992) it is not ethical to plan with a person if the plan does not confront the person's exclusion and aim to create a more diverse, just and inclusive community.

How can person-centred planning be tailored for young people with autism?

The language of PCP can be abstract, using terms such as 'dreams', 'wishes' and 'gifts'. Any system implemented for those with moderate to severe autism needs to be tailored accordingly with specific questions, such as, 'What do you think you are good at?', 'What things do you like to do?'

There is also an emphasis on making planning meetings inclusive and involving as many people as possible. However, if the meetings are too busy this is not necessarily positive for those with an ASC so care needs to be taken to address this issue and make sure meetings are low in arousal, particularly where the involvement of the person with an ASC in the meeting is being encouraged.

The person-centred planning process is generally seen as being autism friendly, as approaches tend to use lots of visual aids (for example, writing down on large sheets of paper the person's strengths or gifts, their dreams or plans for the future) so this helps the person's understanding of what is happening. However, for some people too many visual aids can be over-stimulating and, for those with severe autism, may not serve a significant purpose.

Recognising and valuing each person's special interests is also important; professionals and services often label people with autism as having 'obsessions' rather than talents and gifts. If these talents are used as a focus the person can be supported in a positive way.

It is important that all those involved in the meetings are prepared to use a wide range of communication techniques. All must demonstrate a willingness to supplement the spoken word by using objects, photographs, line drawings, symbols or signs. Writing, drawing, miming, drama and other art forms are all ways of communicating which could be used to aid understanding and elicit responses from those with an ASC. Having people present who know the person's preferred means of communication and who can interpret their expressions, is key to inclusion.

Challenges to using a person-centred approach

Although in many ways, person-centred approaches, assessments and care are ideal when working with both adults and children there are also a number of potential challenges that can prevent high quality care support and services from being put into place and actioned. These challenges will have a direct impact upon the quality of life experienced by people with an ASC and their families and carers.

Increased bureaucracy, tighter budgets and restrictive commissioning of services all limit the ability of frontline workers to provide quality care to service users. This is often compounded by a historical lack of communication and co-operation between the various stakeholders, which could include health, social care, education, voluntary sector and private sector organisations. Bureaucracy can be seen as a primary issue of concern by both service users and frontline workers, limiting the time available for care and support. These limitations can cause stress for frontline workers already working in stressful conditions. In response to increasing constraints, many frontline staff work flexibly to better manage the formal structures imposed on them.

Managers' focus on budgets and commissioning means that they often have different concerns to frontline workers. It could be suggested that good management of frontline staff significantly improves the quality of care service users receive.

There is a mixed picture of the training opportunities available to frontline workers. Lack of training and poor supervision can contribute to staff being undervalued, and good quality training for those working with minority ethnic groups is particularly scarce. Systemic and organisational barriers to good quality care are compounded for people from minority ethnic groups. Systems may be harder to access, and language and cultural barriers can intensify these difficulties.

The actual setting in which a plan is laid out can prove problematic too. The use of either social service or healthcare settings may further the 'bad politics' between health and social care providers. Therefore, a more neutral setting may be needed that does not provoke resentment amongst key stake holders. Too formal a setting can sometimes be perceived as threatening by service users and their families.

However, once these potential problem areas are altered to best suit an individual with an ASC, person-centred planning can be highly beneficial.

Carol Povey, head of service quality for the National Autistic Society, says person-centred planning systems are vital for people with autism because autism is a spectrum disorder. 'People with spectrum disorders have very diverse and individual needs, so a plan tailored to the individual is key,' she says.

Conclusion

According to Steve person-centred care is a 'curate's egg': good in parts but not so good in others. Its intentions of putting the person with an ASC and his or her needs at the centre of every aspect of care are good and its pedigree within the service user and disability politics movements is impeccable. However, for person-centred care to work, there must be willing co-operation between all stakeholders, and it must be more than just paying lip service to Government rhetoric. Without this ability and willingness to put Steve and her needs at the centre of every aspect of care then person-centred planning is doomed to failure.

The next chapter focuses on a specific form of person-centred care: that of 'personalisation'.

Key points

- Person-centred approach (PCA) can often involve person-centred assessment, person-centred planning (PCP), person-centred care and person-centred treatment. The emphasis is on the words 'person-centred'.
- The PCA originated out of the American self-advocacy movement of the 1970s and 1980s and has been championed by most, if not all, the various reports such as *Valuing People*, and *I Exist*.
- The service user is the centre of everything that the service provider does. The person-centred approach is based on the idea that 'a one-sized care package' does not fit all.
- There are a number of PCP packages available to assist both the service user and service provider in accessing support in all areas of life.

References

About Learning Disabilities (2010) *UK Government initiative: Valuing People*. Available from: http://www.aboutlearningdisabilities.co.uk/uk-government-initiative-valuing-people.html [Last accessed 06 July 2010]

Advocacy Resources UK (2010) *Fact Sheet 3 – Five Service Accomplishments*. Available from: www.advocacyresource.org.uk/gen2-file.php?id=23 [Last accessed 05 July 2010]

Department of Health (2001) *Valuing people: A New Strategy for Learning Disabilities for the 21st Century*. The Stationary Office, London

Department of Health (2006) *Valuing People Now*. The Stationary Office, London

Jukes M (2009) Striving towards ordinariness within a regulatory system. In Jukes M (ed) *Learning Disability Nursing Practice*. Quay books, London

Mencap (2008) *Death by Indifference*. Available from: http://www.mencap.org.uk/document.asp?id=284 [Last accessed 15 June 2010]

Mind (2010) *A Brief History of the User/Survivor Movement*. Available from: http://www.mind.org.uk/help/people_groups_and_communities/user/survivor_empowerment/a_brief_history_of_the_user/survivor_mo [Last accessed 04 July 2010]

National Autistic Society (2008) *I Exist: The Message from Adults with Autism*. Available from: http://www.autism.org.uk/iexist [:ast accessed 15 June 2010]

Smull M, Burke-Harrison S (1992) *Supporting People with Severe Reputations in the Community*. Virginia National Association of State Mental Retardation Program Directors, Virginia

CHAPTER 14

Personalisation

Introduction

The previous chapter focused on a number of issues around person-centred planning and its applications and implications, such as person-centred care and person-centred assessment. One of the forms of this person-centred approach to care for those with an autism spectrum condition (ASC) is the concept of personalisation.

Steve, who we met in the last chapter, explains what personalisation is and what it means for those with an ASC and their informal carers (their families). The practicalities of personalisation are explored as are its benefits and challenges.

By the end of this chapter you will have gained an understanding of the following issues:

- The meaning for Steve of personalisation as a practical concept.
- How personalisation works for Steve and other people with an ASC.
- The benefits and advantages of personalisation and the disadvantages and challenges for Steve, those who care for her and service planners.

What is personalisation?

> *I just want to control my own life. I like to socialise with other people and meet new friends. I just want to enjoy my freedom. I don't want people to control my life for me, I want to control it myself.*
>
> Carr (2008: 1)

Personalisation is a way of providing care which has, as its starting point, the individual as a person with strengths, needs, challenges, preferences and a range of family and social networks. Direct control of everything to do with Steve's support and care is given to her, and this includes the way this support and care is funded, purchased and delivered.

According to Carr (2008) personalisation 'reinforces the idea that the individual service user is best placed to know what they need and how those needs can be met'. This should mean that Steve is given responsibility for and is able to make her own decisions regarding the support and care that she needs. In order for Steve to make real decisions, relevant information must be presented to her in an appropriate format and manner and with sufficient time for decisions to be made. In this way the provision of care and support services will fit the needs of Steve rather than Steve fitting the needs of the services. Carr (2008) suggests that, previously, service-led approaches often meant that those with an ASC neither received the right support nor were able to shape the kind of help they needed.

However, according to Carr (2008) personalisation is not just about giving people the option to have and control their own budget, although this is an important aspect of it. Personalisation applies to everyone regardless of how their support services are funded, including those who do not receive State welfare benefits. Personalisation is also about having access to information that is in an appropriate format and at an appropriate level, in order to make appropriate decisions.

Carr (2008) succinctly sums up personalisation as the following:

- Finding new collaborative ways of working and developing local partnerships, which produce a range of services for people to choose from, and opportunities for social inclusion.
- Tailoring support to people's individual needs.
- Recognising and supporting carers in their role, while enabling them to maintain a life beyond their caring responsibilities.
- A total system response so that universal and community services and resources are accessible to everyone.
- Early intervention and prevention so that people are supported early on and in a way that is right for them.

Like person-centred care, personalisation can trace its roots back to the disability, user and survivor movements (Carr 2008) as well as the Community Care (Direct Payments) Act 1996. The personalisation agenda has, according to Carr (2008), been influenced by In Control, a social enterprise charity established in 2003. Over 100 local authorities now use the In Control model of self-directed support and individual budgets.

There are several terms used in association with personalisation or to describe the services or activities that reflect the personalisation agenda. Some of these are used interchangeably and some were covered in *Chapter 13*. They include:

- *Person-centred planning*.
- *Patient-centred care* (see Pelzang 2010): Caution must be exercised here

as it could be suggested that patient-centred care relies upon and reflects an illness and disease model and approach to the person, which may not be entirely helpful whilst working with people with an ASC. Having said that, there are areas of commonality between patient- and person-centred care in that both seek to put the individual service user at the centre of care.

- *Person-centred care.*
- *Person-centred support:* A term used by some service user groups to describe personalisation.
- *Independent living*: One of the goals of personalisation is independent living. This does not mean living or doing things on one's own but rather it means having choice and control over where and how one lives and the support, with health, mobility, education and employment, for example, needed to achieve this.
- *Self-directed support:* This term originated with the In Control project and relates to a variety of ways to create personalised social care and as a route to achieving the goal of independent living. The defining characteristics of self-directed support include:
  - The support is controlled by the individual.
  - The level of support is agreed in a fair, open and flexible way.
  - Any additional help needed to plan, specify and find support should be provided by people who are as close to the individual as possible.
  - The individual should control the financial resources for their support in a way they choose.
- *Direct payment:* For more information on direct payment visit the In Control website (www.in-control.org.uk).

It could be said that Carr's summary reads and sounds a bit too much like 'official speak' to be credible. This is how personalisation should and can work, but does it work in the way that it is intended? And does it work for those on the autism spectrum?

Personalisation for people on the autism spectrum

The Social Care Institute for Excellence (SCIE) (2010) suggests that most charities believe that personalisation offers people with autism and their family carers a greater chance of receiving better tailored support and greater choice. The SCIE goes on to suggest that the traditional service-led approach to care has often meant that people with an ASC have not received the right kind of help at the right time. A recent National Audit Office report (2009) found that:

- 82% of third sector organisations questioned and audited said that personal budgets would allow for more direct contact with the individual with an autism spectrum condition.
- 78% said that support would be better tailored to the individual.
- 77% said there would be greater choice.

According to the SCIE (2010), personalisation will benefit people with an ASC as it should offer them more control over their lives, more choice about the health and social care services they receive and how and where these are provided. The needs of people with an ASC vary considerably according to the severity of their condition, so they will benefit from the opportunity to choose services that meet their particular, specific health and social care requirements.

Personalisation should also help people with higher functioning autism and Asperger's syndrome (who are often considered ineligible for social care due to their perceived ability to self-care) as they will be entitled to better signposting and advice services.

The key to personalisation is to approach each person as an individual. Personalisation does not in itself allow a person with an ASC to be treated as an individual, rather treating the person as an individual allows personalisation to work. Individuality must come first; without it personalisation will not and cannot work. Alongside this sense of the person as an individual must come a realisation that a 'one size fits all' approach is not appropriate. Some people with an ASC may need very little social and healthcare support, others some support and a few 24 hour, seven-days-a-week care and support. Therefore, an independent advocate must be offered to act as an impartial guide through the complex maze of the personalisation process. As a first stage, information must be presented in such a way as to enable those with autism or Asperger's syndrome to engage in the personalisation process. Formats could include the use of pictures, mime, drama, objects of reference as well as written and spoken forms of communication. It is vital not to overload service users with information as such overload will lead to confusion, and feelings of intimidation and disengagement.

Having provided information in an appropriate way to each service user, the individual must be helped to understand the information and what it means in terms of which services are available, which are not and how much these services are going to cost. This costing of services is vital in order to enable people to budget.

In Steve's case, once the service information has been presented and understood, the services will be costed and assistance with budgeting will be offered. Next, an independent advocate, along with the multi-disciplinary team, will help her to purchase the variety of support services that she has decided she would like to enable her to engage fully in life.

However, the purchasing of support services is not the end of personalisation as the amount of money that Steve has at her disposal, the way the money is spent and the support services that have been bought must be evaluated. This is to ensure that the service user spends the money properly and appropriately and that the services are actually delivering what they should. This allows for service planning and delivery to be amended and 'fine tuned' so that users receive an optimum service. The whole process is likely to be repeated in subsequent financial years, bearing in mind that as service users gets older their needs will change.

The National Autistic Society has developed a new resource in consultation with people on the autism spectrum that can be used when implementing personalisation. It aims to help people with autism learn about managing their money. It is funded by the Financial Services Authority, as part of its National Strategy for Financial Capability. The resource, *Managing Money*, can be obtained online (www.managingmoney.org.uk), it covers all aspects of managing money, including opening a bank account, budgeting and compulsive spending. It also includes video clips, interactive quizzes, questionnaires, downloadable resources and a virtual cash machine. *Managing Money* includes a workbook which has the same learning content as the website and is available to order free of charge from the National Autistic Society at www.autism.org.uk/shop.

The benefits of personalisation

There are many benefits of personalisation for Steve and other people with an ASC. Perhaps the most obvious is that Steve will be able to control what support she needs and accesses. Previously, any support offered would have been based around the needs and constraints of the service provider. The money followed the services. Steve would have been told what her support needs were, what support (if any) was on offer, and how and when that support would be delivered. Steve would have been the 'done to', not the 'done with', and certainly not the 'doer'. At worst, Steve would not have been part of any discussion or planning around her support needs. At best, she and/or her parents would have been asked their views and these views may or may not have had some influence on any support discussions, planning or provision.

With personalisation, the emphasis is on Steve saying what support services, if any, she needs, and how those services will meet her needs. Steve becomes at least a 'done with' and likely a 'doer'. The money follows Steve and not the service; service providers have to have a very convincing reason why any particular support service Steve requests is deemed either inappropriate or unavailable. Multi-disciplinary teams would thus become accountable to Steve for their decisions regarding needs assessment, planning and service provision. Although many members of the multi-disciplinary team are likely to be public employees and therefore paid by the State, Steve would effectively be their manager. This represents a huge shift in power affecting the relationship between professional carers and Steve. Steve is able to have a say in what happens, when, where, how and why. Thus, Steve and other people with an ASC will be treated as intelligent and articulate adults, even if they do require the support of an independent advocate to ensure their rights are asserted.

A second advantage to personalisation is that statutory service providers may not necessarily be either the cheapest or most appropriate. By being able to 'shop around', support may be purchased for less, which has obvious economic benefits. Individualised care can also lead to improved self-confidence and self-esteem.

In a period of increasingly austere Government spending cuts, it makes sense to utilise a method of funding and purchasing support that is cost efficient and cheaper than that provided by statutory services. It could be suggested that the whole point of personalisation is to purchase care support packages that are so individualised they are unique. Since Steve owns the entire care support process from initial assessment to final fine tuning, this should have the effect of increasing her sense of self-esteem and self-worth as she will be treated as both an adult and an equal member of the team.

The challenges of personalisation

> *People who use social care services say that the service is only as good as the person delivering it. If we are to deliver our vision this means workers who are open, honest...who treat people using services with equity, are non-judgemental and challenge unfair discrimination. The workforce is, therefore, critical to delivery.*
>
> Department of Health (2005: 14)

While there are many positive aspects to personalisation, there are a number of challenges to its full and genuine implementation. These include:

- *Training*. A lack of appropriate training received by care professionals in all aspects of personalisation, equality, diversity and human and civil rights.
- *Communication*. A lack of genuine communication between care professionals is a major issue resulting when care professionals do not, and perhaps sometimes refuse to, sing from the same hymn sheet. Whilst all members of the multi-disciplinary care team are likely to have their own line management and communication systems and channels, the much discussed 'Berlin Wall' between health and social care professionals, for example, will often get in the way of true communication and collaborative working. This may, in turn, result in service users such as Steve getting inappropriate, poor quality or non-existent care and support.
- *A rationing agenda*. The National Consumer Council (2004) suggests that the issues concerning the rationing of budgets need to be addressed. This is even more important now as the UK is still struggling with the effects of the economic depression and the spending cuts initiated by the UK Government in order to improve the economy. Thus, the rationing of funding by geographical area or locality (the so-called 'postcode lottery') will affect the type, level and duration of support available to Steve and others like her. Dittrich (2008) suggests that the 'cartelisation' of social and healthcare support by a small number of large corporate providers could make Steve's individual budget virtually worthless as she will have an increasingly limited choice of support and care provider.
- *Funding*. There is a lack of real funding complicated by rising demands and shifting demographics, ages, geography, patterns and needs of populations.
- *Market growth*. As personalisation becomes embedded within social and healthcare support and provision, there is likely to be a growth in the market for unregulated and untrained personal assistants who should be used with caution (Leece 2007). However, it could be suggested that individual user choice is best supported by having, amongst others, accountability of service providers to service users. Yet, again, Carr (2008) suggests that 'personalisation is likely to require new, more flexible approaches to regulation, be able to adapt to innovative support from new types of providers offering broader opportunities including scope for people to take appropriate risks'.

- *Support*. Steve may not be fully supported to make appropriate decisions regarding purchasing of support services resulting, in part, from a lack of genuine commitment from care professionals, a lack of understanding and communication by and between care professionals and a lack of strong service user groups. Maynard-Campbell (2007) suggests that the idea of nurturing a strong user voice may not be seen as important and that user-led groups are sometimes left to one or two individuals who have reason to champion the cause.
- *Power imbalance*. There may be power imbalance and shift between Steve and the various care professionals who are involved in the multi-disciplinary care team. Historically, economic, political and social power rested with the various care professionals that make up the multi-disciplinary team, with service users like Steve and her family being powerless. One of the consequences of personalisation is the redistribution of power away from service providers and towards the service user. Such power redistribution may cause some anger and resentment on the part of some care professionals which in turn may result in a lack of commitment to the genuine application of personalisation on the part of the care professionals involved.

As can be seen, many of these challenges both follow on and overlap with each other and it will require more than merely paying lip service to Government policy for those like Steve to feel the full benefit of personalisation.

Conclusion

Personalisation, being both a part of and arising out of the person-centred care movement and agenda as well as being Government policy, could and in many instances will have profound implications for empowering Steve and other people with an ASC. Steve is in the driving seat rather than being a mere passenger. However, whilst personalisation presents huge advantages and benefits for Steve, at the same time it presents huge challenges to both support and care agencies and Steve. The role of the nurse and other direct care professionals is, first of all, to understand what personalisation is and then to critically apply it to and with those with an ASC. Remember, support must be dictated by the needs of the service user and not by the needs of the employing organisation.

Key points

- Personalisation is a way of providing care which has, as its starting point, the individual as a person with strengths, needs, challenges, preferences and a range of family and social networks.
- Like person-centred care, personalisation comes under a variety of different names, including personal or individual budgets.
- The key to personalisation is to approach and work with the person with an ASC as an individual and not to adopt a 'one size fits all' approach.
- Personalisation provides a number of benefits and challenges for both the service user and service provider.

References

Carr S (2008) Personalisation: A rough guide. In Social Care Institute for Excellence (ed) *State of Social Care in England 2006–2007*. CSCI, London

Department of Health (2005) *Independence, Well-Being and Choice. Our Vision for the Future of Social Care for Adults in England*. Department of Health, London

Dittrich R (2008) *Putting People First. Briefing Paper 7: The Care Market – Summary of Pre-existing Evidence from Experts and Research*. Available from: http://www.hants.gov.uk/briefingpaper7-2.pdf

Leece J (2007) Direct payments and user-controlled support: the challenges for social care commissioning. *Practice* **19**(3): 185–98

Maynard-Campbell S (2007) *Mapping the Capacity and Potential for User-Led Organisations in England*. Department of Health, London

National Audit Office (2009) *Supporting People with Autism Through Adulthood*. NAO, Norwich

National Consumer Council (2004) *Making Public Services Personal*. NCC, London

Pelzang R (2010) Time to learn: Understanding patient-centred care. *British Journal of Nursing* **19**(14): 912–17

Social Care Institute of Excellence (2010) *Fair Access to Care Services*. SCIE, London

CHAPTER 15

Autism and sensory issues

In the sense of taste we find almost invariably very pronounced likes and dislikes. It is no different with the sense of touch. Many children have an abnormally strong dislike of particular tactile sensations. They cannot tolerate the roughness of new shirts or of mended socks. Washing water, too, can often be a source of unpleasant sensations and, hence, of unpleasant scenes. There is hypersensitivity, too, against noise. Yet, the same children who are often distinctly hypersensitive to noise in particular situations, in other situations may appear to be hyposensitive.

Hans Asperger (1991)

Some adults with Asperger's syndrome consider their sensory sensitivity has a greater impact on their daily lives than problems with making friends, managing emotions and finding appropriate employment.

Attwood (2006: 290)

Introduction

When asked, most people are likely to say that they are sensitive to, enjoy or dislike certain forms of sensory stimulus. For example, some people may like the taste of burnt toast whilst not liking the tactile sensation of clothing made out of nylon, others may retch at the smell or sight of burnt toast but love the feel of nylon clothing against their skin. A person's sensory profile, what they like and what they dislike, and how it impacts upon understanding and interaction with other people, the environment and the world is personal and unique to each individual. This applies equally to those with an autism spectrum condition (ASC). Indeed, there is now a growing realisation and understanding that sensory stimuli and how a person with an ASC responds or reacts to different stimuli could form a major part of the 'autistic profile' and, as such, can be added to Wing's 'autism triad'.

By the end of this chapter, the reader will have a basic understanding of the following:

- How the various forms of sensory stimuli impact upon 'neuro-typicals'.
- How the various forms of sensory stimuli impact upon those with an ASC.

- The behaviour expressed by those with an ASC as a result of sensory under-stimulation and over-stimulation.
- Nurses' understanding of the sensory profiles of those with an ASC and resulting nursing interventions for this client group.

What are sensory stimuli?

The short answer to this question is: any form of stimulus that impacts upon the human senses. There are generally considered to be five human senses:

- *Sight:* Visual images are picked up and changed into tiny electric currents by the rod and cone cells situated at the back of the eye. These electrical currents are carried by the optic nerve fibres to the area of the brain that processes visual stimuli (the occipital lobes of both cerebral hemispheres).
- *Hearing:* Sound pressure moves tiny hairs in the inner ear which causes the release of a neurotransmitter at their base. The neurotransmitter, in turn, generates a tiny electrical signal that travels to the auditory part of the brain through the cochlear nerve.
- *Smell:* The current produced by the olfactory epithelium that occupies a small area in the roof of the nasal cavity is transmitted along the axons of the olfactory receptor cells (which form the olfactory nerves) to the olfactory bulbs, where they synapse with sensory neurons of the olfactory tract. Because the sense of smell is closely linked to memory it is more likely than other senses to trigger an emotional response.
- *Taste:* Individual gustatory receptor cells located in the tongue respond to four taste sensations: sweet, bitter, sour, and salty. All other tastes arise from a mixture of these four tastes in combination with olfactory sensations associated with the substance tasted. These receptor cells change each particular taste sensation into a tiny electric current. These currents are transmitted to the area of the brain that processes taste.
- *Touch:* The somatic (general) senses collect information about cutaneous sensations, such as touch on the surface of the skin, pain, heat and proprioception. These sensations are transmitted to the brain by various nerve fibres.

However, some schools of thought include two more senses:

- *Instinct or intuition:* (often known as 'sixth sense') The word 'intuition' comes from the Latin word '*intueri*', which is often roughly translated as meaning 'to look inside' or 'to contemplate'. It is not a sense in the same way as the five senses given above. However, instinct or intuition could be argued to be the means by which subtle information from the sensory system is rapidly processed alongside aspects of memory and which allows the person to subconsciously anticipate a future action or event.

- *Balance:* The senses of balance, posture and movement result from a complex interplay between the senses of sight, hearing and touch along with a number of receptor cells and fibres that are located in the vestibular part of the inner ear, the skeletal muscles and the limb joints. The information they transmit to the brain allows us to locate ourselves in space in relation to other objects. Without such a complex interplay, simply standing still would be impossible.

Thus, each human sense is linked and to a certain extent reliant upon all the other senses in order to provide a whole picture for the brain to receive and process. For example, the simple act of sitting and eating a meal involves the senses of balance, sight, touch, smell and taste. These interact with previously established memory structures to allow the brain to register the phenomenon we know as eating.

Sensory impact in those with an ASC

The sensory differences between those with and those without an ASC are not in the actual sensory mechanism: the sense organs function in exactly the same way in both. However, the differences lie in how these sensory signals are processed by the brain and, possibly, the precise location of this processing.

It could be that within the sensory areas of the brain of so-called 'neuro-typicals' there exists a filtering or dampening mechanism that attenuates incoming sensory signals to such a level that the sensory areas situated around the thalamus are able to process these signals comfortably, with ease and without going into 'cerebral melt-down'. Such sensory filtering or dampening mechanisms are arguably absent in those with an ASC. Thus what the sensory areas of the brain in those with an ASC receive is raw, unattenuated and often distorted sensory signals and data. To put it another way, think of the brain as a radio or 'hi-fi'. The 'volume' in the brains of those without an ASC is set very low; however, in the brains of those with an ASC it is set full on. Thus, sensory input into the visual cortex, for example, is so intense as to be often painful.

Each sense and the effects of over- or under-stimulation are outlined below.

Sight

About one person in five, according to Attwood (2006), experiences visual perception issues. People with an ASC may be hyposensitive or hypersensitive.

Hyposensitivity

- Light and dark may be perceived differently; images are darker or may lose features or sharpness.
- Some may concentrate on peripheral vision because their central vision is blurred; others say that a main object is magnified and things on the periphery become blurred.
- There may be poor depth perception which may result in problems with throwing and catching objects; 'clumsiness'.

Hypersensitivity

- There may be distorted vision, such as objects or environments appearing smaller or larger than they really are, and objects and bright lights appearing to jump around. These sensations could even be painful.
- Images may be fragmented as a consequence of too many sources of visual stimuli and information.
- Sources of light, such as reflections and flickering fluorescent lights, can be confusing and can cause headaches.
- There may be a focus on and an intense fascination for specific and often tiny details which may give more pleasure than looking at something as a whole. Those who are artistic can often produce paintings of photographic realism (Attwood 2006). This intense fascination may also provide sensory pleasure. Attwood (2006) suggests that love of symmetry in art and architecture may result from visual hypersensitivity.

Hearing

The most common sensitivity is to very specific sounds and 70–85% of people with an ASC are affected (Attwood 2006). Attwood suggests that there are three types of sound that this group of people tend to find unpleasant and possibly painful: unexpected sounds such as a dog barking or a fire alarm, high pitched sounds such as the small electric motors found in many domestic appliances (food mixers, vacuum cleaners, hair dryers, etc.), and complex sounds such as shopping malls or noisy social gatherings.

Hyposensitivity

- Sounds may only be heard with one ear, the other ear either having only partial hearing or no hearing at all. This has been confused in the past with deafness (Attwood 2006).
- Particular sounds may not be acknowledged (sensory tune-out).
- Crowded and noisy places may be enjoyed or banging doors or objects may give pleasure.

Hypersensitivity

- The volume of noise may be magnified and surrounding sounds distorted and muddled.
- There may be an inability to cut out particular sounds which may lead to difficulties in concentration.
- A lower hearing threshold, which makes people particularly sensitive to auditory stimuli, for example hearing conversations in the distance, may be evident.

Smell

> *Smells like dogs, cats, deodorant and aftershave lotion are so strong to me I can't stand it, and perfume drives me nuts.*

Attwood (2006) suggests that over half of those with an ASC have smell sensitivity.

Hyposensitivity

- There may be no sense of smell and a failure to notice extreme odours.

Hypersensitivity

- Some smells can be intensified and overpowering.
- There may be toileting problems as the person with an ASC may not be able to tolerate the smell of his or her own urine or faeces.
- There may be a dislike of individuals who use distinctive perfumes, shampoos or have strong body odours, etc.
- There may be advantages including being able to recognise food that has gone off or that a friend or family member is unwell. People with an ASC may become wine experts (Attwood 2006).

Taste

Attwood (2006) suggests that over half of those with an ASC have a taste sensitivity.

Hyposensitivity
- Very spicy foods may be enjoyed.
- People who are hyposensitive may eat anything and everything: soil, grass, leaves, faecal matter.

Hypersensitivity
- Some flavours and foods are too strong and overpowering: some people will only eat bland food.
- Certain food textures may cause discomfort: some people will only eat smooth foods such as mashed potatoes or ice-cream.

  I had a big problem with food. I liked to eat foods that were bland and uncomplicated.

  I was supersensitive to the texture of food and I had to touch everything with my fingers to see how it felt before I could put it in my mouth.

  Canned asparagus was intolerable due to its slimy texture.

  Some personal examples of taste sensitivity as cited by Attwood (2006: 283)

Touch

Sensitivity to some forms of touch and tactile experiences occurs in over half of all those with an ASC (Attwood 2006). This can be an extreme sensitivity to particular types of touch, areas of the body touched or the amount of pressure applied. Some of those with an ASC may not be able to tolerate very light touch but will relish deep pressure. Temple Grandin is an excellent example of this:

> *As a baby I resisted being touched and when I became a little older I can remember stiffening, flinching and pulling away from relatives when they hugged me.*
>
> *As a child I wanted to feel the comfort of being held.*
>
> Temple Grandin, as cited by Attwood (2006: 278)

Grandin went on to make a very successful career designing equipment that produced, through applying deep pressure, the feelings of peace and calmness in cows just before they were slaughtered.

Hyposensitivity

- Holds others tightly.
- Has high pain threshold; does not feel pain or extremes of temperature.
- Engages in self-harming.
- Enjoys heavy objects on top of them.

Hypersensitivity

- Touch can be painful and uncomfortable and those with an ASC will often withdraw from touch, which can have a grave effect on their interactions and relationships with others. This could, in adults, include an aversion to or withdrawal from intimate or sexual contact.
- An aversion to or withdrawal from activities that involve tactile elements.
- Dislike of having anything on hands or feet.
- Difficulties in brushing and washing hair. This could extend to having a hair cut, the sensations of which could cause pain (for example, the vibrations of the electric clippers against the skin; the confusing sound of the clippers as transmitted through the skull as well as through the ears).
- Only likes certain types of clothing or textures. May dislike the feeling of any type of clothing on some or any part of the body and may, as a result, take clothing off inappropriately. Again, this may have an impact on the wardrobe the person may have.

Balance

Those people who have problems with the vestibular system that affect their sense of balance may be said to be 'gravitationally insecure' (Attwood 2006). They may have a feeling of disorientation and anxiety if they have to change body position rapidly or if their feet leave the ground. For example, someone could feel sick when going on a fast-moving fairground ride or could even feel sick when watching them. Other people with an ASC are known to positively enjoy the movement of such rides.

Hyposensitivity

- The need for rocking, swinging, spinning.
- Enjoyment of rapid movement.

Hypersensitivity

- Difficulties in activities that include movement, such as sport.
- Difficulties in stopping quickly after or during an activity.

- Travel or motion sickness.
- Difficulties with activities where the head is not in an upright position, or where feet are off the ground.

Pain and temperature

Hyposensitivity

- Not feeling or registering pain that those without an ASC may find intolerable.
- Not feeling or registering either hot or cold (weather).
- Not feeling or registering hot or cold (food, drink, fire).

Hypersensitivity

- A very low threshold or tolerance to pain, thus feeling pain that those without an ASC would not.
- A very low tolerance to changes in temperature.

Attwood (2006) suggests that those with an ASC are more likely to be hypo- rather than hypersensitive to pain and temperature.

Impact on nursing interventions

Sensory issues can have a major impact on the interaction between nurses and those with an ASC and on nursing interventions for this client group.

First it is important to carry out an in-depth sensory assessment. Attwood (2006) suggests that specific aspects of sensory sensitivity could be included in a prospective screening assessment for very young children. Attwood also says that many of the current ASC screening assessments do ask questions around sensory sensitivity as it is a recognised feature of 'severe autism', and a history of unusual sensory perceptions is considered to be one of the diagnostic features of ASC (Attwood 2006).

Any sensory assessment should cover:

- Both hypo- and hypersensitivity to sensory experiences.
- Sensory distortions and sensory overload.
- Sensory 'tune-outs'.
- Unusual sensory processing, such as synaesthesia.
- Difficulties in identifying the source channel of sensory information.

(Attwood 2006: 274)

A number of sensory assessments is available:

- *The Sensory Behaviour Schedule*: This 17-item screening questionnaire is designed to provide a profile of sensory issues and associated behaviour.
- *The Sensory Profile*: This 125-item questionnaire measures the degree that children present all aspects of sensory processing.
- *The Sensory Profile Checklist (Revised)*: This 232-item questionnaire for parents to complete identifies sensory strengths and weaknesses.

However, the inherent weakness in all of these sensory assessment tools is that they are intended to be used to highlight sensory issues and associated behaviour in children. There do not appear to be any similar sensory assessment tools that can be used with adults with an ASC. It could be that as children develop and mature into adulthood they learn to deal with any sensory issues in more appropriate ways; they may also learn to adapt and mellow. Thus, providing an accurate and in-depth sensory profile in adults can be problematic. There is a need to either adapt existing sensory assessment tools or design new ones that can be used with adults.

Having completed a thorough assessment and produced an in-depth sensory profile, there are a number of strategies that can be used, remembering that each person with an ASC is a unique individual and that a 'one size fits all' approach is unlikely to work.

Sight

It may be possible to avoid placing the person with an ASC in a situation where there is intense or disturbing visual stimuli and sensations. Another approach is to use tinted non-optical lenses in glasses in order that certain colours and hues are muted, to improve visual perception and reduce perceptual overload and visual disturbances. An example is Irlen filters. Visual therapy that has been developed by behavioural optometrists to retrain the eyes and associated brain structures, can also be used although, according to Attwood (2006), there is no empirical evidence to suggest that such therapy actually works.

Hearing

It may be possible to avoid exposing the person with an ASC to sounds that he or she considers uncomfortable or painful. For example, if the sound of the vacuum cleaner causes discomfort or pain then it may be possible to hoover when he or she is not around. The discrete use of physical barriers, such as ear plugs, could also be suggested. Likewise, the use of specific forms or types of music could be used to instil a sense of calmness, for example, some classical music and Gregorian or plainchant is known to have a calming effect on mood and behaviour (Barber 1999). It may also help to explain the cause, reason and duration of any sound that is perceived to be uncomfortable or painful. The reduction of background noises, such as other people's conversations may also be useful.

There are two specific therapies that can be used to reduce auditory sensitivity:

- Sensory Integration Therapy (Ayers 1972).
- Auditory Integration Therapy (Berard 1993).

There appears to be a lack of empirical data about either of these therapies, although there is some anecdotal evidence to support their use.

Smell

Having identified through a thorough assessment process which smells the person with an ASC is sensitive to, it may be possible to avoid situations where the person is exposed to them. Programmes of desensitisation and sensory integration therapy may also be fruitful.

Taste

It is important not to use force to either compel or prevent someone eating something. To use such force is unprofessional and unethical. It may be useful to seek the advice of a dietician in order to improve or change a person's diet or the range of food that they will tolerate. Again, a programme of systematic desensitisation could be followed for people of all age groups. Sensory integration therapy may also be useful.

Touch

Family members and care professionals need to be aware of the effect that certain tactile experiences will have on the person with an ASC. Therefore, try to avoid situations or activities that will over-stimulate and cause the person to become 'tactile defensive'. According to Attwood (2006) Sensory Integration Therapy can be used to reduce tactile defensiveness although there is a lack of empirical evidence to support its use. Family members and friends can also reduce the frequency and duration of signs and gestures of affection or greetings such as hugs or handshakes. Prepare the person with an ASC that a hug or handshake is imminent by informing him or her. Understand that some people are far more sensitive to a light than a deep touch.

Balance

Understanding and working with the sensory profile of the person with an ASC is vital. For those who are hypersensitive to movement, try to avoid sudden movement or activities that may affect or compromise their physical balance.

Pain and temperature

Again, understanding and working with the sensory profile of the person with an ASC is vital as is close and attentive observation of that person. Everybody is different, therefore it is important to know and understand what is normal for the person with whom you are working. It may also be useful to assist the patient or service user to know and understand when they are in pain and to manage the feeling appropriately. To this end, it may be useful to seek the assistance of a psychologist.

Conclusion

According to Attwood (2006), one of the attributes of ASC is a hyper- or hyposensitivity to specific sensory stimuli with hypersensitivity often leading to sensory overload, anxiety and associated 'behavioural melt-down'. Attwood (2006) suggests that

> *...very sensitive sensory perceptions, especially for sounds, can cause the person with an ASC to worry when the next painful sensory experience will occur...the sensory sensitivity will create a feeling of anxiety.*

Such anxiety will, in turn, heighten sensory perception. Thus anxiety and sensory over-stimulation have a symbiotic relationship. Such over-stimulation can and does occur across all senses. However, this 'sensory soup' is not always unpalatable and can be quite an enjoyable experience for some people.

Much of the current research and work on sensory issues involves children, there being comparatively little work being undertaken on the sensory profile and needs of adults (particular older adults). Thus there is a need to carry out intensive work including engaging in research and designing sensory assessment and intervention programmes for adults with an ASC.

The over-riding role of nurses and other healthcare professionals is, in the first instance, to understand how sensory stimuli will affect each and every person with an ASC through active listening and a thorough and holistic assessment. Not to listen, not to understand, not to act on what the patient is saying is tantamount to failing that person.

Key points

- Input data from the various sense organs (sight, hearing, smell, taste, touch, balance) may be processed slightly differently within the brain of a person with an ASC.
- Some people with an ASC are likely to be hypersensitive to these stimuli whilst others are likely to be hyposensitive.
- It is vital to carry out a sensory assessment as part of a holistic assessment of the person with an ASC.
- There are a number of strategies that could be implemented that will work with each person's sensory profile.

References

Asperger H ([1944] 1991) Autistic psychopathy in childhood. In Frith U (ed) *Autism and Asperger Syndrome*. Cambridge University Press, Cambridge

Attwood T (2006) *The Complete Guide to Asperger's Syndrome*. Jessica Kingsley Publishers, London

Ayers J (1972) *SensoryIntegration and Learning Disabilities*. Western Psychological Services, Los Angeles, CA

Barber C (1999) The use of music and colour theory as a behaviour modifier. *British Journal of Nursing* 8(7): 443–8

Berard G (1993) *Hearing Equals Behaviour*. Keats Publishing, New Canaan, CT

CHAPTER 16

Nursing interventions for independent adults

Introduction and aims

There are many people who have an autism spectrum condition (ASC) who are dependent to a greater or lesser extent on autism-specific services. *Chapter 9* focused on many nursing, health, social and holistic care needs. There are, however, many who live independently of intensive support and come into contact with autism support services only occasionally. This chapter focuses on the holistic needs of independent adults in a number of key life areas. By the end of the chapter the reader will have a basic understanding of how nurses and other healthcare professionals can work with people with an ASC in the following areas:

- Before, during and after diagnosis.
- Access to healthcare.
- Access to social care.
- Relationships.
- Employment.
- Social skills.
- Residential issues.
- Bereavement.

These will be placed within the context of the autism strategy *Fulfilling Lives* (Department of Health 2010) and the draft autism guidance that arose out of this strategy. The 2009 Autism Act and the 2010 Autism Strategy are explored in *Chapter 19*).

Before, during and after diagnosis

> *For many adults, receiving a clinical diagnosis of autism is an important step towards a fulfilling life.*
>
> Department of Health (2010: 33)

> *Currently, diagnosis can be a complex and lengthy process. Adults with autism talk of having to battle hard – sometimes for years – to get a diagnosis, and then finding that diagnosis is being challenged when they try to access services.*
>
> Department of Health (2010: 33)

Box 16.6. Case example: Bob

Bob, a degree-educated married man in his late 40s, has a teenage daughter who was recently diagnosed with Asperger's syndrome. Bob comes into the GP practice where you work as a practice nurse to keep a previously arranged blood pressure monitoring appointment. During the course of this appointment, Bob tells you that he thinks he may have autism.

Not all those who have an ASC are diagnosed in infancy and childhood; some are diagnosed much later in life. Many of those who have an ASC do not have or may not want, for a whole host of reasons, a formal diagnosis.

In order to make a diagnosis simpler and easier to obtain the Autism Strategy (Department of Health 2010) recommends the appointment of a lead professional to develop diagnostic and assessment services for adults with an ASC.

How, then, would the practice nurse in the scenario in *Box 16.1* engage with Bob? The first thing is to listen to Bob and not dismiss his concerns; acknowledge that he may know more about autism than you do. Secondly, compile a list of psychiatrists and psychologists who have had specific training, experience and expertise in the complex area of autism diagnosis in adults. Remember, diagnosing ASCs in adults is not the same as diagnosing these conditions in children. Therefore, psychiatrists who have the skills and expertise necessary for diagnosing children may not be the most appropriate professionals to diagnose adults. The National Autistic Society (NAS) may have a list of suitably qualified and experienced diagnosticians. Bob may have to be informed that the local health authority does not fund an 'out of geographical area' diagnostician and, therefore, he may have to fund the diagnosis himself. If Bob would like to pursue a diagnosis for himself he may appreciate having some idea of the diagnostic process so that he can prepare himself. Again, such information should be obtainable from the NAS.

Emotional and psychological support may be needed during the diagnostic process, so be available. Similarly, it is neither appropriate nor safe to leave Bob floundering without support if it is found after an in-depth and holistic assessment that he does not fit onto the autism spectrum. Bob may well need to come to terms with this non-diagnosis, and appropriate support and guidance must be offered.

Post-diagnosis information and support needs to be offered at the point of diagnosis. In many circumstances, the immediate needs are for:

- Information about autism: What it is and how it affects those who have the condition.
- Information about sources of help for the individual and his or her family. This could include telephone helplines, possible welfare benefits and local support groups.

While many adults who are diagnosed do receive this kind of information, particularly where the diagnosis is made by a specialist service provider, too many do not, and have to search hard for support (Department of Health 2010).

Having gone through the diagnostic process, Bob will almost certainly need appropriate information regarding the support resources that are available for him. This should be fairly in-depth; a single four-sided A5 leaflet is not enough and may well leave those affected by the diagnosis feeling neglected, confused and angry. Following diagnosis the person with an ASC and his or her carers (if any) must be offered a full and holistic strength and needs assessment (Department of Health 2010).

Access to healthcare services

Those with an ASC are as likely to require and access healthcare services and support throughout their lives as anyone else (Barber 2001). Adults with an ASC may need to access GP practices, community health centres, outpatients, A and E departments, medical and surgical wards, obstetrics and gynaecology departments, dental departments and mental health facilities, to name a few. It is neither realistic, helpful nor appropriate to lay down sets of guidelines that could be applied to each and every healthcare facility, each and every situation and each and every person with an ASC. To attempt to write such a set of guidelines would deny people with an ASC their individuality. Some people may be more adept than others at handling the often unwritten social demands and expectations inherent in accessing public services.

However, there are a number of measures that can be implemented that do not take a great deal of time or resources but that would make the experience of accessing healthcare facilities far less stressful.

Training

> *I have attended a two day workshop on autism spectrum conditions. I now know everything that there is to know about autism. Your child does not have autism.*
>
> Claim made by a social worker as overheard by a parent of a young man with an ASC

Training of health and social care staff in ASC forms a major aspect of the Department of Health's Autism Strategy. In order to offer suitable and appropriate services and care to those with or who are affected by autism spectrum conditions it is vital to recognise any knowledge gap and take active steps to fill it. In order to do this, there are increasing numbers of training courses available for healthcare professionals. These range from short one-day 'tasters' to postgraduate degrees in autism spectrum conditions, such as those offered by the University of Birmingham's School of Education.

Short courses are offered by many mental health, community care and primary care NHS Trusts. Likewise many voluntary and independent sector organisations such as the Cambian Group, the National Autistic Society, Sunfield and Autism West Midlands offer short courses for care staff and parents of those with an ASC. The latter are generally relatively inexpensive or free of charge and have the added advantage of parents, teachers, nurses and doctors learning together on equal terms. This can lead to a cross-fertilisation of experiences, practices and ideas. In addition, many local parent-run autism support groups may be prepared to come and give talks to care staff. However, a note of caution must be struck here: attendance at a one or two day conference, awareness or training session *does not* make you an expert. These short training courses are only intended as very brief, basic, introductory tasters and awareness sessions.

Communication

The key to verbal communication with those with an ASC is to keep such communication short, concise, to the point and honest. Many of those with an ASC have major problems in processing large amounts of information and can only process and therefore understand, half a dozen words out of 30 or 40; the remainder will not be processed and will be lost. This can often cause great frustration to both the person with an ASC and the care staff working with him or her. Again, many people with an ASC have problems being able to focus on the person speaking to them and will often find background noise or other people's conversations a source of major distraction and disruption. Therefore, in order to facilitate verbal communication, try to find somewhere quiet and as free from distractions as possible.

Many people with an ASC have a very literal understanding of verbal communication. If told to 'pull your socks up', a person with an ASC may be confused and say that he is not wearing any socks. Therefore, language should be used carefully. Likewise, many of those with an ASC may not be able to recognise or understand body language. Therefore, verbal communication must be consistent with the body language used by the speaker.

Another area of communication that has arguably been greatly neglected in terms of service provision to those with an ASC is the communication that should, but often does not, take place between care professionals. Interprofessional communication is vital if those with an ASC are to experience the same high quality health services, care and treatment that other people would expect to receive.

Punctuality

If Bob, who we met earlier, is offered a 9.30 am appointment at his local GP practice, hospital outpatient department or local health centre then this must mean that he is seen at 9.30. People with an ASC are far less likely to be able to cope with the uncertainty and unpredictability of being offered an appointment at the same time as half a dozen other patients. The unpredictability of not knowing when he will be seen will increase anxiety and therefore the likelihood of adverse behaviour being exhibited. This will obviously not be possible in A and E departments, for example. However, a simple and on-going explanation as to the likely length of time that the person will have to wait along with reassurance may be all that is necessary to prevent increased anxiety and 'behavioural melt-down'.

Low arousal environments

Many people with an ASC are unable to cope with an over-stimulating environment, such as a clinic or ward where there are lots of people and noise, where there is too much activity or where there are too many visual stimuli. This may require the use of a quiet side room where the person with an ASC can feel safe and comfortable. Again, arranging appointments at quieter times may be all that is needed to prevent over-stimulation, increased anxiety and possible 'behavioural melt down'.

Pre-appointment/pre-admittance visits

It may be possible for those with an ASC to be offered the opportunity to visit the hospital ward or department, health centre or health clinic a few days before admission or appointment. The purpose of such a visit would be to introduce the person to the clinical area, its staff, routines, noises and smells. The person would thus be able to understand, accurately anticipate and predict what is going to happen during his or her appointment, admission or clinical procedure. Such understanding would lower anxiety and thus decrease the likelihood of adverse behaviour. It is accepted that this may take up valuable staff time but it should result in a less anxious and therefore calmer patient. There are a number of dental practices that arrange such pre-appointment visits by patients with an ASC with good results.

Availability of information before and during the appointment/admission

The provision of precise and specific information that details exactly what will happen to the patient during his or her hospital or health centre appointment or admission is very useful in decreasing anxiety levels. It must be remembered that people with an ASC need a higher level of predictability than many people without an ASC. This requirement for predictability could be met through such a provision of information. It must also be remembered that many of those with an ASC may not be able to process written information. Therefore, the use of other media including interactive CD ROMS incorporating virtual tours of wards, departments or procedures, DVDs, audio cassettes or even story books could all be used to good effect. These communication methods may not require a huge investment of time or money and could be hugely beneficial.

Time

Finally, extra time must be taken to reassure and support patients with an ASC if they need it, remembering that not everyone with an ASC may need such support in all clinical settings or all of the time. It may involve just sitting down with the patient in quiet stillness.

Access to social care services

Strictly speaking, social care could be argued to be the realm of the social worker rather than the nurse. However, nurses and other healthcare professionals may be involved in helping those with an ASC to assess, plan, meet and evaluate their social care needs. This may include nurses working within community mental health and learning disability teams and others employed by national autism support organisations, such as the NAS, and regional support organisations, such as Autism West Midlands. The areas of social care support could include assistance with the following:

- Budgeting.
- Obtaining social welfare benefits.
- Obtaining and keeping accommodation.
- Purchasing furniture.
- Healthy eating.
- Access to and use of public transport through 'travel training' schemes.
- Employment.
- Learning activities.
- Leisure facilities.

In all of the above areas of assistance, which is by no means an exclusive list, the person with an ASC must be a central member of the multi-disciplinary team (MDT) and not peripheral to assessing, planning, implementing and evaluating support. Full involvement as an equal member of the MDT is a major aspect of personalisation which was the subject of *Chapter 14*.

Much of this assistance revolves around communication and social interaction issues and requires a full, thorough and in-depth analysis of the person's strengths and needs.

The role of the nurse or healthcare professional is to be:

- Fully involved as the advocate of the person with an ASC if he or she needs it.
- Aware of what services are available for the person with an ASC to access in order to improve the quality of his or her life.
- Aware of who to go to or who to refer the person with an ASC to for help.

A simple database or folder comprising information about appropriate services and contacts could be useful and may be all that is needed.

Relationships

Whilst those with an ASC have the same right to engage in emotional, romantic and sexual relationships as anybody else, many choose not to do so. This is only to be expected, given the issues regarding social interaction, social communication and social imagination that form an integral part of the personality of those with an ASC. Many do not see the need for such relationships, whilst others try to avoid them due to uncertainty and anxiety. The choice not to engage in emotional and sexual relationships on the part of those with an ASC must be recognised, respected and supported. However, it may be useful for the healthcare worker to be aware of the signs and symptoms of loneliness and isolation and be in a position to suggest other types of social interaction and engagement based on the person's interests.

However, some people with an ASC do feel the need for and will engage in short, medium and long-term emotional and sexual relationships with others. Such relationships could and sometimes do include marriage and/or having children.

The role of the healthcare professional may include:

- Teaching the person appropriate social communication, interpersonal and interaction skills and offering support.
- Running antenatal and parenting classes specifically targeted at the needs of people with an ASC.
- Being aware of and supporting the social, communication and relationship needs of the non-ASC partner.

One way of helping a non-ASC partner could be to help set up and facilitate a partners' support group. For information regarding one such group that exists in the Birmingham area contact: aspartnerswestmids@yahoo.co.uk.

Employment

Many, if not most, of those with an ASC who are 'independent' are able to gain and keep employment, with much of this employment being based around their specific interests. For example, those who have a passion for all things to do with computers may be employed within an IT role; those who have a unique artistic or musical creative ability may become professional artists, musicians or composers.

Employment may, however, present a number of difficulties.

- *Social communication:* those with an ASC may experience difficulties in

engaging in conversations in appropriate ways with work colleagues. Some may find it difficult to understand and engage with other people's need to discuss the previous evening television programmes, for example. Social banter and verbal innuendo may also pose major difficulties for people with an ASC.
- *Social interaction:* partly as a result of communication difficulties, those with an ASC may experience problems with engaging and interacting with other people; for example, being aware of other people's body language and need for personal space, as well as appropriate means of social interaction.
- *Social imagination:* being able to understand the thinking and perspective (theory of mind) of work colleagues, and the tendency of many people with an ASC to see the world in 'black and white' with no intermediate shades of grey, may cause problems.

The healthcare professional may be involved in the following:

- Supporting those with an ASC in being aware of his or her own interests, strengths and weaknesses and therefore what types of employment to seek.
- Supporting the person throughout the job application process and disclosing his or her ASC status to employers and colleagues.
- Alerting the employer and future colleagues around the needs of the new employee who has an ASC and drawing up work-based support strategies with the full knowledge and consent of the individual involved.
- Supporting the person with an ASC through the provision of individualised support strategies which could then be delivered either on a one-to-one basis or in a group setting.

Social skills

I can speak on matters for resolution and matters for discussion in front of 1500 or so of my nursing peers and colleagues at RCN Congress, no problems! But you put me with the same nurses at a social event during Congress and I freeze. I'm a fish out of water.

There are likely to be many adults with an ASC living independently who need support in order to access social and leisure facilities and to know how to communicate and interact appropriately with others. Support may also be needed around self-esteem and self-value in order to counteract the 'can't do it, therefore won't do it' mentality that can often prevent meaningful social interactions. Pubs, football matches, swimming pools and music concerts, for example, are arenas for social interaction that most of us take for granted and can cope with without difficulty. For those with an ASC, these can be fraught with problems due to a lack of predictability and a lack of understanding. Therefore, one-to-one or small group coaching in language, communication and social interactions may be necessary in order for those with an ASC to be able to participate fully in social activities and enjoy a good quality of life.

Residential issues

Many adults with an ASC live independently without any help or support. However, many will need some support in choosing and obtaining the right accommodation in terms of size, price and location. My Safe House (www.mysafehouse.info) is a voluntary sector organisation that was set up specifically to enable those with a disability to own their own home and it can provide useful information. Support with budgeting in order to pay bills on time and buy food may also be needed as well as the communication and interpersonal strategies needed to deal effectively with 'cold callers' and doorstep sales people. The role of the nurse is to know to whom to refer the service user/patient for support. This is likely to be a social worker, however, a GP practice, health centre nurse or community psychiatric nurse may be involved in providing one-to-one or small group sessions that focus on the skills needed to live independently.

Bereavement

End of life, dying and death of the individual with an ASC, his or her parents or family member, children or friends may be particularly problematic due to emotional issues, communication and information processing skills. People with an ASC will have their own way of coming to terms with their own and others' mortality and must be given assistance to do so. Support must be offered in acknowledging one's own mortality and preparing for death and bereavement. This can be done in the following ways:

- Advanced directives (living wills) could be discussed as a means of documenting what sort of healthcare support people with an ASC may need when they near the end of their lives.
- Those with an ASC must be supported to grieve at the death of a parent or other family member or friend in their own individual way.
- Be aware of how this grieving process may impact on the person's own

mental health and be able to offer (or refer the person for) appropriate mental and emotional health support.

- It may be helpful to have a list of the contact details of care professionals who work in the area of end of life, dying, death and bereavement. Such care professionals may well include learning disability and mental health nurses and faith community leaders.

Please note, the emphasis here, as elsewhere, is on offering and not imposing such support.

Conclusion

This chapter has covered a wide range of issues in an attempt to cover the major aspects in the lives of those with an ASC who are independent and who may require support. Such support, which is likely to focus on social communication, social interaction, social imagination and self-help skills, must be offered and not imposed; some with an ASC may not require any help, others minimal help and others more intensive help. Support may be time-limited and focus on working on and resolving specific issues whilst other areas of support may be more long-term and may even be life-long. Any support that is offered must be culturally and ethnically sensitive and take into account the fact that needs will change over time; a one size approach is not inappropriate. Such holistic support will, if based on a thorough assessment of needs, only serve to enrich the lives of all those with an ASC and those associated with them.

Key points

- Many adults with an ASC are likely not to have a formal diagnosis.
- Appropriate, correct and sensitive information regarding all therapy and support options must be made available before, during and after diagnosis.
- Appropriate training on all aspects of ASCs must be made available and attended by healthcare professionals in order to optimise support and care.
- Those with an ASC may need support with relationships, communication, employment, housing, healthcare and leisure.
- There are a number of ways that more able adults can be supported whilst they access health and social care facilities.

References

Barber C (2001) The training needs of registered nurses engaged in work with people with an autistic spectrum disorder. *Good Autism Practice* **2**(2): 86–96

Department of Health (2010) *The Sutism Strategy: Fulfilling and Rewarding Lives*. Department of Health, London

CHAPTER 17

Nursing interventions for informal carers

Box 17.1. Mother and son jump to their deaths

CCTV footage shows last minutes of missing woman
Eight-second gap between two figures seen falling

Two grainy 'ant-like' figures clamber over a security railing on the eastern footpath of the Humber bridge. Moments later one is seen tumbling towards the treacherous waters 30 metres (100ft) below. Eight seconds pass, then the other figure falls too.

Police specialists were trying yesterday to enhance 30 seconds of poor-quality CCTV footage, increasingly convinced that it shows how a desperate single mother and her 12-year-old autistic son jumped to their deaths from Britain's biggest suspension bridge.

Martin Wainwright
The Guardian
April 19, 2006

Introduction

For the past 50 years it has been UK Government policy that wherever possible, people who have mental health problems or a disability should be cared for in the community rather than in an institution (Percy Commission 1957; DHSS 1971). Since the 1990s however, a series of UK Government reports and initiatives have recognised that poverty, additional expenditure and low income have often been linked to the lives of families caring for a child or adult with a disability (Russell 2005). The role of the statutory services is now seen as being to support informal caregivers so that they can continue to look after their dependents in the community (DHSS 1981). Based on UK census data, Drever et al (2003) reported that 57.7 million people were resident in households in April 2001 and approximately 10% of these were informal carers.

Up until now, this book has focused on the lives, experiences and needs of those with an autism spectrum condition (ASC). However, their parents, grandparents, aunts, uncles, siblings, or children (collectively known as 'informal carers') may frequently need help in order to meet the needs of their family member.

This chapter explores:

- The experiences of mothers, fathers and partners who care for a person with an ASC whilst assisting that person to access health and social care.
- The personal feelings and health issues of these caregivers.
- Ways that healthcare professionals can assist informal carers to look after the person with an ASC.

By the end of this chapter you will have an awareness of:

- What makes for a good or bad experience for caregivers while accessing healthcare.
- The impact on informal caregivers of caring for a person with an ASC.
- What caregivers expect of healthcare staff.
- The role of the nurse and other healthcare professionals in supporting caregivers.

Definitions of an informal carer

According to the website of Carers UK, a major national informal carers' organisation (www.carers.org.uk), and Doran et al (2003) there are around six million informal carers currently in the UK. This equates to around 10% of the current UK population. An informal carer is anyone who looks after or cares for a family member or friend without being paid or trained to do so. This is in contrast to 'formal' or professional carers, such as nurses, doctors, social workers or religious ministers. Volunteers (who are placed with a person with a disability by a voluntary sector organisation or faith community) or personal assistants are not seen as informal carers. According to Carers UK, informal carers save the State around £87 billion a year in services and support that it would otherwise have to provide. This equates to each carer saving the State £14500 per year. Carers come from all social classes and economic backgrounds and from all age groups, from seven or eight-year-olds caring for their parents or siblings through to people in their 90s.

Demographic and age information of the estimated 6 million informal caregivers currently living in the UK are shown in *Boxes 17.2* and *17.3*.

It is not known for certain how many people in the UK have an ASC and, therefore, how many caregivers are involved in the lives of those with an ASC.

Box 17.2. Demographic information on carers

- 1 adult in 8 (6 million) (12.5% of the population) is providing informal care.
- 1 household in 6 contains a caregiver.
- 3.5% of adults (1.7 million) spend more than 20 hours a week giving care.
- 23% of all caregivers have been caring for between 5 and 19 years and 24% have been caring for more than 10 years.
- 18% of caregivers look after more than one person.

Box 17.3. Age of carers

- Peak age of caregivers is in the 45–64 age range.
- 11.4% (114000) of children aged between 5 and 14 provide informal care.
- 12% of those aged over 65 provide informal care.
- Of these, more than one-third provide more than 50 hours of care a week.
- Fewer than one-third of caregivers over 65 years of age are in good health.
- 44000 caregivers are aged over 85.

Data gathering methods

Much of the data in this chapter were obtained through a joint approach of a qualitative, non-standardised questionnaire, an informal one-to-one interview with five parents of young people with an ASC, and a group discussion/interview/focus group involving five partners of adults with an ASC. Both questionnaires and interviews involved open-ended questions that attempted to explore the parents' and partners' experiences, both good and bad, of accessing healthcare resources and facilities for the person with an ASC. Any physical, emotional, mental and spiritual health issues that arose out of caring for someone with an ASC were also explored. The interview subjects were all known to the interviewer and the interviews were carried out in the subjects' own homes as this allowed for an informal atmosphere and gave the subjects control over what was discussed.

All the questionnaire and interview participants, whose names have been changed in order to protect their identities, were known to the author through a number of forums. Whilst this could have led to bias and an identification with the subjects this was avoided through producing and, as much as possible, keeping to a questionnaire and interview script. Again, due to the small number of subjects and the way that the questionnaires and interviews were conducted, it could be suggested that the information elicited has only anecdotal value. However, whilst this may be true, Coad et al (2006) suggest that even anecdotal evidence is evidence and has value as such.

Qualitative rather than quantitative structures were used throughout as what was being examined was people's experiences, which were highly personal to each participant. It was felt that quantitative structures would not have elicited the experiential stories and data that were essential for this chapter.

General issues around caring

There are a wide number of issues around caring for a family member or friend who has a disability. Some of these will affect those caring for a person with an ASC whilst others may not. These can include the carer experiencing some or all of the following:

- Economic poverty.
- Disability discrimination by proxy or by association.
- Physical health issues.
- Mental health issues.
- Emotional health issues.
- Spiritual health issues.

Economic poverty

Many people who take on a caring role find that they may have to either leave their paid employment, work part-time or take 'less demanding' employment in order to meet the care needs of the person they are looking after. This will, inevitably mean a decrease in financial income whilst financial outgoings either stay the same or, in some cases, increase due to the cost of caring. Whilst there is 'Carers' Allowance', a welfare benefit that can be claimed by those who are caring for a minimum of 35 hours per week, this is currently pegged at £52.30 a week, currently about a quarter of the national minimum wage.

Disability discrimination by association

Many carers experience discrimination due to the fact that they are carers. For example, there is anecdotal evidence to suggest that employees who are carers may be treated less favourably than others in terms of flexibility of working times (start and end times and meal breaks) which has a direct impact on their caring roles. Again, some experience difficulties in finding suitable employment that will allow them to combine employment and caring, or experience negative attitudes from potential employers. Others experience difficulties accessing services due to their caring responsibilities, for example, inflexible appointment times at GP practices, out-patient or other hospital departments. Such discriminatory practice is now illegal under the Equality Act 2010 but hospital staff still need to be aware through on-going professional development of the needs of carers, the necessity to make services 'user friendly' and the consequences if they do not.

Physical health issues

There is a high occurrence of muscular-skeletal problems including both acute and chronic back pain and broken bones among those who provide informal care. This is likely to be as a result of poor or inappropriate manual handling techniques. Whereas care professionals attend annual training courses with accredited trainers lasting one or two days on the subject of manual handling, many informal caregivers receive only 15–20 minutes of being shown the correct techniques for manual handling by a community nurse (Carers UK 2010a), and this is usually in relation to the use of hoists.

Mental health issues

There appears to be a higher than normal incidence of mental health issues experienced by informal carers (Carers UK 2010b). Such issues include depression, physical and mental exhaustion, self-harm, excessive use of alcohol and thoughts of and even attempted suicide. These can often be compounded by stress and mental and physical exhaustion. According to Carers UK (2010b), many carers can all too easily get caught in a cycle of resentment and guilt: resentful that their life is no longer their own and guilty for feeling like this. These feelings will often increase the likelihood of the carer experiencing periods of depression.

Emotional health issues

Not only will carers' physical and mental health be likely to deteriorate as a result of caring, so will their emotional health. The often high demands of caring for a person with a disability, juggling the needs of other family members, trying to hold down paid employment and trying to meet their own needs can often lead to stress and emotional burnout. Trying to care for another can be humbling, rewarding and even exhilarating; it can also be incredibly exhausting, isolating and lonely. It is not unheard of for friends and family to stop visiting and to stop providing support. Statistically, those families that have a 'disabled' member are also more prone to experiencing marital problems, including separation and divorce than 'non-disabled' families.

Spiritual issues

As noted above, caring can be both very rewarding and very isolating. Within most if not all world religions, expressing care, love and support for others in need is seen to be good, even holy and to be praised. Within the Christian faith for example, caring can often be seen as helping to carry the Cross of Christ and as such is a holy calling. Therefore, there is now a growing awareness and understanding of the spirituality of disability and caring. However, carers can feel ignored and forgotten by their individual faith communities. This can be a cause of great pain and sadness and can lead carers to question and even lose their faith.

Experiences of carers for people with an ASC

This chapter has so far focused on issues around the needs of those who are informal carers in general rather than exploring the specific needs of informal carers of those with an ASC. The experiences of those who have a family member or friend with an ASC will have many, but perhaps not all, of the issues already highlighted.

The following views were expressed by a small number of parents and partners of those with an ASC who kindly participated in either one-to-one or small group discussions or responded to an emailed questionnaire. The questions focused on carers' positive and negative experiences of accessing and using medical and health services and support for the person with an ASC. The author would like to thank those who participated for their time and input into this chapter.

Box 17.4. Comments from informal carers

My teenage son with autism recently had to go into hospital for an operation. Most of the nursing staff could not understand my son's behaviour and when I told them that he has autism they just grunted. They had no knowledge, awareness or understanding of autism and were not prepared or willing to learn. I ended up doing all of my son's personal care whilst he was at the hospital. There was only one nurse on this ward who was prepared to listen and she was brilliant, even making up a bed for me so that I could be with my son during the night.

I had to take my son who has autism and who can be a bit noisy to see his GP a while ago. Whilst he was in the surgery consulting room, the GP said 'Can't you keep him quiet?' I just looked at this GP and replied, 'If you know how, then tell me as I would love to know.'

...We wanted to have been listened to. For nurses to have done their jobs properly. For nurses to have communicated....

...I would like to see more training, compassion and understanding. Nurses and doctors need to learn how to communicate properly with people. They need to learn how to be flexible. They need to learn how to listen....

...Specific services for adults. At the moment, there is very little that my son and I can access, not even respite. What little support we get will disappear when he becomes an adult and this scares me....

We would like information specifically on employment, social skills, relationships, independence and stress management.

When questioned, all the interview and questionnaire participants agreed that they had encountered both helpful and unhelpful healthcare professionals.

Ms A, who has a teenage son with Asperger's syndrome said:

Behavioural aspects of my son were not dealt with. The nurses and doctors were very dismissive. I did not feel that I had been listened to. I was and felt blamed for his autism. The speech and language therapists were not trained, knew nothing about autism and could not deal with my son's autism. One particular speech and language therapist went off long-term sick due to the stress of having to deal with his autistic behaviour. Most staff were untrained when it came to autism, did not understand, did not want to know. I felt that J had been failed right down the line. We sought a diagnosis because we wanted to manage his behaviour, not to label. We went to our GP when J was 18 months old but we were constantly fobbed off. Medical consultants need to learn how to communicate with people. All healthcare professionals need to listen to the parents and not dismiss them. We would have valued more input from care professionals who need to be properly prepared before medical appointments.

When asked about any problems that were experienced recently, Mrs B responded:

Yes. A few weeks ago, C had to go into our local hospital for an exploratory test. He had to have this done by GA [general anaesthetic] and that was only after I kicked up a fuss. I knew that he would not be able to tolerate having the test done under a local. When he came around after his GA, he was left on his own. I was not allowed to be at his side. He was left cold and scared. He had to 'phone me on his mobile for me to ask the nursing staff to get him a blanket. I asked the nursing staff whether they had been briefed that C had autism/Asperger's and was told very rudely 'yes'.

When asked about receiving information about ASC from healthcare professionals, Mr D replied:

We received virtually no information from any healthcare professional about autism, Asperger's syndrome and how to manage it. We had to find the information ourselves with no help from care professionals. We knew that there was something wrong with J but we had to get his diagnosis privately for which we had to pay. We only had a three-hour session at our local hospital about autism and that was it. We were given no written information about behaviour management. We did join a local autism support group and we did receive some help from his primary school but that was it. I did attend a small number of short courses including one on control and restraint.

However, one respondent, Mrs D, who was a nurse working in neurology services as well as an informal carer, was full of praise for all the nursing and healthcare professionals encountered by her 8-year-old daughter who had an ASC and could not fault their work.

Mrs E, also a nurse, when asked what positive experience she had had with care professionals in the past, said that she had an excellent rapport with a psychiatrist who helped with diagnosing Asperger's syndrome in her daughter at the age of 14 years. However, when asked if she had any negative experiences of healthcare professionals she said that because her daughter's Asperger's was mixed with learning disability they had to fight for a diagnosis. One locum psychiatrist asked her many complicated things about voices in her daughter's head and spoke in terms she did not understand. When asked what could have been improved, Mrs E said she needed time to ask questions and take on board how she felt. Also, care professionals needed to be open to the idea that having a diagnosis is okay and can be beneficial. When asked whether she or her husband had received any information on ASC from the psychiatrist who diagnosed her daughter, Mrs E replied that she had not. She also suggested that follow-up information and services would have been really useful. Mrs E said that she had experienced neither positive nor negative attitudes and practices by healthcare professionals towards her daughter.

Mrs E said:

> *As a nurse myself I know there are LD [learning difficulty] nurses around but for autism, there is nothing in pre-registration nurse training as I understand it. Nurses do not know or understand about this condition and as such do not know how to communicate. They are more likely to label someone as abrupt, awkward, and unemotional. It would be good if a nurse was placed in certain areas like special schools, colleges, etc. to understand more of the condition, However I don't believe there is any capacity for this to happen. Also a family link worker who can help support with educational, health and social issues. Links with educational establishments are a must. A specialist worker can help work with the individual to help them face what autism means to them.*

Experiences of carers who have an ASC

Whilst the above section focused on the views of those who are providing care for a family member who has an ASC, it must not be forgotten that some people who have an ASC are themselves carers of others. For example, one person with an ASC who is in her 40s and known to the author is a carer for her husband who has depression and for her teenage daughter who also has

Asperger's syndrome. Such a situation is unusual but is not unheard of. Due to the communication, interaction and imagination difficulties experienced by those with an ASC, extra support may need to be offered to both the carer and the cared for. For example, the carer with an ASC may require support in a whole range of areas:

- Actually knowing what care to provide, in what circumstances, how, when and why.
- Knowing what welfare benefits to claim and how and when to claim them.
- Knowing how to work with a wide range of health and social care providers and services.
- Being able to recognise and understand the needs and intentions of the person they are caring for.
- Being able to recognise and understand the subtle forms of language and communication employed by other members of the multi-disciplinary team.
- Knowing where to access emotional and psychological support for themselves.

Much of this support, which revolves around issues of advocacy, can be discussed and put in place during a full, in-depth and holistic carer's assessment. However, such an assessment must be always offered to but never imposed on the carer with an ASC, or any other carer for that matter. Again, being able to recognise and understand the different and often hidden agendas of the various members of the multi-disciplinary team can often pose problems not only for carers who have an ASC but for other carers as well. The provision of support for carers is not always as 'black and white' as it may appear; there are large grey areas when it comes to forming political alliances and this can often be problematic not only for carers who have an ASC but for other carers as well. Such differing agendas can often be an inevitable part of working within a multi-disciplinary environment.

Role of the nurse and other healthcare professional

As can be seen from the comments made by some of the carers who were questioned, there appears to be a lot of anger that needs to be understood and dealt with by nurses and other healthcare providers. There are several roles that the nurse, doctor and other healthcare professional can undertake when working with informal carers to deal with such anger. These will often include being aware of:

- The likelihood that, at some point, you will be meeting and working with people who are informal carers.
- The need to listen to informal carers.
- The issues around disability and caring for a person with a disability.
- Any differing agendas between carer and the person being cared for and between informal and professional carers.
- The various forms of support resources that could be made available for informal carers.

In addition, healthcare professionals can help by:

- Running informal carer friendly services.
- Facilitating carer support groups.
- Being prepared to act as advocate for informal carers.

Whether you are working in learning disability, mental health, paediatrics, GP practice, health centre or anywhere that has a high throughput of patients or service users you are likely to meet and work with informal carers. Your first role is, therefore, to be aware of this. Secondly, and perhaps most importantly, you need to listen to and understand informal carers rather than dismiss or ignore them. Quite often, carers are likely to know more about the needs of their family member than you do; they rather than you are the experts in their family member's care. Therefore, humility and an acknowledgement that you do not know about all their problems and are not able to provide all the answers may go a long way to defuse a possibly emotionally angry and volatile situation.

Along with listening to the carer, try to understand what it is like to have a disability or to be a carer. Many healthcare organisations run short courses or seminars on various aspects of caring and it may be useful to invite a person with a disability and a carer to speak at these seminars or courses. Contact local disability or carer support groups and ask for information as to what it is really like to live with a disability. Most acute hospitals have a staff library, so carry out a journal research project on life with a disability and reflect on this information.

There can be differences in the agendas held and followed by those with a disability and those who care for them, so try to understand these differences. Those with a disability and those who care for them may have differing and even opposing views of what services they need or would like to access. This is quite normal and to be expected, particularly when the person with a disability tends towards independence and is assertive. Whilst it will not be your role to interfere and take sides where there are powerful family dynamics at play, it may be your role to act as mediator and broker. Therefore, it is important that you are able to understand the various perspectives of the stakeholders involved. The same applies when there are differing agendas followed by the various care professionals. It is not unusual for nurses, doctors and social workers to follow and promote their own different agendas with ensuing power struggles. There may be competing demands between service users, carers and professional service providers. When this happens, which it almost certainly will, take a step back and remember why you are there, before you start to champion particular sides.

One of your most important, and perhaps easiest, roles is to compile a comprehensive database of information, resources and contacts that could be used to support family and friends who care for and support a person with an ASC. The National Autistic Society, conferences and training courses and local autism support groups would be a useful place to begin such a compilation.

Since informal carers may not be able to attend healthcare appointments that are timed and located to meet the needs of the healthcare organisation, try to offer appointments for carers at times and places to suit them. Whilst this may prove difficult from an organisational perspective, offering 'carer friendly' services will repay dividends in terms of carers keeping appointments.

There may be a dearth of friendly and accessible support groups for carers of those with an ASC in your local area. Talk to carers to obtain their views and if they express a need for such a support group then offer to help start one. This may simply involve providing a meeting space in your local child development centre, GP practice or health centre, providing basic refreshments such as tea, coffee and biscuits, and providing basic administrative support such as the use of a photocopier. Remember, it is unlikely to be part of your role to run a support group as this takes power away from carers. However, keeping a 'watching brief' and helping to run the first couple of support group meetings may be required.

Finally, as has been implied in much of the above, act as advocate on behalf of both carers and people with an ASC. At all times, remember why you are there and whose needs you are there to meet. The person with an ASC and his or her carer are central and not peripheral to what you do.

Conclusion

This chapter has sought to highlight the various support needs of informal carers in general and those who care for a family member or friend who has an ASC in particular. Many of the experiences reported by family carers have been positive but more have not, and whilst there have been many reports of positive attitudes and practice adopted by care professionals, there have also been many that have been negative. Ultimately, your role is to be aware of the needs and work with rather than against families and friends of those with an ASC in such ways as to prevent the recurrence of the suicide of a mother and child as reported in *Box 17.1*. To fail to take seriously responsibility in this area would be to fail not only this young mother and others like her but also the person with an ASC.

Key points

- There are around 6 million people who care for a family member or friend. These are 'informal carers'.
- A series of UK Government reports and initiatives have recognised that poverty, additional expenditure and low income have been linked to the lives of families caring for a child or adult with a disability.
- Other issues experienced by informal carers of those with an ASC include disability discrimination by association, social and spiritual isolation, and physical, mental and emotional health issues.
- The experiences of informal carers, including those who have an ASC, at the hands of nurses are very mixed.
- The role of the nurse includes being aware of and understanding the needs of informal carers, the provision of accurate and appropriate information, running informal carer friendly services, facilitating carer support groups and being prepared to act as advocate for informal carers.

References

Carers UK (2010a) *Backcare*. Available from: http://www.carersuk.org/Information/Helpwithhealth/Backcare [Last accessed 23 October 2010]

Carers UK (2010b) *Coping with Stress*. Available from: http://www.carersuk.org/Information/Helpwithhealth/Copingwithstress. [Last accessed 23 October 2010]

Coad J, Hardicre J, Devitt P (2006) How to search for and use 'grey literature' in Research. *Nursing Times* **102**(50): 35

DHSS (1971) *Better Services for the Mentally Handicapped* (CMND 1683) HMSO, London

DHSS (1981) *Growing Older* (CMND 8173). HMSO London

Drever F, Doran T, Whitehead M (2003) Health of young and elderly informal carers: Analysis of the UK Census data. *British Medical Journal* **327**(7428): 235

Percy Commission (1957) *Royal Commission on the Law Relating to Mental Illness and Mental Deficiency*. (CMND 169) HMSO, London

Russell P (2005) *A Guide to Support for Adult Learners Caring for Disabled Children or Other Family Members*. The Nuffield Foundation, London

Wainright M (2006) A mother and son smiling at the station. Then two specks on the edge of a bridge. *The Guardian* **April 19th**

CHAPTER 18

Autism spectrum conditions and welfare benefits

And God said: 'I may be omnipotent and omniscient but that does not mean that I can understand and find My way around the welfare benefits system. It's got Me stumped.'

Introduction

The UK welfare benefits system is incredibly complex: which is the best benefit to claim, how and when can it be claimed, what are the criteria for claiming each benefit and what are the advantages and disadvantages of claiming specific benefits?

Welfare benefits are usually thought to be the remit of social workers rather than nurses, doctors and other healthcare professionals. Whilst this may be correct, if nurses and healthcare professionals are to provide holistic care and support for people with an autism spectrum condition (ASC) they must be able to:

- Know the right person to go to for information and advice.
- Provide correct and accurate information on the main welfare benefits available to both those on the autism spectrum and their families/informal carers.

It is not be unusual for nurses, doctors and other healthcare professionals to be the first port of call for those with an ASC and/or their informal carers for help with the welfare benefits system. Healthcare professionals who work in GP practices and local health centres and community mental health and learning disability teams are particularly likely to be consulted.

In this chapter, Steve (the young lady we met in *Chapters 13 and 14*) will act as an example to help you to have a basic understanding of:

- The welfare benefits that are available for her and other people who are on the autism spectrum.

- The purpose of each benefit.
- The criteria for claiming each benefit.
- How to claim each benefit.

The author is indebted to the Child Poverty Action Group (2005) for the information in this chapter.

What welfare benefits are available?

There are innumerable welfare benefits that Steve, her family and other people on the autism spectrum can claim. The main ones are:

- Disability Living Allowance (DLA).
- Carers' Allowance (CA).
- Employment Support Allowance/Incapacity Benefit.

Other, more minor, benefits include:

- Council Tax Benefit.
- Housing Benefit.
- Jobseekers Allowance.
- Social Fund.
- Tax credits.

Other benefits applied locally include:

- Free school meals.
- Access to respite care services.
- Travel training.
- Small grants for holidays and specific care, and living/household equipment, such as cookers, fridges, freezers, washing machines and so on, are made by various voluntary sector organisations. For further information on these visit the websites of the National Autistic Society, Carers UK and the Princess Royal Trust for Carers. Social workers may also be able to provide information.

The local social work/social service team should be able to provide information regarding these benefits.

Disability Living Allowance (DLA)

The DLA is a non-contributory, tax-free benefit that provides cash help towards extra costs that Steve and others like her may face on a daily basis. The DLA is for those with physical and/or learning disability and/or mental health issues, under the age of 65 when they claim, with a disability severe enough to need help with personal care or have difficulties with mobility, or both. It is not a benefit for people who act as carers, for example Steve's parents, but is for those who have a disability, such as Steve. By non-contributory is meant those claiming this benefit do not have had to pay National Insurance contributions and the benefit is not affected by any other income or savings that Steve and her family may have. The DLA, although one single benefit, comprises a care component and a mobility component. Those on the autism spectrum who are aged over 65 cannot claim the DLA but can claim Attendance Allowance. Attendance Allowance is pegged to the age of male retirement, so when the retirement age rises the age at which Attendance Allowance takes affect may well also rise.

The DLA's care component has three rates at which it can be awarded. The rate depends on what and how much claimants can do for themselves and how much help they need:

- *Lower rate:* This is for claimants who need help with personal care for some of the day.
- *Middle rate:* This can be claimed if help with personal care or supervision is required frequently throughout the day or if the claimant is on dialysis.
- *Higher rate:* This can be awarded if help with personal care or supervision is needed throughout most of the day and also during the night.

The DLA's mobility component is for those who experience difficulties in walking. Such difficulties may include one or a combination of either physical, psychological or emotional issues. There are two rates to the mobility component depending on the level of difficulty.

- *Lower rate:* This is for those who are 5 years of age and over and who can walk but need guidance or supervision from another person when walking out of doors in unfamiliar places, environments and situations. This is to avoid danger or harm to the person because they may have problems with their behaviour, have a sensory impairment, a speech or language disorder or may need someone to keep a close eye on their condition.

- *Higher rate:* This is for those who are aged 3 years or over and where any of the following applies, even if the person concerned is using mobility equipment:
  - Claimants cannot walk at all.
  - They can only walk for short distances without severe discomfort.
  - The effort of walking could threaten their life or seriously affect their health.
  - They have severe sensory impairment.
  - They are entitled to the highest rate of the DLA's care component and they have a severe mental impairment (learning disability and/or mental health) and have severe behavioural problems.

Carers' Allowance (CA)

Carers' Allowance is a benefit for people who care on an 'informal' basis for those with a severe disability. It is not a benefit for the person with a disability. An 'informal carer' is someone who is looking after or caring for a family member or friend without being hired or paid to do so. This is in contrast to 'formal' or professional carers such as nurses, doctors, support workers, social workers or religious ministers who are hired, trained and paid to provide care. It is, however, not unusual for a person to be both a professional and an 'informal' carer. Only those who act as an 'informal' carer can claim Carers' Allowance, even though they may as their 'day job' be a professional carer. Therefore, Steve cannot claim for Carers' Allowance, but her parents can. Carers' Allowance is not based on the level of the carer's personal savings or whether or not the carer has made any National Insurance contributions through having previously had a paid job. However, the level and amount of the carer's personal income is taken into account as it is assumed that the person claiming the allowance is providing more or less full-time care. The value of Carers' Allowance is currently £53.10 a week. Whilst this equates to only £1.52 per hour for a 35-hour working/caring week, it can act as a gateway to other benefits.

Employment Support Allowance(ESA)/Incapacity Benefit

Employment Support Allowance (which superseded Incapacity Benefit in October 2008) is paid to people who are incapable of paid work of any kind over any duration. The focus is on capability rather than incapability to work and it seeks to assess capability of claimants for work-related activity. In order to claim this benefit the person claiming must have either paid or been credited with sufficient

National Insurance contributions or have become incapable of work as a youth. This is not to be confused with sickness benefit – Statutory Sick Pay (SSP) – as SSP is intended for short-term sickness only, although SSP could form the basis of a claim for ESA if the illness or health condition is likely to become very long term. The ESA focuses now on enabling the claimant to return to some sort of employment.

Council Tax Benefit

Council Tax Benefit is paid to people with a low income who pay council tax. It is paid whether or not the person claiming is available for or in paid work and may be paid in addition to other benefits.

Housing Benefit

Housing Benefit is paid to people with a low income who pay rent. It is paid whether or not the person claiming is available for or in paid work and may be paid in addition to other benefits.

Jobseekers' Allowance (JSA)

JSA (which has superseded Unemployment Benefit) is a benefit for people who are unemployed or who work for less than 16 hours a week. The JSA can also act as a gateway to other welfare benefits or locally agreed discounts.

Social Fund

The Social Fund is a Government fund that makes two types of payment:

- Sure Start Maternity Grants, funeral expenses and cold weather payments and Winter Fuel Payments.
- Discretionary community care grants, budgeting loans and crisis loans to meet a variety of needs, such as the purchase of a cooker, bed, chairs, tables, fridges, etc.

Tax credits

This comprises Child Tax Credits and Working Tax Credits. Both these are intended to top up low family income but are separate from the benefits system.

Eligibility for benefits

The previous section indicated which welfare benefits could be available for Steve, her family and other 'informal carers' who may look after her now or in the future. This section indicates in more depth the entitlement that Steve and her family may have to these benefits, how they qualify and what they must prove in order to get these benefits.

Disability Living Allowance (DLA)

- Steve must be living in the UK and not subject to immigration control.
- There is no lower age limit for claiming the care component of the DLA. However, to qualify for the higher rate mobility component the claimant must be aged over 3 years but under 65, and for the lower rate mobility the claimant must be aged over 5 years but under 65 and must have had the disability for more than 3 months.
- Steve must be able to take advantage of outside journeys in a car or public transport in order to claim the mobility component.
- For the higher rate mobility component, Steve must have a physical disability that means she is either:
  - unable, or virtually unable, to walk
  - both deaf and blind
  - was either born without feet or legs or is a double amputee
  - has a severe 'mental impairment' and severe 'behaviour problems'.
- For the lower rate mobility component, Steve must demonstrate that although she can walk she is unable to walk unsupervised, even in familiar environments.
- For the lower rate care component, Steve must be able to demonstrate that she is:
  - 16 years of age or older.
  - So severely disabled either physically or intellectually that she cannot prepare and cook a main meal if she has the ingredients (the 'cooking test').
  - So physically or mentally disabled that she requires support from another person for a significant portion of the day in order to carry out basic care needs such as getting up from bed in the morning, washing, dressing, and going to and staying in bed at night.
- For the middle rate care component, Steve must be able to demonstrate that she requires:
  - Frequent attention throughout the day from another person in order to

carry out basic bodily functions such as toileting, washing and dressing, or
 - Constant supervision throughout the day in order to avoid substantial danger or harm to herself, or
 - Repeated or prolonged support at night in relation to carrying out bodily functions, or
 - Somebody to be awake at night to watch over her.
- For the higher rate care component, Steve must be able to demonstrate that she requires frequent attention throughout both the day and night in connection with bodily functions or to prevent danger or harm.

Carers' Allowance (CA)

To qualify for Carer's Allowance, Steve's parents or siblings must meet the following criteria:

- Steve must be 'cared for' regularly and substantially. In practical terms this means that her parents or siblings must be supporting or caring for Steve for at least 35 hours per week in 22 of the previous 26 weeks.
- Caring and supporting here may involve supervising Steve as well as practical assistance. This could also include time spent in preparing for Steve to come and stay if she is living away from home (for example, in a residential college) or is returning from a holiday, or cleaning up after her visit.
- However, this '35 hours a week caring' rule must be consistent. It is not enough to demonstrate that Steve's parents or siblings are providing more than 35 hours a week during some weeks and less than 35 hours a week in others.
- The '35 hours a week caring' must be spent on Steve alone and must not be split between Steve and anyone else who may be living in the family home.
- Steve's parents or siblings can still receive Carers' Allowance if they have a week or two's break from caring (if, for example, Steve goes into respite care) providing they do not breach the '22 out of 26 weeks caring' rule.
- Steve's carer (be it a parent or sibling who is claiming Carers' Allowance) must not be 'gainfully employed'. By this is meant that, although Steve's carer can have an outside paid job, he or she cannot earn more than the lower earnings limit for National Insurance contributions which was in force at the end of the week that was worked. In the year 2010–2011 this amounts to £95 per week after tax and National Insurance deductions.

Employment Support Allowance ESA/Incapacity Benefit

To qualify for ESA/Incapacity Benefit, Steve must prove that she:

- Is a UK resident.
- Is assessed as incapable of work due to health reasons for more than four working days.
- Is not over the current pension age.
- Is not entitled to Statutory Sick Pay (SSP).
- Has paid or been accredited with sufficient National Insurance payments to cover ESA/Incapacity Benefit.
- Qualifies as someone who became incapable of work in youth. Steve must be over the age of 16 years and be incapable of work for 196 consecutive days (28 weeks, a week being Monday to Sunday inclusive) and not in education or training for more than 21 hours a week, or
- Not over pension age when she became incapable of work.

Whilst Incapacity Benefit has now been superseded by the Employment Support Allowance the above criteria are still valid.

Council Tax Benefit

To qualify for Council Tax Benefit, Steve must prove that she:

- Is liable for council tax.
- Has a low income.
- Has savings and capital worth less than £16000.
- Is not a full-time student.
- Is not in receipt of rents from someone who lives in her house.
- Is a UK resident and not subject to immigration control.

Housing Benefit

To qualify for Housing Benefit, Steve must prove that she:

- Is on a low income.
- Has savings and capital worth less than £16000.
- Pays rent.

- Will spend the benefit money on rent.
- Is a UK resident and not subject to immigration control.

Jobseekers' Allowance

To qualify for Jobseekers' Allowance, Steve must prove that she:

- Is not in full-time work.
- Is capable of work.
- Is not in education or training.
- Is available for and is actively seeking work.
- Is below the pension age.
- Is not in receipt of Income Support.

Social Fund

- Steve would have to prove financial hardship in order to claim from the Social Fund.
- The Social Fund is a strictly limited fund and, being discretionary, there is no legal entitlement to a payment.
- Most payments are in the form of a loan which is recovered through deductions in other benefits.
- There is no right of appeal to an independent tribunal.

Working Tax Credits

To qualify for tax credits, Steve must prove that she:

- Is in full-time paid work (or her partner is).
- Has a sufficiently low income.
- Is currently and ordinarily resident in the UK and is not subject to immigration control.

How to claim benefits

There are a number of ways to claim the benefits that are highlighted in this chapter. Possibly the first point of call would be to contact a social worker for help and advice. A second point of call could be the local Citizens Advice Bureau

(CAB) as CABs may employ the services of a social welfare benefits advisor or worker. A third option would be to consult the *Welfare Benefits and Tax Credits Handbook* that is published annually by the Child Poverty Action Group. This handbook should be available from disability employment advisors who are attached to Jobcentre Plus offices, good bookshops, local libraries, or hospital and university libraries. The Government website, Direct-Gov (www.direct.gov.uk) and the Department for Work and Pensions (www.dwp.gov.uk) have much useful information on the various social welfare benefits that are available and how to claim them.

To claim welfare benefits, there is usually a lengthy and often in-depth form that needs to be completed. These can be obtained as follows:

Carers' Allowance

- Carers Allowance Unit
  Palatine House
  Lancaster Road
  Preston
  Lancashire PR1 1HB
  01253 856123
  0800 88 22 00 (Open 08.30–18.30 Monday to Friday and 09.00–13.00 on Saturday for general benefits enquiries)

- www.dwp.gov.uk (for on-line claims)
- www.direct.gov.uk/carers (for on-line claims and information)

Disability Living Allowance

- Department for Work and Pensions
  PO Box 14
  Heywood
  Lancashire OL10 2FN
  08457 123 456
  0800 88 22 00 (Open 08.30–18.30 Monday to Friday and 09.00–13.00 on Saturday for general benefits enquiries)

- www.dwp.gov.uk (for on-line claims)
- www.direct.gov.uk/disability (for on-line claims and information)

Jobseekers' Allowance/Employment Support Allowance/ Incapacity Benefit

Information on how to claim for Employment Support Allowance can be obtained from your local Job Centre Plus and its Disability Employment Advisor.

Housing Benefit/Working Tax Credit/Council Tax Benefit/Social Fund

Information on these benefits and how to claim them can be obtained from local neighbourhood community offices and social workers.

Summary

Although most people with an ASC and their families have a social worker (or, at least, access to a social worker), some may not. This may be because they feel that they do not need one, do not know how to get one or be in the process of obtaining or being allocated one. Therefore, healthcare professionals may be the first people with whom people with an ASC and their families come into contact and may be asked for help and advice. This is likely to be the case if the healthcare professional works as part of a community mental health or learning disability team, as a school nurse, a community or district nurse or as a GP practice nurse. Therefore, it is worth obtaining copies of the claim forms for all the various welfare benefits that people with an ASC and their families could claim and to become familiar with them. If you do not understand the benefits forms you will be less likely to be able to assist those who come to you for help. Welfare benefits claim forms are not easy to understand with most running to between 30 and 40 pages. They often use complex, confusing and even contradictory language. One of your roles may be to 'interpret' and present the contents of these claim forms and associated information packs into more easily understood and simpler language. This may involve using alternative communication methods such as audio tapes, CDs, or pictures or other visual formats.

Conclusion

The welfare benefits system is incredibly complex and difficult to understand. Many healthcare workers may question the need to know about them but knowledge and understanding of the benefits that Steve and her family can claim is vital if one is to deliver holistic care. One of the roles of the healthcare professional is to obtain welfare benefits information and present it in a way that is simple and easy to understand for people with an ASC and their carers.

Key points

- The UK welfare benefits system is extremely complex and difficult to negotiate.
- There are a number of welfare benefits that a person with an ASC or their families can claim. The main benefits are Disability Living Allowance, Carers' Allowance and the Employment Support Allowance.
- More minor welfare benefits include: Council Tax Benefit, Housing Benefit, Jobseekers Allowance, Social Fund, Tax Credits.
- There are a small number of locally administered benefits that may be of use to those with an ASC and their families.

References

Child Poverty Action Group (2005) *Welfare Benefits and Tax Credits Handbook*. Child Poverty Action Group, London

CHAPTER 19

The Autism Act 2009 and the Autism Strategy 2010

Jo Delrée, RNLD, BPhil

Introduction

The Autism Act 2009 is the first disability-specific piece of legislation to be passed in the UK. It is seen by many as the victorious culmination of years of campaigning that highlighted the dearth of provision for people, particularly adults, with autistic spectrum conditions (ASCs). The passing of the Act means that an awareness of the lack of provision is no longer enough – services have a legal duty to make provision for those with autism, including those who have previously been excluded from receiving services because of restrictive and seemingly arbitrary eligibility criteria.

The Act lays out the need for 'guidance' to be issued that will describe the duties and responsibilities of service commissioners and providers, particularly in the areas shown in *Box 19.1*. This guidance has been published in the form of

Box 19.1. The Autism Act 2009

(5) Guidance issued under this section must in particular include guidance about:

- The provision of relevant services for the purpose of diagnosing autistic spectrum conditions in adults.
- The identification of adults with such conditions.
- The assessment of the needs of adults with such conditions for relevant services.
- Planning in relation to the provision of relevant services to persons with autistic spectrum conditions as they move from being children to adults.
- Other planning in relation to the provision of relevant services to adults with autistic spectrum conditions.
- The training of staff who provide relevant services to adults with such conditions.
- Local arrangements for leadership in relation to the provision of relevant services to adults with such conditions.

Box 19.2. Key areas for action in the Autism Strategy

- Increasing awareness and understanding of autism.
- Developing a clear, consistent pathway for diagnosis of autism.
- Improving access for adults with autism to the services and support they need to live independently within the community.
- Helping adults with autism into work.
- Enabling local partners to develop relevant services for adults with autism to meet identified needs and priorities.

the Autism Strategy *Fulfilling and Rewarding Lives* and an associated first year delivery plan. The Autism Strategy (Department of Health 2010) lays out areas for improvement and change within existing services, with a focus on equality of access, opening up mainstream and existing services rather than creating new autism-specific provision, and aiming not to need significant additional funding. It highlights five 'strands' or areas which must be addressed to fulfil its aims. These are detailed in *Box 19.2*.

Clearly this implies that the impact of the Act and Strategy should be far-reaching, and should have many implications for a broad range of services, covering all age ranges and all areas of health and social care. At the time of writing, with the documents freshly published, and with a recent change of Government and an unstable economic climate, little change has been seen at the ground level. So how can services prepare themselves for their new responsibilities towards the existing population? What will be expected of health and social care services and what can help them to meet this challenge?

Increasing awareness and understanding of autism

The lack of understanding of autism and the impact that this has on the quality of life for affected individuals and their families and carers is well documented (Broach et al 2003, Blackwell et al 2004). In response to this, the Autism Strategy outlines an expansive programme of training and awareness raising.

In line with the key areas for action outlined, workers across public services are targeted for awareness training, including those in the Criminal Justice System (the police, youth offending and probation services), those in employment and benefits advisory services, those in the education system, and health and social care workers. Government departments, business and the public as a whole are also included.

The Department of Health has allocated £50000 of centrally held funds for improving levels of knowledge and understanding of autism. Working with Skills for Health, Skills for Care, the Royal College of Psychiatrists, the Royal College of General Practitioners, the British Psychological Society, the Social Care Institute for Excellence and the Royal College of Nursing, materials for training, including online resources, are being developed (Department of Health 2010). A Statutory Guidance document is to be published which will give best practice examples of training, which should involve parents and carers as well as people with autism.

Health and social care staff

Mental health and learning disability services

In the past, and currently, mental health services have been ill equipped to recognise autistic spectrum disorders. This has lead to misdiagnosis of mental health conditions such as schizophrenia (Bell 2006, Gould 2009), and a form of 'diagnostic overshadowing' where secondary mental health conditions, such as depression, anxiety disorders and obsessive-compulsive disorder develop, in part due to lack of support, and mask the underlying autism (Berney 2006, Rosenblatt 2008). Staff in mental health services need to be made aware of this, and to have adequate training, knowledge and experience of autism to be able to recognise ASC when its presentation is less obvious, and in the presence of secondary diagnoses (Bell 2006, Gould 2009).

There is a common misconception that those who are 'more able', i.e. those with average or above average IQ, need less support; this is absolutely not the case (Holliday Willey 2006, Rosenblatt 2008). Many people with autism have no learning disability but have significant support needs which, left unaddressed, contribute to poor mental health (Blackwell et al 2004, Dowell et al 2007). If eligibility criteria allow, and with appropriate training, mental health nurses/teams may be well placed to deliver some of this support in order to maintain mental health and prevent future ill health. This would reduce the need for intensive (and costly) 'crisis' intervention at a later date (Rosenblatt 2008).

Although it is not possible to give exact figures, it is thought that approximately 50% of people with autism also have a learning disability (Tsakanikos et al 2007).

The Department of Health has now made a commitment to establish a Public Health Observatory to establish this figure, amongst others.

Currently, a large amount of the support available to those with autism, and a significant proportion of autism expertise, comes through learning disability services (Broach et al 2003). But, in both mental health and learning disability services, the knowledge base varies from place to place, and tends to be lead by individuals with an interest in autism rather than by policy or strategy. The Autism Act (2009) clearly lays out that this needs to change; staff must be trained and strategies must be developed to support people with autism.

The Autism Strategy describes the need for an improvement in the basic level of understanding throughout services, from ground staff to commissioners, but for certain individuals across the disciplines to train to become the 'expert' for that service, providing information and support to colleagues.

Who that should be will be a local decision, dependent upon existing structures and services. The challenge for mental health and learning disabilities services is to find the most effective way of using training and 'expert' individuals to maximum effect. This may be a matter of better information sharing, developing clearer pathways or 'signposting' to more appropriate individuals and services.

Primary and secondary healthcare

A National Autistic Society survey found that just 36% of GPs felt that they had sufficient information to assess the likelihood of a patient having an autistic spectrum disorder, and the National Audit Office (NAO) (2009) reported that 80% of GPs did not feel they had sufficient knowledge of the condition. If this is the case it is reasonable to extrapolate that this same group would not have sufficient practical knowledge nor experience of the condition to effectively diagnose and treat physical health complaints. It has long been known and documented that people with learning disabilities suffer from health inequalities (Michael 2008). This would naturally apply to the estimated 50% of the autistic population who also have learning disabilities. Once more, in the absence of any concrete figures pertaining to health in people with autism in particular, we can extrapolate from this and conclude that people with autism are likely to suffer from the same discrimination and poorer quality healthcare compared with the general population, in both cases resulting from a lack of knowledge (Mencap 2007, O'Hara et al 2010).

Currently, 24% of training plans for NHS staff do not address the needs of individuals with autism (NAO 2009), and the efficacy of that training must be questioned since the same report notes that a lack of knowledge of autism was noted in staff across local services. This must change, and the only way to achieve this is through good quality training tailored to meet the needs of the individual disciplines from expert practitioners, as described in the Autism Strategy and required by the Autism Act (2009).

Awareness raising of simple, practical measures, such as using double appointments, or those at the very beginning or very end of the day to avoid the anxiety of waiting, and gathering information about the individual's level of understanding and preferred strategies to support communication can make a world of difference. These should be as much the focus of training as theoretical and psychological perspectives. Including non-medical staff, such as receptionists and security staff, is also vital, as these people are often the first point of contact and can be instrumental in achieving a successful health appointment.

The use of health liaison nurses, working within mainstream services, has been proposed as a cost-effective way of providing information and expertise on learning disability (Department of Health 2007, 2009). A similar role, or perhaps additional training for existing health liaison posts, could be considered for providing information and advice on autism.

A further recommendation is to ensure that staff who carry out NHS continuing healthcare assessments are trained in autism; where this has not been the case people with autism who have comparatively high support needs have been denied care (Rosenblatt 2008).

Local authorities

The difficulties faced by people with autism in obtaining a thorough and accurate assessment of need are well documented (Dowell et al 2007, Rosenblatt 2008, NAO 2009). The reasons for this become clearer considering that Rosenblatt's (2008) study found that local authorities do not think that care managers receive sufficient training in autism in their initial professional training (71%), nor in their post-qualification training (67%), and 76% of local authorities do not have an autism training strategy at all.

Seventy percent of local authorities did not cover high functioning autism in their training for staff assessing under Fair Access to Care Services (NAO 2009). People with high functioning autism and Asperger syndrome often appear to be very able at a first meeting, and to an untrained assessor may not seem to need support. Verbal ability can often be taken to mean high levels of ability in the activities of daily living, which is often not the case in autism (NAS 2009).

Clearly there is a role for the higher education establishments who provide social work training to ensure that the social workers and care managers of the future understand autism. Such a role could include looking towards offering modules for continuing professional development, working in conjunction with colleagues in practice, and for clear training and guidance to be given to those who undertake assessments of any kind. This would apply equally to staff in transition services (Dowell et al 2007).

Other public services

Given that this chapter is directed towards healthcare professionals, these services will not be covered in depth. However it is useful to know what can be expected for and from colleagues in other areas.

Criminal Justice

> *In the criminal justice system, police officers, probation services and courts may all be unaware of the communication challenges posed – leading to overly heavy-handed responses to incidents.*
>
> (Department of Health 2010)

The need for a better understanding of autism through training, and for developing techniques for communication and intervention in criminal justice settings is well known (Welsh Assembly 2006, Bishop 2008, Benton and Sharp 2009). The use of 'attention' cards, alerting criminal justice staff if individuals have an ASC has been used successfully in some areas (Welsh Assembly 2006, Benton and Sharp 2009).

Employment and benefits services

> *A particular area where adults with autism have highlighted the need for increased awareness is among employment and benefits advisers.*
>
> (Department of Health 2010)

Measures have been taken to provide training for disability employment advisors in some areas, and the Strategy clearly states the expectation that this is rolled out. The same applies to personal advisers working for Jobcentre Plus; training is being made available online, and through tutorials, etc.

Education

> *Educational settings which do not make adjustments for people with autism can make it harder for adults with autism to complete courses and gain qualifications, as well as missing out on the social aspects of college life.*
>
> (Department of Health 2010)

The Act and Strategy note the difficulties that people with autism experience in accessing further and higher education, when often a small adjustment can be the difference between success and failure (Breakey 2006). The Act notes that the Disability Discrimination Act (2005) can be used where adjustments have not been made, to ensure that educational establishments understand their responsibilities. Again, information and staff training are often the key to success.

Clear diagnostic pathways

Current evidence clearly shows the difficulties that people experience in obtaining a diagnosis of autism, especially for adults and those who have high-functioning autism or Asperger's syndrome (Blackwell et al 2004, Rosenblatt 2008). Research evidence suggests that 74% of primary care trusts understand that there are difficulties around adult diagnosis, and it is common for there to be a lack of specialist diagnostic services (Rosenblatt 2008). Many adults go through their lives suspecting, or even knowing that they have an ASC, but are unable to get a diagnosis – and without a diagnosis they are unable to access the support services that they need (Blackwell et al 2004, Dowell et al 2007, Rosenblatt 2008). This in turn can lead to mental ill-health (Blackwell et al 2004, Dowell et al 2007), which clearly has a cost implication.

The other issue with this under-diagnosis of adults is a pragmatic one. If people are not diagnosed, services cannot know whom they should be supporting, and hence the services are not there for that population (Dowell et al 2007).

The Strategy aims to 'increase capacity' around diagnosis, and ensure that every area has a clear diagnostic pathway; this is not currently the case. NICE are developing clinical guidance that can be used to support NHS bodies to do this. The Strategy cites good practice examples to guide other areas (e.g. Liverpool, etc.).

Clearly this will mean that appropriately placed professionals will need additional training to be able to diagnose, but it is equally important that any practitioner who will potentially come into contact with people in need of support or services is able to recognise potential signs of autism, and is able to refer to an appropriate colleague.

Again, although NICE guidance will be published, exactly how this pathway is put in place and what it looks like will be left to local commissioners to decide. This is to allow for existing structures to be made use of, as ever, in the interests of economy. However, it is strongly recommended that an Autism Lead is appointed to direct diagnostic and support services, as it has been shown that this has a significant effect on outcome for individuals with autism (Department of Health 2010).

Improving access to services

A NAS survey found that 40% of adults with autism were supported by their parents in the family home, and of those who lived in their own homes, 44% received support from family members (Rosenblatt 2008). The same survey found that 76% of these family carers did not receive any support from the local authority, and 68% had not received a carers' assessment. This may be forgivable if the people in question felt well supported and all involved believed that this was the best solution and were coping well, but this is not the case. The majority of adults with autism report that they do not receive enough support, and that this has a direct impact on their quality of life and anxiety levels and can cause significant mental health problems (Dowell et al 2007, Rosenblatt 2008). Obviously this raises ethical considerations regarding quality of life, but there are also practical considerations; who will support these adults when their parents die? What are the cost implications of treating these preventable mental illnesses? Rosenblatt (2008) highlights the need for preventative services, which may be infrequent or low intensity, but which prevent more significant problems from building up over time.

There is a huge need for social support services. They tend to be viewed as being less important than physical/personal care support services, and are almost certainly cheaper, but they are of paramount importance to the well-being of people with autism (Dowell et al 2007).

The Autism Strategy acknowledges the difficulties that people with autism face in accessing appropriate services that meet their needs even when suitable services do exist, which frustratingly, they often do. There are services currently operating which provide suitable structures to support people with autism, but are not currently able to do so.

This is in part due to a lack of understanding of the condition within various services as discussed, but also due to restrictive eligibility criteria. The issues around accessing mental health services are a case in point.

The Autism Strategy recognises this and uses the Disability Discrimination Act (2005) to push forward the need for mental health services to adapt to meet the specific needs of people with autism:

> *To reinforce the requirement under the DDA [Disability Discrimination Act] that services should make reasonable adjustments for adults with autism, the 2010/11 NHS Standard Contract for Mental Health and Learning Disability Services includes, for the first time, specific reference to adults with autism.*

Under this contract, services will be required to demonstrate what reasonable adjustments are made for people with autism. The Department of Health has committed to producing guidance as to what these adjustments might be, in terms of adaptations to the physical environment, and methods of communication used. One would hope that this would extend to adapting diagnostic tools to accommodate the communication and understanding of those with autism (Bell 2006, Berney 2006).

This, it is hoped, will counter the well-known problem encountered by those with Asperger's syndrome and high-functioning autism of 'falling between two stools' whereby neither mental health nor learning disability services are able to meet their needs due to the restrictions of eligibility criteria. The Government has known about this for some time, and state that this is

> *...unacceptable and contrary to the intention of Government policy.*
>
> Department of Health (2006: 7)

Despite this, 45% of local authorities do not have a clear strategy for dealing with this problem at present (Rosenblatt 2008).

Similarly, in learning disability services the NHS Standard Contract for 2010/11 mentions autism specifically for the first time, and the same requirements under the Disability Discrimination Act (2005) will apply to learning disability services.

It is hoped that this will open services to those with autism that were previously unavailable due to restrictive, IQ-based eligibility criteria. For instance, the Autism Strategy states:

> *...many of the changes set out in Valuing Employment Now are designed to benefit adults with autism even if they do not have a learning disability.*

A move towards criteria which take into account overall social and adaptive functioning, and which consider what supports the individual needs and whether the service is able to provide for this would be more useful and is supported by the Autism Strategy.

The aim of the Autism Act and Strategy is not necessarily to develop services specifically for people with autism, although this may be necessary in some instances, but rather to open up existing services to a group of people who desperately need support (Department of Health 2010). It is stated, however, that it may be necessary to develop specialist services so that people with autism are able to access mainstream services.

Access to employment

The barriers preventing more able people with autism from being employed are raised again and again as one of the biggest problems that people feel that they face (Blackwall et al 2004, Rosenblatt 2008). Currently, only 15% of adults with autism are in full-time employment (Rosenblatt 2008), despite evidence that there is considerable scope for the inclusion of this group in the workplace (Blackwall et al 2004). This group is currently reliant on State benefits, when they could be, and for many people very much want to be, employed. The Government paper *Building Britain's Recovery: Achieving Full Employment* (Department for Work and Pensions 2009) aims to have 80% of people of a working age employed. Thus the wishes of people with autism, the Autism Act and Strategy and Government directives and guidance, including *Valuing Employment Now* (Department of Health 2009) seem to be in accordance with one another – helped by the potential saving to the State.

However, considerable change is required to make this a reality. The improved awareness of Jobcentre Plus employees, mentioned previously, is a step in the right direction but much more needs to be done to fully open up the world of employment to people with autism. Again, appropriate training for employers is vital, and the Strategy goes on to outline various other supports: better suited pre-work training, job coaching, internships under Project Search (Department of Health 2010), or more open recruitment procedures using practical tests or work trials rather than the traditional work interview (Hendrickx 2009).

Although employment may not at first seem to be within the remit of health professionals, holistic models of health and health promotion recognise the importance of work on physical and psychological health (Naidoo and Wills 2009). The social contact that is associated with employment can be extremely beneficial to this group, as can the status and self-esteem that are attached to paid work (Hendrickx 2009).

As well as the practical measures suggested, perhaps what is needed is a shift in our understanding as practitioners, which takes into account what people with autism say. Employment is important to their overall well-being, and the issues which prevent it must be addressed as a priority.

Planning for and meeting local need

The National Audit Office (2009) found that 75% of local councils did not have a commissioning strategy for autism. One of the biggest issues with regard to developing such a strategy and planning services for people with autism is the fact that we do not know how many people we are planning for, although the currently accepted prevalence rate is thought to be approximately 1% (Baird et al 2006). The Autism Act now requires both learning disability and mental health services to capture and provide data regarding the prevalence of autism among those that they serve to inform local planning. This is clearly a critical first step to planning.

This information, alongside the information captured within Joint Strategic Needs Assessments (JSNAs), should be the basis of local planning, the Strategy says. And there is a positive change already it would seem:

> *The Care Quality Commission report, The State of Healthcare and Adult Social Care in England 2009, found that 83% of local authorities surveyed were now considering the needs of adults with autism in JSNAs, commissioning strategies and plans.*
>
> (Department of Health 2010)

Estimates of the number of adults with autism in each area are to be published shortly as part of JSNA core data sets, and these figures can be compared to the number of people known to services to give an indication of unmet need. This information will determine how localities proceed. It should be noted that the Strategy clearly states that the Director of Adult Social Services must ensure that there is a joint commissioner/senior manager who has a clear responsibility for adults with autism, as per previous guidance (Department of Health 2010).

Once more, the Strategy makes clear the intention that any autism strategy and resultant services become part of existing processes and partnerships, making the best use of financial and human resources in that area. It is recommended that commissioners work with *Valuing People* regional leads and deputy regional directors, learning disability partnership boards and mental health local implementation teams and the third sector, to ensure that functions are not replicated, and for effective future monitoring. It also stresses the importance of involving people directly affected by autism in decision making and planning, citing the requirement to do this under *Creating Strong, Safe and Prosperous Communities* (Communities and Local Government 2008).

While the Strategy is clear that what local strategies look like may differ depending on existing services and local need, it does pledge to identify and promote best practice, and cites examples as such to help local planning, and requires that a first year delivery plan be produced detailing possible structures.

Conclusion

The Autism Act and Strategy are without doubt a welcome first step towards changing and improving service provision, particularly for adults with autism. But it would be naïve to believe that any changes will happen quickly.

The Autism Act requires that planning and leadership of autism services adhere to the guidance issued – but there is still little legal weight that can be applied to service provision itself.

In addition, current budget cuts in health and social care mean that it will be difficult for local authorities to develop new services. Despite suggestions in the Strategy that there will not be any need for additional funding, autism expertise is not going to arrive for free: training must be provided, expert practitioners must be consulted or employed, and there is a need for at least some new specialist services. This in a climate where adult mental health services are notoriously underfunded, and learning disability services are likely to face severe funding cuts.

But, there are some improvements that will cost very little, in particular changing eligibility criteria and allowing access to appropriate existing services and supports. With training and the will to do so, small changes could have an enormous impact.

People with autism and their families, friends and supporters have been fighting for appropriate provision for a long while. The fight is not over, but perhaps we have gained some ground.

Key points

- The Autism Act 2009 is the first disability-specific piece of legislation to be passed in the UK.
- The Act lays out the need for 'guidance' to be issued that will describe the duties and responsibilities of service commissioners and providers.
- The Autism Strategy (2010) which followed the Autism Act puts a responsibility on service providers to increase awareness and understanding of autism, develop a clear and consistent diagnostic pathway, improve training opportunities for healthcare professionals, improve service access for those with an ASC, help adults into work, and engage in strategic level commissioning of autism services at a local level.
- Guidance as to how these responsibilities were to be implemented was issued in Autumn 2010.

References

Autism Act 2009 London, HMSO

Baird G, Simonoff E, Pickles A, Chandler S, Loucas T, Meldrum D, Charman T (2006) Prevalence of disorders of the autism spectrum in a population cohort of children in South Thames: The Special Needs and Autism Project (SNAP). *Lancet* **368**(9531):179–81

Bell D (2006) Betwixt and between: The barriers to the diagnosis of Asperger's syndrome for those working in the field of adults with learning disabilities. *Good Autism Practice* **7**(1): 54–62.

Benton C, Sharp M (2009) West Midlands Forum on the Criminal Justice System and the Autistic Spectrum. *Good Autism Practice* **10**: 1

Berney T (2006) Psychiatry and Asperger syndrome. In: Murray D (ed) *Coming Out Asperger*. Jessica Kingsley Publishers, London

Bishop D (2008) An examination of the links between autistic spectrum disorders and offending behaviour in young people. *Internet Journal of Criminology*. http://www.internetjournalofcriminology.com/Bishop%20%20Autistic%20Spectrum%20Disorders%20and%20Offending%20Behaviour%20in%20Young%20People.pdf [Last accessed 07 April 2011]

Blackwell J, Chaplin C, Lindsay K (2004) *A Place in Society*. National Autistic Society, London

Breakey C (2006) *The Autism Spectrum and Further Education: A Guide to Good Practice*. Jessica Kingsley Publishers, London

Broach S, Camgöz S, Heather C, Owen G, Potter D, Prior A (2003) *Rights in Reality: How people with autism spectrum disorders and their families are still missing out on their rights*. National Autistic Society, London

Broach S, Potter D, Heather C, Prior A, Mustapha S (2003) *Autism: Rights in Reality*. National Autistic Society, London

Communities and Local Government, Her Majesties Government (2008) *Creating Strong, Safe and Prosperous Communities*. HMSO, London

Department of Health (2006) *Better Services for People with an Autistic Spectrum Disorder: A Note Clarifying Current Government Policy and Describing Good Practice*. HMSO, London

Department of Health (2007) *Good Practice in Learning Disability Nursing*. HMSO, London

Department of Health (2009) *Valuing People Now*. HMSO, London

Department of Health (2010 *The Autism Strategy: Fulfilling and Rewarding Lives*. HMSO, London

Department for Work and Pensions (2009) *Building Britain's Recovery; Achieving Full Employment*. HMSO, London

Disability Discrimination Act 2005. HMSO, London

Dowell E, Johns N, Cooper A (2007). *Autism and Independence: A guide for local authorities: Enabling adults with an autism spectrum disorder to achieve greater independence*. National Autistic Society, London

Gould J (2009) Autism and mental health. *Mental Health Today* **Suppl**: 1–2

Hendrickx S (2009) *Asperger Syndrome and Employment: What People with Asperger Syndrome Really Really Want*. Jessica Kingsley Publishers, London

Holliday Willey L (2006) Pretending to be normal: Living with Asperger syndrome. In: Murray D (ed) *Coming Out Asperger*. Jessica Kingsley Publishers, London

Mencap (2007) *Death by Indifference*. Mencap, London

Michael J and the Independent Inquiry into Access to Healthcare for People with Learning Disabilities (2008) *Healthcare For All: Report of the independent inquiry into access to healthcare for people with learning disabilities*. HMSO, Lodon

Naidoo J, Wills J (2009) *Foundations for Health Promotion*. Balliere Tindall, London

National Audit Office (2009) *Supporting People with Autism Through Adulthood*. HMSO, London

National Autistic Society (2009) *If I Tell Them How They Feel Then They'll Understand*. National Autistic Society, London

O'Hara J, McCarthy J, Bouras N (2010) I*ntellectual Disability and Ill Health: A review of the Evidence*. Cambridge University Press, Cambridge

Rosenblatt M (2008). *I Exist: The message from adults with autism in England*. National Autistic Society, London

Tsakanikos E, Sturmey P, Costello H, Holt G, Bouras N (2007) Referral trends in mental health services for adults with intellectual disability and autism spectrum disorders. *Autism* **11**(1): 9–17

Welsh Assembly Government (2006) *Identifying and Supporting People with Autistic Spectrum Disorders within the Youth Justice System in Wrexham and Flintshire*. Available from: http://wales.gov.uk/topics/housingandcommunity/research/safety/autisticjustice/?lang=en [Last accessed 07 April 2011]

CHAPTER 20

Decision making: Consent

Karen Lesley Sanders MA, RGN, RNT

Medical treatments such as artificial nutrition, invasive investigations, drug therapies, surgical procedures, intravenous hydration and medical treatments for organ failure(s) due to disease, trauma and old age are readily available within today's healthcare system and offer considerable benefits to vast numbers of people. However, some people might choose not to receive such treatments if their disease or injury cannot be reversed, or their quality of life maintained or improved. In law within the UK competent adults (aged 16 years or over), having had sufficient time to deliberate, have the right to make voluntary, uncoerced decisions, based upon adequate information, to accept or refuse a proposed course of medical treatment which will directly affect them. They do not have a legal right to withhold consent, and thus refuse basic nursing care.

Over recent years in the UK decision making regarding the provision of medical treatment and care has evolved slowly from paternalism via an autonomous approach, towards an emphasis on patient choice, 'independent choice', 'self-rule'. Autonomy is the ability or capacity to make informed choices, free of coercion or unwanted interference, based on one's own personal beliefs and values in all areas of one's life. Gillon (1985a) offers an interpretation which can be directly applied to nursing practice:

> *Personal autonomy allows one to think, decide and act on the basis of such thought, making decisions freely and independently, developing personal interests, setting and achieving personal goals, and giving meaning and coherence to such life.*

Individuals' inability to make decisions or their inability to control their actions or both, as a result of illness, psychological impairment and physical or mental disability will diminish each individual's autonomy. Nurses must always strive to eliminate barriers that may hinder a patient's autonomy, remembering however that they must work within professional boundaries defined by the Nursing and Midwifery Council Code of Professional Conduct (2008), the organisational milieu, and in responce to the needs of all patients. This means that total patient autonomy is not reconcilable with the limitations of the real world and the present healthcare system.

Since 2007, all adults (aged 16 years or over) in England, Wales and Scotland are to be presumed to have decision-making capacity and are therefore afforded the right to make decisions for themselves (Mental Capacity Act 2005, Adults with Incapacity (Scotland) Act 2000). Patient autonomy, the patient's right to make decisions, can only be legally disregarded when individuals are found to be incompetent to make decisions and thus protect themselves from harm. As a result society assumes responsibility for providing protection (Mental Capacity Act 2005, Adults with Incapacity (Scotland) Act 2000). Both Acts are designed to protect people who are competent and those who lack the ability to take decisions for themselves due to mental capacity difficulties.

The Mental Capacity Act 2005 (MCA 2005), which came into force in England and Wales during 2007, gave adults (aged 16 years or over) with capacity, the legal right to consent to, and also refuse medical treatments. The MCA was fully implemented on 1 April 2009, when the Deprivation of Liberty Safeguards came into force.

The MCA 2005 aims to support people with impaired capacity so that they can make decisions for themselves, but where they cannot take decisions, to provide a protective framework for decision-making for those who have to make and implement 'best interests' decisions on their behalf.

The Department for Constitutional Affairs has stated that the MCA Act 2005

> *... affects over 2 million people in England and Wales including the elderly, those with dementia, learning disabilities, mental health problems, a stroke and head injuries who lack the capacity to make their own decisions.*
>
> (Young and Bonnerjea 2007: 2)

The five statutory principles underpinning the MCA 2005 demand a new approach to healthcare provision:

- A person must be assumed to have capacity unless it is established that he or she lacks capacity. A lack of capacity is to be established as a last resort.
- A person must not to be treated as unable to make a decision unless all practicable steps to help him or her to do so have been taken without success. People with impaired capacity must be empowered to make their own decisions. Maximising their ability/capacity to make decisions must be a first priority of care. Would the person have a better understanding if the information was explained or presented in a different way? All available methods of communication must be employed.

- A person is not to be treated as unable to make a decision merely because he or she makes a decision judged to be unwise by others, e.g. relatives and/ or healthcare professionals.
- An act done, or a decision made, under this Act on behalf of a person who lacks capacity must be made in his or her best interests. Until the MCA 2005 came into force there was no clear legal authority for people to act on behalf of those who lack capacity. There was no legal status for 'next of kin'. This meant that family/significant others had no legal decision-making powers for adults with incapacity, nor any right to be consulted about their care. There were only limited ways in which a person could ensure that their wishes about treatment could be taken into account after they had lost the capacity to make decisions. The MCA 2005 has created the following: new proxy decision makers and advocates; a new court, 'the Court of Protection'; a criminal offence, 'The wilful neglect and ill-treatment of a person who lacks capacity'; and a statutory framework for advance decision making.
- Before a 'best interest' decision is made and an action taken, it is necessary to consider whether the outcome of the proposed action can be as effectively achieved in a way that is less restrictive of the person's rights and freedom of action.

Prior to the MCA being implemented patients reported that they found it difficult to ensure that their healthcare choices were understood, respected and followed, both in real time and in the long term. They reported fearing that if and when they lost their ability to communicate or make decisions, that their choices would be ignored or not recognised, that they might be over-treated or receive inappropriate treatments. Some claimed that due to their condition (old age, learning disability, mental health problem), they were automatically labelled as incompetent – unable to make decisions and protect themselves from harm.

Consent is

> *...a voluntary and un-coerced decision made by a sufficiently competent or autonomous person, on the basis of adequate information and deliberation, to accept rather than reject some proposed course of action that will affect him or her.*
>
> Gillon (1985b)

An adult patient who is competent and fully informed of the consequences has a right to refuse treatment even if such refusal is likely to result in death (House of Lords 1994).

How do I assess whether an adult is competent to make decisions?

The MCA 2005 provides comprehensive frameworks to establish whether an adult (aged 16 years or over) is competent to make decisions and to make decisions on behalf of adults who lack the capacity to make decisions. To determine if a person has the capacity, is competent to make a particular decisions, the following two-stage test must be used.

- *Stage 1*: Does the person have an impairment of, or a disturbance in the functioning of, their mind or brain? If so
- *Stage 2*: Does the impairment or disturbance mean that the person is unable to make a specific decision? This is established by asking whether the person is able to:
  - Understand the relevant information about the decision to be made.
  - Retain that information in their mind.
  - Use that information as part of their decision making.
  - Communicate their decision (verbally, using sign language, pictures or any other means).

Failure to achieve any of the above must lead to a decision that the person concerned lacks the capacity to make decisions, and is not competent. Lack of capacity can no longer be established merely on the basis of age, appearance, condition (mental health problem, learning disability, dementia, head trauma, etc.), any aspect of behaviour (apathy, excitability) or decisions judged to be irrational or unwise by others.

For most day-to-day decisions, the decision maker will be the person who is directly concerned with the person at the time the decision needs to be made, usually the care or treatment giver. This means that different people will be involved in assessing a person's capacity to make different decisions at different times during a day, e.g. a care worker might need to assess if the person has capacity to consent to be washed, a nurse if the person has capacity to consent to have a wound dressing changed, and a doctor if the person has capacity to consent to have a kidney biopsy.

What should I do if a person whose capacity is in doubt refuses to undergo an assessment of capacity?

Firstly ask if the person understands why the assessment is necessary. Further explanation may be necessary. The person cannot be forced to undertake the assessment. The use of threats and/or force is not acceptable, e.g. if the person refuses to open the door to his or her home, it cannot be forced. If there are serious worries about the person's mental health, it may be possible to get a warrant to force entry and assess the person for treatment in hospital, but the situation must meet the requirements of the Mental Health Act 1983 (section 135). Simply refusing an assessment of capacity is in no way sufficient grounds for an assessment under the Mental Health Act 1983.

If a person lacks the capacity to make a decision, the assessment can usually take place as long as the person does not object to the assessment, and it is in the person's 'best interests'.

I believe a person lacks capacity, what should I do?

Ask the following questions:

- Does the person have all the relevant information he or she needs to make the decision?
- If the person is making a decision that involves choosing between alternatives, does he or she have sufficient information on all the different options?

It is very difficult for patients to take an active part in the decision-making process if they do not have or understand the necessary information needed to make the choice.

- Would the person have a better understanding if information was explained or presented in another way?
- Are there times of the day when the person's understanding is better?
- Are there locations where the person may feel more at ease?
- Can the decision be put off until the circumstances are different and the person concerned may be able to make the decision?

Mental Capacity Act Code of Practice (2005) Section 4.36

When caring for adults with chronic conditions it is important to review the person's capacity to make decisions from time to time since people can improve their decision-making capabilities. In particular, people with an ongoing condition may become more able to make some, if not all, decisions, for example people with learning disabilities will learn new skills throughout their life, improving their capacity to make certain decisions.

If patients lack the capacity to make decisions and protect themselves from harm, then by law all decisions taken on behalf of the person must be taken in his or her 'best interests'.

'Best interests' is as objective a test as possible of what would be the person's choice/decision if competent, having taking into consideration all the relevant factors.

How might I establish a person's 'best interests'?

A person's best interests can be established by considering the following.

Encourage participation: do whatever is possible to empower and encourage individuals to take part in, or to improve their ability to take part in making the necessary decision.

Identify all relevant circumstances: within the time available, and circumstances permitting, try to identify all the things that individuals who lack capacity would take into account if they were making the decision for themselves:

- Their past and present wishes and feelings. These may have been expressed orally or in writing (e.g. advanced decision, healthcare records and advanced care planning) or through behaviour or habits.
- Their beliefs and values (e.g. religious, cultural, moral or political) that would be likely to influence the decision(s) in question.
- Any other factors they would be likely to consider if they were making the decision or acting for themselves.

Consult relevant others: if it is practical and appropriate, consult all relevant people for their views about the person's best interests in order to establish whether they have any relevant information about the person's wishes and feelings, beliefs and values. In particular try to consult:

- Anyone previously named by the person as someone to be consulted on either the decision in question or on similar issues.

- Anyone engaged in caring for the person, including paid carers, social workers, healthcare professionals and family members.
- Close relatives, friends or others who take an interest in the person's welfare and may be able to provide valuable information, e.g. the person's past behaviour and abilities and the types of decisions he or she can currently make. However their personal views and wishes about what they would want for the person must not influence the decision to be made.
- Any Lasting Power of Attorney appointed by the person.
- Any deputy appointed by the Court of Protection to make decisions for the person.
- For a person where there is no-one who fits into any of the above categories, an Independent Mental Capacity Advocate (IMCA) must be consulted when decisions about major medical treatment to be undertaken or where the person should live, are to be made.

Avoid discrimination: do not make assumptions about someone's best interests based solely on their age, appearance, condition or behaviour.

Assess whether the person might regain capacity (e.g. after receiving medical treatment): if so, can the decision wait until then? If this is the case, wait and let the person decide.

If the decision concerns life-sustaining treatment: it must not be motivated in any way by a desire to bring about the person's death. The decision must not be made based upon any assumptions that the person's quality of life is/will be poor and unacceptable. Euthanasia is illegal in the UK.

Avoid restricting the person's rights: is there any other option that may be less restrictive of the person's rights, if so choose that option.

When consulting with others, confidentiality must be maintained. It might therefore not be appropriate to share all information gained with everyone involved in the process of establishing 'best interests'.

Who makes the 'best interests' decision?

Many different people may be required to make decisions or act on behalf of the person who lacks the capacity to make decisions for him or herself. The person making the decision is referred to as the 'decision-maker'. It is the decision-maker's responsibility to work out what would be in the best interests of the person who lacks capacity.

For most day-to-day actions or decisions, the decision-maker will be the person directly involved with the person and the action at the time the action is needed. For decisions involving the provision of medical treatment, the doctor will be the primary decision-maker in consultation with the other healthcare professionals (physiotherapist, occupational therapist, speech therapist, nurse, etc.) responsible for carrying out the particular treatment(s). For decisions involving the provision of nursing or paid care, the nurse or paid carer will be the decision-maker. If a Lasting Power of Attorney has been appointed and registered by the person, or the court has appointed a deputy, the attorney or deputy will be the decision-maker, for decisions within the scope of their authority.

Carers, whether family members or not, paid or unpaid, trained or not, are unlikely to be experts in assessing capacity. They, along with health professionals are protected from liability (their actions are lawful) when providing care and treatment to the incompetent person, if, as the decision-maker, they have a reasonable belief that the person lacks capacity at the time the decision was made and that the act or decision was made in the person's 'best interests'. Therefore it is very important that a record of the assessment of competency and the 'best interests' decision is made by the decision-maker and stored in the person's healthcare record. It should clearly outline:

- Why the person was assessed to be incompetent to make the decision in question.
- How the person's 'best interests' decision was reached; the process.
- What were the reason(s) for reaching the 'best interests' decision.
- Who was consulted to help establish what the person's 'best interests' were and why.
- What particular factors were taken into account and why.

Prior to the MCA coming into force, the courts had decided that some decisions relating to the provision of medical treatment were so serious that in each case, an application should be made to the court for a declaration that the proposed action was lawful before that action was taken. Cases involving any of the following decisions should now be put in front of the Court of Protection for approval.

- Withdrawal of artificial nutrition and hydration from patients diagnosed as being in a permanent vegetative state.
- Organ or bone marrow donation from a person who lacks capacity.
- Non-therapeutic sterilisation of a person who lacks capacity (e.g. for

contraceptive purposes). Such cases continue to require to be put in front of the court as before.

- Doubts or dispute about whether a particular treatment or intervention is in the 'incompetent' person's best interests.
- Cases involving ethical dilemmas in untested areas.

What is an 'advance decision'?

An 'advance decision' is a document made by a competent person in anticipation of becoming incompetent in the future who may require medical treatment(s) and/or care. Within the document individuals record their desire to refuse or accept specific treatments which might be prescribed for them, in specific circumstances. For example, a person might use an advance decision to refuse artificial nutrition in the event that he or she becomes permanently unconscious.

Advanced decisions cannot be used to demand specific treatments or receive procedures that are against the law, e.g. euthanasia. Nobody has the legal right to demand specific treatment that healthcare professionals consider to be clinically unnecessary, futile, inappropriate or not in the person's 'best interests', whether such persons are competent or not.

Advance decisions come into force when the person becomes incompetent. In some parts of the world such decisions are known by other names: 'advance directives'; 'living wills' or 'advance statements'. An advance decision is legally binding only if it satisfies the following criteria required by the MCA 2005. It must:

- Provide details of the specific medical treatment(s) and care that is acceptable or is refused. This may be expressed in layman's terms.
- Be made only by persons who are 18 years or older (different from all other elements of the MCA 2005).
- Be made only by persons who currently still have capacity as defined by the Mental Capacity Act.
- Be in writing; a specific form is not needed, any piece of paper is sufficient.
- Be signed by the patient. If the patient is unable to sign, it needs to be signed on their behalf by another person (18 years and older) in the patient's presence and in the presence of a witness (18 years and older).
- Be signed by the witness (18 years and older) in the presence of the patient.
- Be verified with a statement to the effect that the advance decision should apply even if life is at risk, if applicable. Some patients may choose to

use their advanced decision to refuse life-sustaining treatment(s). Others may not. This statement can be included in the document itself or can be a separate statement, in which case the patient and a witness must also sign the separate statement.

Healthcare professionals should not delay emergency treatment to look for an advance decision if there is no clear indication that one exists. If it is clear that a person has made an advance decision that is likely to be relevant, healthcare professionals should make every effort to assess its validity and applicability as soon as possible. Sometimes the necessity for emergency treatment decisions will make this impracticable.

An advance decision is invalid if the patient:

- Has withdrawn the advance decision at a time when he or she had capacity to do so. (A patient with capacity can withdraw an advance decision at any time either in writing or verbally; no formal procedures are required.)
- Has created a Lasting Power of Attorney after creating an advance decision, which gives their attorney the power to give or refuse consent to the treatment(s) proposed.
- Since making the advance decision, has acted in a way that is clearly inconsistent with the existing advance decision.

An advance decision is not applicable if:

- At the time, the patient still has the capacity to make decisions.
- The treatment in question is not the treatment specified in the advance decision.
- The circumstances are different from those that may have been set out in the advance decision.
- There are reasonable grounds for believing that circumstances exist which the patient did not anticipate at the time of making the advance decision, and which would have affected his or her decision. For example, if the refused treatment has developed significantly since the time the patient created the advance decision.

Whilst an advance decision should set out the treatment being refused, an advance decision refusing all treatment in any situation, for example, one that explains that a person holds a particular religious or personal belief may be valid and applicable.

If the advanced decision is not considered to be binding and applicable it should be used when attempting to establish the person's past and present wishes, feelings, beliefs and values when making a decision regarding the person's 'best interests'.

If healthcare professionals are satisfied that an advance decision exists and that it is valid and applicable to the present circumstances, but fail to follow its directions, they run the risk of being charged with battery or arrested under the criminal charge of assault and under the new statutory criminal offence of 'the wilful neglect and ill-treatment of a person who lacks capacity'.

What is a 'Lasting Power of Attorney'?

The MCA 2005 created a new proxy decision-maker, the 'Lasting Power of Attorney' to replace the previous system of 'Enduring Power of Attorney'. The MCA 2005 allows a competent person, who is 18 years or older (described in the Act as a 'donor') to appoint one or more other competent person (described in the Act as an 'attorney') to make decisions for them should they lose the capacity to make decisions in the future. The attorney can be appointed to make financial decisions, or decisions about welfare and healthcare. The previous Enduring Power of Attorney system did not allow the attorney to make welfare or healthcare decisions.

In order to be appointed as an attorney under Lasting Power of Attorney, a person must be at least 18 years of age and competent. The Act does not impose any further restrictions on an attorney appointed to make health or welfare decisions. In order to be able to legally fulfil the requirements of Lasting Power of Attorney, the donor, whilst he or she is competent, must register the Lasting Power of Attorney with the Office of the Public Guardian. Those not registered in this manner have no legal powers to make decisions on behalf of the donor. Donors must use the relevant specific form (prescribed in the regulations) to register Enduring Powers of Attorney and Lasting Powers of Attorney. There are different forms for Enduring Powers of Attorney, Lasting Powers of Attorney (relating to property and affairs) and Lasting Powers of Attorney (relating to personal welfare).

Healthcare professionals should obtain details of the 'incompetent' person's Lasting Power of Attorney from the Public Guardian if necessary. This can be obtained from: www.direct.gov.uk/en/Governmentcitizensandrights/Mentalcapacityandthelaw/Mentalcapacityandplanningahead/DG_185924.

An attorney has the power to give consent to any treatment that is specifically refused in an advance decision, if the donor has appointed the Lasting Power of

Attorney after creating the advance decision, and has given the attorney the specific power to give or refuse consent to the treatment in question, the Lasting Power of Attorney will take precedence, and the advance decision becomes invalid.

An attorney does not have the power to give consent to any treatment that is specifically refused in an advance decision if the advance decision was created after the Lasting Power of Attorney was appointed.

Donors may confer on their attorney(s) the power to give or refuse consent to life-sustaining treatment, provided that an express statement is included in the Lasting Power of Attorney document to that effect (and subject to conditions set out in the MCA 2005).

Attorneys do not have the power to demand specific forms of medical treatment that healthcare staff do not believe are necessary or appropriate for the donor's particular condition.

Who is the Public Guardian?

The Public Guardian is an individual who works with the Office of the Public Guardian whose role it is to:

- Register Enduring and Lasting Powers of Attorney.
- Supervise deputies and work with other organisations such as social services (if the person who lacks capacity is receiving social care).
- Review reports from deputies and attorneys acting under a Lasting Power of Attorney.
- Investigate concerns about how attorneys and deputies are acting, including making reports to the Court of Protection (www.direct.gov.uk/en/Governmentcitizensandrights/Mentalcapacityandthelaw/Mentalcapacityandplanningahead/DG_185924).

What is the Independent Mental Capacity Advocate (IMCA)?

The aim of the Independent Mental Capacity Advocacy Service is to provide independent safeguards for incompetent people who have no-one else (other than paid staff) to support or represent them or be consulted when certain important decisions need to be made on their behalf (Adult Protection). The IMCA must be involved when an NHS body is proposing to provide major medical treatment (e.g. decisions about providing, withholding or stopping serious medical treatment, and care reviews). The IMCA must also be involved when an NHS or local authority is arranging where the person should live or a change of accommodation in either a hospital for longer than 28 days, or a care home for more than eight weeks is being proposed.

The IMCAs must be independent of the NHS body and local authorities. However, they have the right to see relevant health and social care records. Any information or reports provided by an IMCA must be taken into account as part of the 'best interests' decision-making process. All IMCAs must have specific experience and have completed appropriate IMCA training before commencing their role and must act in accordance with the principles of the MCA 2005.

In order to fulfil their role, IMCAs:

- Should get the views of all professionals and paid workers providing care or treatment for the person who lacks capacity.
- Should get the views of anybody else who can give information about the wishes and feelings, beliefs or values of the person who lacks capacity.
- Should obtain any other relevant information they think will be necessary to make a decision.
- Must find out what support a person who lacks capacity has had to help them make the specific decision.
- Must try to find out what the person's wishes and feelings, beliefs and values would most likely be, if the person had capacity.
- Should find out what alternative options are available.
- Should consider whether getting another medical opinion would help the person who lacks capacity.
- Must write a report on their findings for the local authority or NHS body concerned.

What is the Court of Protection?

The Court of Protection is a new specialist court created by the MCA 2005. Its purpose is to ensure that the MCA legislation is adhered to. The new Court of Protection replaces the old court of the same name, which only dealt with decisions about the property and financial affairs of people lacking capacity to manage their own affairs. The new court deals with serious decisions affecting healthcare and personal welfare matters, as well as property and financial affairs previously dealt with by the High Court under its inherent jurisdiction.

The Court of Protection is a superior court of record and is able to establish precedent (it can set examples for future cases) and build up expertise in all issues related to lack of capacity. It has the same powers, rights, privileges and authority as the High Court. When reaching any decision, the court must apply all the statutory principles set out in the MCA. In particular, it must make a decision in the best interests of the person who lacks capacity to make the specific decision.

If a best interests decision is disputed (there is genuine doubt or disagreement) and there is no way of resolving the dispute, the person(s) challenging the decision may be able to apply to the Court of Protection to ask it to decide what the person's best interests are. There will usually be a fee for applications to the court.

The Court of Protection has powers to:

- Decide whether a person has capacity to make a particular decision for him or herself.
- Make declarations, decisions or orders on financial or welfare matters affecting people who lack capacity to make such decisions.
- Appoint deputies (Court Appointed Deputies) to make decisions for people who lack the capacity to make decisions for themselves.
- Decide whether a Lasting Power of Attorney or Enduring Power of Attorney is valid.
- Remove deputies or attorneys who fail to carry out their duties.
- Make declarations as to whether a person does or does not have capacity to consent to, or refuse treatment at the time the treatment is proposed and whether an advance decision is valid and applicable to the proposed treatment in the circumstances that have arisen.

The Court does not have the power to overturn a valid and applicable advance decision.

What is a Court Appointed Deputy?

In some circumstances it is not practical or appropriate for the Court of Protection to make a single declaration or decision.

If the court thinks that the incompetent person is likely to lack capacity to make decisions in the future and therefore needs somebody to act on their behalf in their best interests, it can appoint a deputy to act for that person. A Court Appointed Deputy for welfare and health will only be needed in complex/difficult situations were there is no other way of determining the best interests of a person who lacks capacity. For example where:

- Someone needs to make a series of linked welfare decisions over time and it would not be beneficial or appropriate to require all of those decisions to be made by the court. An example could be someone (such as a family carer) who is close to a person with profound and multiple learning disabilities who might apply to be appointed as a deputy with authority to make all such decisions.
- The most appropriate way to act in the person's best interests is to have a deputy, who will consult relevant people but has the authority of the court to make the decisions.
- There is a history of serious family disputes that could have a detrimental effect on the person's future care unless a deputy is appointed to make all the necessary decisions.
- The person who lacks capacity is felt to be at risk of serious harm if left in the care of family members. In these rare cases, welfare decisions may need to be made by someone independent of the family, such as a Local Authority officer. There may even be a need for an additional court order prohibiting those family members from having contact with the person.

In the majority of cases, the deputy is likely to be a family member or someone who knows the person well. However, the court may decide to appoint a deputy who is independent of the family (e.g. where the person's affairs or care needs are particularly complicated). This could be the Director of Adult Services in the relevant local authority or a healthcare professional. The Office of the Public Guardian has a panel of professional deputies, who are solicitors who specialise in this area of law and who may be appointed to deal with both property and healthcare affairs should the court decide that would be in the person's best interests. A Court Appointed Deputy cannot make decisions about life-sustaining treatment.

Summary

Seeking consent from a competent person or acting in the best interests of an incompetent person can at times be a personal and professional challenge, particularly when decisions that appear irrational, or unwise are made. However failure to respect the patient's wishes or failure to comply with the MCA 2005 may result in an arrest under the new criminal offence of 'the wilful neglect and ill-treatment of a person who lacks capacity'.

Key points

- Over recent years in the UK decision making regarding the provision of medical and nursing treatment and care has evolved slowly from paternalism towards an emphasis on patient choice.
- Since 2007, all adults (aged 16 years or over) in England, Wales and Scotland are to be presumed to have decision-making capacity and are therefore afforded he right to make decisions for themselves.
- The Mental Capacity Act 2005 aims to support people with impaired capacity so that they can make decisions for themselves.
- Where they cannot take decisions, the MCA aims to provide a protective framework for decision making for those who have to make and implement 'best interests' decisions on behalf of other people.
- A person must be assumed to have capacity unless it is established that he or she lacks capacity. A lack of capacity is to be established as a last resort.
- A person must not to be treated as unable to make a decision unless all practicable steps to help him or her to do so have been taken without success.

References

Adults with Incapacity (Scotland) Act 2000. www.legislation.gov.uk/asp/2000/4/contents

Gillon R (1985a) Autonomy and the principle of respect for autonomy. *British Medical Journal* **290**: 1806–8

Gillon R (1985b) Autonomy and consent. In: Lockwood M (ed) *Moral Dilemmas in Modern Medicine*. Oxford University Press, Oxford

House of Lords (1994) *Select Committee. Report on Medical Ethics*. HMSO, London

Nursing and Midwifery Council (2008) *Standards of Conduct, Performance and Ethics for Nurses and Midwives*. NMC, London

Young M, Bonnerjea L (2007) *Mental Capacity Act 2005*. DCA and Department of Health, London

Resources

British Medical Association (2007) *Mental Capacity Act. Guidance for Health Professionals*. Available from: www.bma.org.uk/ethics

Guidance for Restrictive Physical Interventions. Department of Health and

Department for Education and Skills. Available from: www.dh.gov.uk/assetRoot/04/06/84/61/04068461.pdf. For guidance on using restraint with people with learning disabilities and autistic spectrum disorders

Guidance on the Deprivation of Liberty. Available from: www.bild.org.uk/humanrights/docs/The Deprivation of Liberty Safeguards and You.pdf

Mental Capacity Act (2005) Available from: www.legislation.gov.uk/ukpga/2005/9/contents

Mental Capacity Act (2005) Code of Practice (2007) Available from: www.dca.gov.uk/menincap/legis.htm

Office Of The Public Guardian. www.publicguardian.gov.uk/mca/mca.htm.uk/ www.direct.gov.uk/en/Governmentcitizensandrights/Mentalcapacityandthelaw/Mentalcapacityandplanningahead/DG_185924

CHAPTER 21

Autism: An anarchy too far?

Introduction

Language inhabits a funny old world, amongst other oddities, decadent could mean having 10 teeth.

One of the issues alluded to throughout this book is how changes in language and philosophy have affected the development, understanding and treatment of autism spectrum conditions (ASCs). In this chapter, autism and Asperger's syndrome will be viewed in the context of language and linguistic and philosophical constructs. In other words, how autism and Asperger's syndrome as conditions are defined and understood by language and philosophy.

This chapter will take both the author and the reader out of familiar territory, out of their comfort zones, and into areas that could be challenging. However, it is vital to understand the symbiotic relationship that language, philosophy and ASCs have and how changes in one affect changes in the other.

At the end of this chapter you will have a basic understanding of:

- ASCs as a form of anarchy and anarchism.
- The changes in language connected to ASCs.
- How these changes affect how autism and Asperger's syndrome are perceived by both those with and those without these conditions.
- How changes in perception affect developments in language and philosophy.
- How these changes affect the support services available to those on the autism spectrum.

Autism as anarchy

Anarchy and anarchism may seem to be somewhat strange terms to apply to ASCs. According to Mautner (1997), anarchy has two meanings: 'a condition of political and social disorder especially if due to absence of government control' and 'the political condition advocated by anarchism'. Mautner (1997) further defines anarchism as: 'a theory or a political movement that interprets the ideals of human freedom...so as to exclude all relations of domination'. Early anarchists such as Godwin, Proudhon and Bakunin (all from the late 18th and early 19th centuries) focused on property and its ownership and control by a very small but wealthy, and therefore powerful, elite. For the purpose of this chapter, language will be seen and discussed in terms of property in much the same way as the early anarchists would have viewed 'bricks and mortar' and Marx would have viewed and talked about 'human labour'.

Anarchism reached its high water mark in the first two decades of the 20th century but declined after that, although it is far from being a 'spent force', as demonstrated by the existence of anarchist websites. The Conservative Government of the 1980s and 1990s, with its intention to roll back and minimise the effect and control of the State over individuals is often seen as a form of libertarian anarchism. Such libertarian anarchism can still be seen in many of the policies of the current Coalition Government.

What has this got to do with ASCs and nurses? Surely, if anything, those with autism are far removed from the ideas of anarchy and anarchism. It could be suggested that, as a result of the way that their brains have been 'wired', they are 'control freaks', needing predictability, sameness, routine and control over their world. People with autism and Asperger's syndrome have different ways of interpreting, interacting and connecting with other people and the environment in which they live, work and have meaning and, therefore, are not concerned with physical, financial, social or intellectual property and who owns or controls it.

However, anarchism and ASCs do have a number of points of contact, a number of areas where they could be seen as overlapping.

The idea central to anarchism of excluding all forms of domination could, if interpreted very loosely, be seen as meaning, on a human level, a person with a free spirit who ploughs his or her own furrow in life and who revels in this state of 'free spiritedness'. People with free and unique spirits who interpret, interact, connect and engage with the world and its people on their own terms could be seen as anarchic. Could this describe the state of being autistic? Many gifted and unique individuals who have ploughed their own furrow, including Bill Gates (the founder of Microsoft) and Einstein, have Asperger's syndrome or high functioning autism.

When one talks of having an 'anarchic sense of humour', what is meant by this? Thinking back to the early 1970s, the television comedy programme Monty Python as an example of anarchy in humour. In journalism, the underground and counter-culture *Oz* magazine published in the late 1960s and early 1970s was seen in terms of anarchy (see the *Oz* UK obscenity trials in 1971). Indeed, it could be argued that anything that attracts the epithet of 'counter-culture' or 'underground' could loosely be seen as embodying certain aspects of anarchy. Therefore, one arrives at the ideas of 'autism as underground', 'Asperger's syndrome as counter-culture', 'ASCs as anarchy', even if such links and ideas are somewhat tenuous.

If one comes to see autism as an expression of anarchy, what of those who provide direct support and care for this group? Does that make them anarchists by association? The answer is yes if, in order to provide genuine and holistic support and care that follows the agenda of those with an ASC, nurses and healthcare professionals start to see, interact and engage with the world through their eyes. If we begin to accept that there may be different priorities to life than the daily soaps, worrying about how our hair looks and trying to remain 'forever youthful', if we start to dance to the sound of a different drum, then yes.

Changes in language connected to ASCs

The last section tried to use language in order to define, connect or align autism and Asperger's syndrome as forms of anarchy, even if very loosely. In order to so define autism, the issue of language development and use and its relationship to the development in the understanding of ASCs becomes both interesting and central. In many ways, developments in language regarding autism reflect similar developments in language regarding learning disability and mental health.

Decades ago, the words 'imbecile', 'retard', 'defective' and 'lunatic' were not only commonly used but also became embedded in popular language. Hospitals for those with a learning disability or mental health issue were often known as 'lunatic asylums' or 'hospitals for the mentally defective'. 'Aberrant behaviour' was often, even if unofficially, linked to the phases of the lunar cycle, particularly the full moon (Barber 2010). Imbecile and lunatic even became legal categories in the 1913 Mental Deficiency Act. They also became, and to a certain extent remain, terms of insult, ridicule and even fear and hate, as do 'defective' and 'retard'.

The words defective and retard, however, deserve closer scrutiny. As well as being seen and used as forms of verbal abuse, defective, retard, and feeble minded, amongst others, became part of the lexicon of the social control and eugenics movements. The term eugenics was first used by the geneticist Francis Galton (1822–1911). Galton's aim was to bring about a general improvement in the human population by socially controlling human reproduction (Mautner 1997). Desirable physical and mental qualities could, over time, be increased and undesirable qualities decreased by selective breeding. Selective breeding was brought about through a combination of education, segregation, abortion and sterilisation. Eugenics saw those with a mental deficiency (learning disability, mental health problem or ASC) as well as people with a physical disability and the poor as predatory, parasitic and dangerous to the quality of the human race (Gilbert 2009). Segregation was seen as central to the eugenicists' policy in order to prevent procreation.

Eugenics as social control has been labelled 'social Darwinism', whereby survival of the fittest is assured and the weak go to the wall (Mautner 1997). In the UK, eugenics theories and practices had their heyday in the late 19th and early 20th centuries and had some very high profile supporters, including Winston Churchill (Gilbert 2009), and led to the Royal Commission on the Care and Control of the Feeble Minded in 1908. This Commission led onto the Mental Deficiency Act in 1913 which in turn led to the building of many of the old 'mental subnormality hospitals', such as South Ockendon (Essex), Ely (Cardiff) and Monyhull (Birmingham). This led to the segregation of those with a learning disability from society in general and along gender lines (the latter being to prevent pregnancies amongst those with a learning disability).

Eugenics fell out of favour and became discredited from the mid-20th century onwards. However, the ideas of eugenics have been reactivated by developments in biomedicine, particularly in relation to embryo selection, genetic engineering and genetic counselling and testing. There is some anecdotal evidence that if antenatal tests indicate the existence of a disability in the fetus, termination of pregnancy is offered as a matter of course and pressure is applied to 'coerce' women into accepting a termination. Research has lead to an increasing number of tests that could indicate the presence (or otherwise) of various genetic conditions, including ASCs with the results of these tests forming the basis of genetic counselling.

This, however, is not a 'pro-choice'/'pro-life' issue as such but rather an issue of whether society in general and the medical and nursing professions in particular values disabilities or differences. It is about whether people with disabilities, including those with autism, are valued by society and by the medical and nursing professions. It is about the use, control and ownership of language to subjugate and oppress certain people on the grounds of their disability.

Even in the 1960s and 1970s, the nursing profession followed the dominant language and philosophical ideology around disability; the qualification held by nurses working with those who had a learning disability was RNMS (Registered Nurse – Mental Subnormality). In other words, those with a learning disability (and those with an ASC) were 'mentally subnormal', they fell below 'normality' and, therefore by implication, 'desirability'. During the 1980s and 1990s the mental subnormality nurse qualification gave way to mental handicap which in turn gave way to learning disability. Although many people on the autistic spectrum do not fit comfortably within the learning disability camp, many would have been tarred with the same linguistic brush.

How changes in language affect how autism and Asperger's syndrome are perceived

There are many ways in which changes in language use and structure can influence how those with an ASC are perceived by both others and themselves. The 'discursive space', the space occupied by philosophical debate, is rather murky here. The debate around autism, its value and consequent service provision, is split down the middle: those with an ASC and their families being in support of all things autism, and others, including service providers, economists, philosophers and ethicists, could be argued to be anti-autism. Historically, this did indeed reflect the pattern of debate. However, this 'discursive split' is somewhat simplistic and artificial. It could be suggested that many service providers and academics support all things autism whilst many of those with an ASC and their families hate autism with a passion and, given the chance, would support the eugenics position of segregation and sterilisation of all those with an autism condition. Whilst very few people are openly advocating a return to this position, the biomedical/biosocial model of service provision is far from dead. One has only to look at the American Autism Research Institute's (ARI) website (http://www.autism.com/) to see the promotion of the biomedical approach to autism. The ARI appears to believe firmly in and promote the idea that autism is 'curable' and cites those who were 'formerly autistic' who believe that they have been 'cured' of autism. Hence, it could be suggested that the ARI views ASCs not only as diseases but as diseases to be cured.

The recurrent debate around genetic testing and autism is an example of this model in action. It could be suggested that the underlying aim of genetic testing is to offer those being tested 'genetic counselling' as to the risk of having a child with an ASC in any future pregnancy or, if already pregnant, a termination of pregnancy. Indeed, it could be argued that this is the reason for pre- and antenatal screening. Dig a little deeper and one hits the ongoing debate around the value of those with a disability within society. Disability is still viewed and held negatively, with those with a disability being perceived as 'deviant' and certainly far from perfect. Do parents really want to bring another 'handicapped' child into the world? Think of all the pain and misery that the child will have to endure throughout his or her life. Think of the cost of looking after the child. Will the child have a poor quality of life? These are rather crass questions to be asking at the beginning of the 21st century, surely we have moved on.

However, despite this, the control, ownership and use of language surrounding disability in general and ASCs in particular have changed for the better and this has brought about changes in how those with autism are viewed and valued. These changes have been a slow, gradual evolution brought about in part by the growing vociferousness of service users and disability and advocacy movements. Along with the change from 'mental sub-normality' with its inferences of invalid (literally lacking validity as a human) and deviance, to 'learning disability' has seen the move from:

- Segregation to inclusion.
- Dependency to rights.
- Being a drain on society's resources to being active contributors to society's resources and wealth.
- Being a human trapped inside an impenetrable shell to being a person who happens to view and interact with the world and with other people in different but often creative and unique ways.

As language continues to develop, so, too, will the value perception of those with an ASC.

How changes in perception affect developments in language and philosophy

The previous section focused on if, and how, changes in language meaning and use affects people's perception of those with an ASC. This section looks at the issues of language and perceptual changes from the opposite end of the linguistic and conceptual telescope: what effects do changes in the perception and understanding of autism have on the control, ownership and use of language as property and of philosophical, economic, political and policy debates.

As *Chapter 3* on the history of autism and ASC suggested, the 'autistic image' has changed over the decades:

- From one of 'educational, social, economic and political defective' with rather draconian methods employed to prevent those so labelled from escaping and infecting the rest of society.

- Via the situation where the person with an ASC is seen as a bit of a 'misfit' and just, perhaps barely, tolerated.
- To where the person with an ASC is seen as a unique and gifted individual who just happens to be differently abled and who interacts with the world and those who live in it in a different way to what might normally be expected or seen as appropriate.

Such a change in imagery has, it could be argued, lead to a change in language from one of rejection, defect and segregation to one of disability, '*dif*ability' (a term used by Wendy Lawson to describe that she is 'differently abled'), value and inclusion. Such a change in language, imagery and therefore action on the part of society has been bought about largely by the user, self-advocacy and disability political movements. These have in turn led to a number of critical reports by voluntary sector organisations such as Mencap (*Death by Indifference*; Mencap 2007) and the National Autistic Society (*I Exist*) (NAS 2008). This latter is important as it focuses specifically on the experiences and lives of adults rather than children with an ASC. These changes have been supported by the 'consumer movement' started in the 1970s by, among others, the American consumerist Ralph Nader who coined the phrase 'the consumer is king'; those who use health and social care services get to say what these services include and how they are delivered. Services follow and fit in with the needs of service user rather than the service user fitting in with the needs of service provider.

However, when one discusses changes in perception, from whose standpoint is this perception being discussed? Are these perceptions held by those with an ASC or by 'neuro-typicals'? Again, not everyone who has an ASC perceives their autism in the same way. Some welcome and celebrate their difference whilst others despise it. Some do not see themselves as having a disability at all, or at least will so water down the language and meaning associated with autism-as-disability that disability as a concept will quietly disappear. Others accept the label of disabled with all its ramifications and consequences.

Thus, differences in the perception of the construct, meaning and lived experience of autism by both those with and those without the condition has led to differences in the construction, meaning, use and ownership of language as property. The same also applies in reverse: those who own or who have power over language as property claim the power to alter the meaning of language and perceptual constructs. The key concept here is: who owns and controls language and its varied meanings? Do those with an ASC own language and, therefore, own how autism is defined and perceived by both themselves and others? Do so-called 'neuro-typicals' own language and, therefore, claim and own the power to impose a concept, construct and understanding of ASCs? Is such an imposition malicious, oppressive or benevolent? To what end? After all, those who own language, it could be suggested, are also likely to own the power to ascribe meaning and perceptions and, through these, control. This applies to 'autism-as-a-language construct' as it does to any other condition, concept or construct.

How these changes affect the support services available to those with an ASC

> *If you state 'autism spectrum disorder' rather than 'autism spectrum condition' when claiming benefits and social service support, you are more likely to get that support.*
>
> Advice given to a parent of a teenager with an ASC by a social worker

In many ways, both the language used to frame ASCs and the perceptions about these conditions have led to huge changes in the services that are provided. As a direct result of pressure and lobbying from those with an ASC and their supporters there have been a number of public initiatives:

- *I exist* (NAS 2008). This document highlights the experience and needs of adults with an ASC. These adults had, until recently, been forgotten, since the focus of autism debates and services had been on children.
- The Autism Act (Department of Health 2009). This Act focuses specifically on the needs of adults with an ASC (see *Chapter 19* for a more detailed discussion of the Autism Act 2009).
- *The Autism Strategy: Fulfilling and Rewarding Lives* (Department of Health 2010). The strategy arose out of the 2009 Autism Act and focuses on seven specific areas of life (see *Chapter 19* for a more detailed discussion of this strategy).
- *The Autism Guidelines*. The guidelines arose out of the Autism Strategy and seek to provide guidelines for health and social care service commissioners and providers as to how to implement the seven specific areas highlighted in the Strategy. The national Autism Steering Board that is charged with drawing up the final draft of these guidelines is headed by Paul Burstow (MP and currently Minister of State at the Department of Health) and includes as equal members two people with an ASC and two parents of those with an ASC.

Both the Autism Strategy and the Autism Guidelines took the initial form of public consultations in which those with an ASC and their families and carers were actively encouraged to participate. Thus, it could be argued that those with an ASC were exercising their collective voice, their collective 'political muscle' in order to get the Autism Act passed as law and then implemented in such ways that could only enhance their personal, collective, private and public perception of autism. It would appear that those with an ASC owned the property that is language and meaning associated with autism both in terms of a condition and a disability; they owned the discourse and the means by which this discourse was carried out. Autism has come of age.

Or has it? Just because the Autism Act became law in 2009 does not mean that it will be implemented in full by the current or any future Government. Just because there is an autism strategy called *Fulfilling and Rewarding Lives* does not mean that it will be implemented and funded in full.

The language used throughout the autism guidelines consultation process betrays great weakness. In the draft guidelines and associated consultation questions, the word that is used most frequently to denote action is 'should', whereas the far stronger word 'must' is conspicuous by its absence. To take one example:

> *When an adult is diagnosed with autism, healthcare services* ***should*** *inform the relevant local authority adult services department promptly. The diagnosing professional* ***should*** *inform diagnosed adults of their right to request a community care assessment.*
>
> Topic 3: Assessment of needs for relevant services (emphasis added)

According to the online versions of both the Cambridge and the Oxford dictionaries 'must' and 'should' have different meanings:

- 'Should' is used to indicate a suggestion, what is probable, what is possible, a conditional mood, conjecture or hope.
- 'Must' is used to indicate something that is necessary, insistence, an obligation.

A document that is couched in terms of what is probable and possible does not have the same authority as a document that is couched in terms of insistence, duty and obligation. The use of such arguably weak language could result in delays and the watering down of the guidelines.

The influence of language and perception of ASCs on public understanding and policy can be counteracted, however, by the re-emerging interest in the thinly veiled field of eugenics. The following all stand testimony to such new eugenics:

- Genetic testing and counselling with its emphasis on prevention of autism.
- The language of guilt and control which is used to underpin the offering and even imposition of genetic testing and counselling.
- The possibility of offering a termination of pregnancy if an ASC is discovered *in utero*.
- The arguably premature reports of the death of the medical model with its language of social control and deviance.

Conclusion

The relevance of this chapter to clinical practice can be questioned, and it may appear merely to be a somewhat confusing and rambling exercise in introspection; of academic and intellectual navel gazing. However, it has hopefully forced a re-evaluation of how one uses language to refer to a disability and to those with a disability within an autism context. If one has a poor understanding of how language shapes and forms and therefore controls the disability of autism, how can one avoid repeating the mistakes of the past? How can one provide holistic services and care for those with an ASC? How can one truly and honestly be involved and share in all aspects of their joys, frustrations, pain and their past, present and future lives? How can one truly and honestly stand at the side of those with an ASC in solidarity? To fully engage with those with an ASC, nothing less than a commitment to and willingness to perceive, understand and join with autism as anarchy and those with an ASC as anarchists is required.

References

Barber C (2010) A review and application of monthly circadian rhythms. *Journal of Psychiatric and Mental Health Nursing* 17:274-279

Department of Health (2009) *The Autism Act*. HMSO, London

Department of Health (2010) *The Autism Strategy: Fulfilling Lives*. HMSO, London

Gilbert T (2009) From the workhouse to citizenship: Four ages of learning disability. In Jukes M (ed) *Learning Disability Nursing Practice*. Quay Books, London

Mautner T (1997) *Penguin Dictionary of Philosophy*. Harmondsworth, Penguin

Mencap (2007) *Death by Indifference*. Mencap, London

National Autistic Society (2008) *I exist*. National Autistic Society, London

Key points

- Language and philosophy have affected the development, understanding, treatment and support of autism spectrum conditions (ASCs).
- The idea central to anarchism of excluding all forms of domination could, if interpreted very loosely, include a person with a free spirit who ploughs his or her own furrow in life and who revels in this state of free spiritedness, such as do many of those with an ASC.
- Autism is 'underground' and Asperger's syndrome is counterculture, both of which could be argued to be forms of anarchy.
- In many ways, both the language used to frame ASCs and the perceptions about these conditions have led to huge changes in the services that are provided.
- Language can also be used to impose guilt, discrimination and control over those with an ASC.
- A re-evaluation of how one uses language to refer to a disability and to those with a disability within an autism context is essential if those with an ASC are to take their rightful place as equal citizens within society.

RESOURCES

There are a large number of information and support resources that can be found by entering 'autism resources' into any internet search engine. A selection of these resources is given below.

Autism and Asperger's Support
Website: http://www.iser.com/autism-aspergers-support.html
A website and blog set up by Dave Angel, a social worker who supports families living with autism spectrum conditions in Portsmouth. A weekly blog is posted.

Autism Research Institute (ARI)
Website: http://www.autism.com/
This American organisation provides support, advice and research into autism spectrum conditions.

Autism Speaks
Website: http://www.autismspeaks.org/
Organisation that provides information and advice on many issues connected with autism spectrum conditions.

Autism West Midlands
18 Highfield Road
Edgbaston
Birmingham
B15 3DU
Tel: 0121 450 7582
Website: http://www.autismwestmidlands.org.uk/
For all issues, help and advice regarding autism spectrum conditions in the West Midlands. Other UK regions may well have their own regional autism societies.

British Institute for Learning Disabilities
Campion House
Green Street
Kidderminster
Worcestershire DY10 1JL

Tel: 01562 723 010
Fax: 01562 723 029
email enquiries@bild.org.uk
Website: http://www.bild.org.uk/index.html
Organisation that works with and supports those who have a learning disability, including those who are on the autism spectrum

Cambridge Autism Research Centre
Website: www.autismresearchcentre.com/
The Centre carries out research studies into autism, Asperger's syndrome and other conditions on the autism spectrum.

Carers UK
20 Great Dover Street
London
SE1 4LX
Tel: 020 7378 4999
Website: http://www.carersuk.org/

Carers Northern Ireland
58 Howard Street
Belfast
BT1 6JP
Tel 02890 439 843
Website: http://www.carersuk.org/northernireland

Carers Scotland
The Cottage
21 Pearce Street
Glasgow
G51 3UT
Tel: 0141 445 3070
Website: http://www.carersuk.org/scotland

Carers Wales
River House
Ynys Bridge Court
Cardiff

CF15 9SS
Tel: 02920 811 370
Website: http://www.carersuk.org/wales
For all issues regarding the voice and support of those who are 'informal carers'.

Good Autism Practice Journal
Editor: Dr Glenys Jones
School of Education
University of Birmingham
Edgbaston
B15 2TT
Email: g.e.jones@bham.ac.uk
Website: http://www.bild.org.uk/03journals_gap.htm

Mencap
123 Golden Lane
London EC1Y 0RT
Telephone: 020 7454 0454
Fax: 020 7608 3254
Learning Disability Helpline: 0808 808 1111
Mencap Direct: 0300 333 1111

Mencap Northern Ireland
Tel: 02890 691351

Mencap Cymru
Tel: 02920 747588
Email: information@mencap.org.uk

Website: http://www.mencap.org.uk/
One of the premium organisations who work with people who have a learning disability. This will also include those on the autism spectrum. Mencap have regional offices and run regional services throughout the UK.

National Autistic Society
393 City Road
London, EC1V 1NG
Tel: +44 (0)20 7833 2299

Fax: +44 (0)20 7833 9666
Email: nas@nas.org.uk
Website: http://www.autism.org.uk/
For all issues, help and advice regarding autism spectrum conditions.

Office for Advice, Assistance, Support and Information on Special Needs
Website: www.oaasis.co.uk/Autism-Info
Organisation offering advice and information on many issues to do with autism spectrum conditions.

Princess Royal Trust for Carers
Unit 14, Bourne Court
Southend Road
Woodford Green
Essex
IG8 8HD
Tel: 0844 800 4361
Fax: 0844 800 4362

Glasgow Office:
Charles Oakley House
125 West Regent Street
Glasgow
G2 2SD
Tel: (0141) 221 5066
Fax: (0141) 221 4623

Wales Office:
Victoria House
250 Cowbridge Road East
Canton
Cardiff
CF5 1GZ
Tel: 02920 221788

Website: http://www.carers.org/
For all issues regarding the voice and support of those who are 'informal carers'.

Son-rise
Website: http://www.autismtreatmentcenter.org/
American treatment programme for children and adults with autism spectrum conditions

University of Birmingham School of Education: Autism Centre for Education and Research (ACER)
School of Education
University of Birmingham
Edgbaston
Birmingham
B15 2TT
Tel: 0121 414 4866
Website: http://www.education.bham.ac.uk/research/acer/index.shtml
Research centre that focuses on research and teaching on education and care for individuals with autism spectrum disorders (ASD).

Index

I

J

K

L

M

N

Y